TITANIC MYTHS, TITANIC TRUTHS

BY

CAPT. DAVID G. BROWN

ALSO BY CAPT. DAVID G. BROWN:

Make Money With Your Captain's License
The Pontoon and Deckboat Handbook
White Hurricane
The Last Log Of The Titanic
Chapman: Piloting & Seamanship (62nd & 63rd Eds.)
The Farm: A Vanishing Way Of Life
Boatbuilding With Baltek DuraKore
Complete Guide To Anchoring & Line Handling
Complete Guide To Boat Maintenance

Titanic Myths, Titanic Truths

Brown, David G. (David Geren), 1944–

Titanic Myths, Titanic Truths / David G. Brown

Includes bibliographic references (p. 245)

ISBN 978-1456461751

1. Titanic (steamship) 2. Shipwrecks – North Atlantic Ocean

Dedication

Gains in transportation safety whether they be in ocean liners, space shuttles, or a family automobiles are the result of tragedy. Human beings do not learn much from success, only from our failures. New laws, regulations, and attitudes to improve safety come at the cost of blood from those who died teaching us better ways of getting to work, walking in space, or crossing the ocean.

The myths that have grown up around *Titanic* are charming, but teach us nothing about the root causes of the accident. For that reason the myths take away the meaning of the sacrifice made by the ship's more than 1,500 victims. We can properly honor them only be learning what went wrong that cold April night and applying that knowledge to future voyages. That is why this book dedicated to those who sail forever in Titanic.

And, for personal reasons I am also dedicating this work to Lowell Lytle who is known and loved by thousands as Captain Smith. He gave me the heart to go back to *Titanic* and bring the truth to light.

Table Of Contents

RESEARCH METHODS & ASSUMPTIONS USED IN PREPARING THIS BOOK

All good history is interpreted history. No one person, nor even a team of historians can know every detail about past events. This is especially true of events that took place before the development of modern electronic devices. *Titanic* sank now a hundred years ago. It left behind only the imperfect memories of the survivors. Since then the wreck has been found and it has provided a few more precious details about what took place. Even so, vast amounts of the story remain shrouded in mystery.

The only way for honest historians to make sense out of these mysteries is to interpret them from a stated point of view. My viewpoint is that of a licensed shipmaster who knows that safety at sea is written in blood. The only way that mariners can learn how to do their jobs better is to study how their predecessors failed. To me there are no villains or heros in the *Titanic* story, only participants.

No one aboard the ship had a crystal ball. On the afternoon before the accident Captain E.J. Smith could not know his ship would strike an iceberg. We have the advantage of that knowledge. Many would-be historians find fault in *Titanic*'s crew for not knowing the future. As a mariner, I know that the only way I can prevent a similar accident in my future is to study how those men of a century ago acted and reacted in their time of peril. If we do not learn from them, the sacrifice of those lives will have been in vain.

Titanic has been described as, "history's first media circus," and it was. Hoopla surrounded the sinking from day one. Wildly embellished newspaper articles of the period make fun reading because so often the facts were not allowed to get in the way of a good story. Even books published during that frenzy are not immune from similar defects. This is why as far as possible I have been avoided both as sources for my research. Instead of lurid newspaper accounts, this book is based primarily upon sworn testimonies taken from the U.S. Senate and British Board of Trade inquiries into the disaster.

True, there were no physical barriers to prevent a witness from lying or giving deceptive testimony to either hearing. However, those who appeared were under the threat of punishment if they perjured themselves. If for no other reason, this makes statements under oath more truthful than news reports or books written years after the event.

The stenographic process of these hearings was also more likely to get a speaker's words correct than the convoluted process of reporter-to-rewrite-to-copy desk process of newspaper reporting. Unlike copy editors, court stenographers also have no interest in "punching up" the testimony. With this in mind, I developed a personal "hierarchy of reliability" to guide my choice of research materials. The following sources are listed in descending order of reliability.

1. Documented evidence obtained from the physical remains of the ship on the bottom of the Atlantic.
2. Sworn testimony taken before a public body where the witness is under threat of punishment for perjury.
3. News accounts whether in newspapers or in hastily-published books about the tragedy.
4. Autobiographical books by survivors written or published years after the event.
5. Interviews done late in the lives of survivors.

Adherence to sworn testimony as the primary source for this work admittedly prevents me from tapping much of the rich lode of newspaper accounts, autobiographies, and interviews published after the tragedy. Undoubtedly, some important historical information has been overlooked as a result. However, it is my conviction that the loss of a few random details is an acceptable price for avoiding egregious errors contained in many of the overblown 1912 accounts of the sinking.

Adding to confusion caused by an exuberant press was a deliberate attempt by the participants to mislead the public about what actually took place. Even in 1912 it was certain as day follows night that officials and companies involved in a disaster would attempt to cast themselves in the best light. They attempted what we call today "public relations damage control." Just as now, the goal was to control public opinion and, ultimately, control history.

Accident investigators are familiar with "spin." That is why they favor information gleaned from impartial voice and data recorders. These devices were invented to help unravel mysteries surrounding a airliner accidents. They are now coming into use aboard ships as well. Investigators are no longer forced to rely upon fallible human memories of events. That was not the case when *Titanic* sank. The ship did not carry anything resembling a modern "black box" accident recorder. The only record of that night are the memories of people who happened to survive. This means our knowledge of those events was skewed by the random hand of death.

Memories of two-thirds of the people who sailed aboard *Titanic* perished on the cold morning of April 15, 1912 and can never be recovered. From the standpoint of history this means that two-thirds of the story cannot be told. This is made all the worse by the fallibility of the memories from those who did survive. Many contained unintentional distortions which even their owners did not recognize..

For example, it turns out that leading stoker Frederick Barrett was wrong about being in boiler room #6 at the time of impact on the iceberg. This mistake does not mean that he did not see the side of the ship open up from the iceberg as he described.

Or, Fourth Officer Joseph G. Boxhall was caught in outright perjury during the British inquiry into the sinking. However, Boxhall's testimony is also filled with provable facts about the ship's navigation. Without this information it would be impossible to reconstruct *Titanic*'s last hours.

Even so, another principle that guides my research is to assume everything survivors said under oath was "true" until proven false by testimony from other witnesses or physical facts. A corollary is that just because one part of a survivor's testimony was false does not mean that everything the witness said was a lie.

ACKNOWLEDGMENTS

George Behe
Capt. Rick Brown
John Chatterton
Capt. Jim Currie
Capt. Trey Elliot
Tad Fitch
Tim Foecke
Edward Goyette
Sam Halpern
G. Michael Harris
Deborah Hopkinson
Denise Hunyadi
Mary Kellogg
V.C. King
Richie Kohler
Dale Limbert
Roger Long
Ken Marschall
Tom McCluskie
Senan Molony
Simon Mills
Rob Ottmers
Gordon Simpson
Michael Standart
Parks Stephenson
Joanne Sutton
David Walker
Capt. Charles Weeks
Bill Willard
Bob Williams
Kirk Wolfinger
Capt. Erik Wood
Bill Wormsted

Not everyone on this list agrees with my conclusions. Some pointedly disagree. But each has added greatly to both the body of knowledge about *Titanic* and my research. Readers are encouraged to look up their books, papers, TV documentaries and internet postings.

AUTHOR'S INTRODUCTION: DEBUNKING THE MYTHS OF TITANIC

The Big Myth: *Titanic* was unsinkable.

The Truth: *Titanic* sank.

Titanic was the largest passenger liner in service when it sank. There is irony in the fact that I have been master of the smallest Coast Guard inspected vessel in today's U.S. passenger fleet (20 feet in length, 14 people). My command is smaller than either of the lost liner's two emergency cutter lifeboats. Despite the disparity in size between my vessel and *Titanic*, experience on the water has taught me about passenger vessels and the crews that sail them. Along the way I've also learned about how passengers react as they place their souls into the hands of people they do not know and boats of unknown quality. I have also gained first-hand experience of the danger a licensed merchant officer faces if he cooperates fully with authorities investigating a marine casualty.

My Master's license has started its fifth renewal, so I've been doing this "captaining" business for more than 20 years. Sure, I've made my share of mistakes. So far none have had the disastrous consequences of the iceberg incident that ended Captain Edward J. Smith's career. Mistakes, of course, are how we learn. Personal errors have taught me that even seasoned professional mariners with the best of intentions can, as sailors put it, "Screw up big time." In Smith's case he and his fellow officers and engineers managed to leave some 1,500 people to their fates in mid-Atlantic on a cold April night. This book attempts to explain how those good men created the most famous maritime disaster of all time.

No ship in history is surrounded by more myths and even deliberate falsehoods than the supposedly "unsinkable" R.M.S.

Titanic. Its designers, builders and sailors certainly never considered the ship as unsinkable. Nor was it the most palatial ship ever built. The ugliest myth surrounding the ship claims poor passengers were locked below to keep the third class away from the lifeboats. These well-known fictions swirl around the real ship like a fog of myth. This fog hides the truth of what took place that unforgettable night a century ago.

Untruths about the ill-fated liner have been told and re-told so often that *Titanic* has now become two ships. The real vessel of steam and steel, elegance and grandeur, life and death, slipped beneath the North Atlantic during the early morning hours of April 15, 1912. The real ship has faded from the public imagination. People have become transfixed by a second *Titanic,* a ghostly vessel on an eternal voyage across a sea of half-truths through a fog of myth. Thanks to hundreds of books and a 1997 blockbuster movie named for the ship, nearly everyone in the Western world knows this mythical vessel. Sadly, those same movies and books have pushed the real ship and the real events even farther from the public imagination.

I became aware of the two *Titanic*s while writing my earlier book, *The Last Log Of The Titanic*. Back in the late 1990s I thought the mythical ship only affected Hollywood movies. Much to my surprise I found the mythical vessel has also come to dominate much scholarly research into the sinking. Some well-meaning "experts" are blissfully unaware of how little they know about the real iron, the real navigation, or the real accident of the real ship. In place of reality they have unwittingly become experts in the myths which surround the phantom vessel.

Discord is as much a part of *Titanic* research as wind and waves are part of seafaring. However, the academic myopia that currently dominates *Titanic* research is an insult to the memories of those more than 1,500 souls who sail forever on the doomed liner. My goal is to set straight as much of the record as I can. *Titanic* was deliberately, if unwittingly, steered directly at the iceberg. First Officer Murdoch did not try to avoid the collision with some fanciful "port around." *Titanic* did not receive a necessarily fatal wound from the iceberg. And, a series of tragic human mistakes both caused the accident and then later allowed the ship to founder.

That is what happened to the real ship built by Harland & Wolff in Belfast, Ireland. But, that famous shipyard was not where the mythical ship of popular imagination was built. Construction of this second and mythical *Titanic* began with over-zealous news reporting during the early morning hours of Monday, April 15, 1912. The heavy lifting building the mythical ship was done by two of the four surviving licensed officers. Second Officer Charles H. Lightoller famously admitted applying "whitewash" to the story during both official inquiries, but especially the one in London. The British inquiry caught Fourth Officer Joseph G. Boxhall in an outright lie about an ice memo he wrote and posted in the chart room.

These men who walked *Titanic*'s bridge had an understandable need to protect their careers. I have great sympathy for them in that regard. About a decade ago a city fireboat nearly ran down my passenger vessel. The fireboat violated at least three key federal rules designed to prevent collisions at sea. For my part, I damaged by power plant "crashing back" the engine in a successful effort to prevent catastrophe. Then, despite damage to my engine I landed my passengers safely without incident.

At the time of the incident the U.S. Coast Guard was forming partnerships with local police and fire departments. It was part of what is now called "homeland security." In that political climate it was apparently deemed wise for the Coast Guard not to blame the fireboat for its actions. So, the blame was shifted to my shoulders even though the official report lauds my actions in preventing an accident. In governmental inquiries, scapegoats are always in high demand.

In 1912 other mariners jumped in to help *Titanic*'s officers defend themselves by obfuscating the truth. Captain Arthur H. Rostron of the rescue ship *Carpathia* willingly assisted Boxhall hide the sizable error in *Titanic*'s distress coordinates. Rostron told Boxhall the coordinates were "splendid" even though he knew they were wrong. Rostron had much to gain from his little white lie. By accepting Boxhall's erroneous coordinates Rostron made it seem he accomplished a breakneck rush through icebergs at an impossibly fast speed. Later, Rostron parlayed fame he gained from rescuing *Titanic*'s lifeboats into commodoreship of the Cunard Line.

Corporations were at risk from the sinking just as much as the ship's officers. Maritime law protected White Star Line by placing strict limitations on monetary damage claims against it arising from the sinking. The company's post-sinking liability was equal to the cash value of the small fleet of wooden lifeboats stored in a New York loft. However, legal restraints on damage claims disappeared if there were a violation of "privity and knowledge" of events surrounding the accident by White Star's corporate officers or directors. Company lawyers must have been upset to learn that managing director J. Bruce Ismay visited *Titanic*'s bridge during the emergency and may have participated in the decision to steam the wounded *Titanic* to Halifax.

The firm of Harland & Wolff was the world's largest shipbuilder in 1911 when it launched *Titanic*. The company prided itself as "shipbuilder to the world." Sheer size meant the company needed a steady flow of "new build" contracts from shipping lines other than White Star to maintain its huge operations in Belfast and elsewhere. The scantlings for *Titanic* had been developed independently by Harland & Wolff. Hull plating thickness and the number of rows of rivets in seams were considerably less than 1912 industry standards. Stories that one of its ships broke apart while sinking could have sent profitable contracts to competing shipyards.

Governments also had concerns. The United States and Great Britain conducted formal inquiries into the disaster. Even though these probes claimed to seek the truth, the two inquiries ignored the real ship in favor of giving the mythical vessel a cachet of government approval. *Titanic* is hardly unique in this regard. The internal explosion of USS *Maine* was *causus bellum* for the United States to go to war with Spain in 1898. In Myth the USS *Maine* was the victim of a Spanish mine. In truth, the U.S. Navy knew at the time that the real explosion was an internal event. The fact the *Maine* blew itself up was concealed from the public during the American rush to war with Spain.

Titanic, of course, was not a war casualty.

Or, more properly, it was not the casualty of a shooting war even though it was in the thick of an economic battle between Great Britain and Germany that presaged World War I. The *Titanic* affair was an embarrassment to Britain because it called into question English commercial supremacy on the seas.

The tragedy was also an American event. J. Pierpont Morgan and his U.S. dollars paid for construction of the Olympic Class vessels. White Star Line was part of the International Mercantile Marine maritime conglomerate put together with money from the American millionaire. Morgan's financial involvement in *Titanic* piqued the interest of Michigan Senator William A. Smith. He saw the tragedy in political terms as an opportunity to gain populist support by exposing the "evils" of super-wealthy capitalists in those pre-income tax days.

There is danger in asking "why" questions about history. Asking "why" begins a never-ending chain of follow-on questions. One "why?" begets another. This chain ultimately probes the mind of God for divine intention. A mere mortal is better advised to ask "what" questions that focus on events aboard the real ship. "What factors allowed boiler room #6 to flood?" is a question that can be answered by studying hard facts and reading eyewitness testimony.

Of course, some "why?" and "what" mysteries surrounding the sinking will always remain unexplained. Too many of the key individuals went down with the ship. We have lost their eyewitness accounts. We know only bits and pieces of survivor memories and reminiscences of what took place. These are seldom backed up by hard evidence and are usually unconnected within the overall context of events. The wreck is too badly disintegrated and fragile to ever be brought to the surface for forensic study. Historians are faced with a jigsaw puzzle with more pieces missing than available.

What follows is the picture of *Titanic* that I see when I assemble those available jigsaw pieces.

CHAPTER 1
FIRE DOWN BELOW

The Big Myth: *Titanic* was ripped open through five compartments. From the outset the damage was fatal to the ship.

The Truth: *Titanic* had uncontrollable flooding only in the first three large compartments. If nothing else intervened, the ship could have been kept afloat "as its own lifeboat."

Red-hot steel and freezing ice plagued *Titanic*'s short life. Most everyone knows about the iceberg, but few are aware that *Titanic* was on fire. An uncontrolled blaze burned in the ship's belly for all but one day of the ill-fated maiden voyage. Coal in a fuel bunker spontaneously ignited on Tuesday, April 2 during the delivery trip to Southampton after the Belfast steaming trials. Nobody knows for certain why the coal started to burn. The best guess is that the wrong grade was loaded at the shipyard of Harland & Wolff. Britain was just getting over a national coal strike and fuel was still in short supply. This was particularly true of "steamer grade" coal preferred in passenger liners. It came in large lumps, had little dust or "slack," and was relatively low in iron pyrites which oxidized in the damp atmosphere of a ship. Oxidation created heat which under the right conditions could cause spontaneous combustion.

It is likely that lower-grade railroad fuel was sent aboard for *Titanic's* steaming trials on Tuesday, April 2, 1912. While not diagnostic of poor coal, black smoke seen pouring from the ship's funnels in photographs of it leaving Belfast is typical of low-grade coal. Railroad coal was smaller in size, had more dust and slack, and would spontaneously combust from pyrite oxidation while in storage. These defects were acceptable on the rails because engine tenders did not carry enough coal to create a significant fire hazard. Locomotives consumed their fuel fast enough that the problem solved itself in one day as coal from the tender was shoveled into the engine firebox.

Railroad coal yards stored the black lumps in large piles which were susceptible to spontaneously catching fire. To prevent that from happening, fuel sellers continuously moved coal piles to break up smoldering hot spots. It is possible that some of the coal loaded in *Titanic* was already hot enough to spontaneously combust when it came aboard. In addition, Belfast had experienced April rains. Pyrites in damp coal oxidized more quickly, increasing the probability of spontaneous combustion. No matter how it happened, one of the ship's bunkers was noted to be "on fire" shortly after being loaded.

The burning bunker was discovered before the ship arrived in Southampton. It was inexplicably ignored for the next week while finishing touches were put on the passenger quarters and provisions were loaded. Nothing was done about the fire on Good Friday or Easter Sunday morning. The bunker was still burning unchecked when the ship finally sailed for New York on Wednesday, April 10. Only then were men put to work digging out the burning coal and feeding it to the furnaces. Work getting rid of the blaze did not begin until after the first passengers came aboard at Southampton. Shoveling out the hot coal continued at Cherbourg and Queenstown.

> *The bunker was a-fire. It was fire. The hose was going all the time.*
>
> Frederick Barrett
> Leading Fireman

No shipboard fire can be dismissed as inconsequential. This was especially true in a vessel with a largely wooden interior such as Titanic. If that wood ignited, the hull could have become an oversize version of a backyard barbecue kettle with passengers taking the place of steaks and ribs. The steel shell plating would have contained any fire and reflected its heat back into the blazing wood. As a result, *Titanic*'s interior would have burned far hotter than any building ashore. Fortunately, that did not happen. The problem was contained to one bunker.

Because the fire did not spread, the smoldering coal must have been confined in a relatively isolated location. That location was also isolated enough not to call attention to itself. The burning bunker escaped detection of government officials who inspected *Titanic* prior to departure. Those inspectors were responsible that the ship was ready in all respects to carry passengers across the open Atlantic Ocean. A ship with an uncontrolled fire should have been detained until the problem was corrected.

Titanic did not sink because of the bunker fire. The blaze gained historical significance only after the ship foundered from striking on an iceberg. The location of the burned-out bunker is an absolute gauge for the size and placement of iceberg damage on the ship's hull. And, the tale told by the fire is more than surprising. Correctly locating the burning bunker proves the actual iceberg damage was significantly smaller than usually believed. It should have been survivable.

Even so, both the American and British inquiries accepted the myth that the ship suffered fatal damage. The official version of events was based on information from leading stoker Frederick Barrett who would appear a most credible witness. He had been assigned to boiler room #6 at the time of the accident and was probably the only survivor to actually see the iceberg break open the hull. "We have it in Barrett's evidence," naval architect Edward Wilding said in London when he estimated damage extended from the peak, "to number 5 boiler section."

Myth: Firemen Frederick Barrett pinpointed the exact location of the bunker fire inside boiler room #5.

Truth: Barrett agreed the fire was in boiler room #5, but only after he was "led" to that conclusion by the questions he faced.

Too many historians have assumed that Barrett pinpointed the exact location of the fire. He did not. In America he never mentioned the blaze. Barrett did discuss it in London, but of his own volition he never specified exactly which bunker had the fire. Rather, his memories were steered by carefully formulated leading questions from The Solicitor-General, attorney Thomas Lewis representing the British Seafarers' Union, and a Mr. Cotter representing the Union of Stewards. They focused Barrett's attention by asking questions which presupposed that boiler room #6 had major flooding and that additional water was coming into an empty bunker of #5. The way in which Barrett was led is illustrated by British inquiry question 1965 and the stoker's answer.

1965 (The Solicitor-General) Let us understand it you said that the bunker in No. 5 had got some water coming into it?
Mr. BARRETT: Yes. But the hole was not so big in that section as it was in No.6.

A little later attorney Lewis resumed the interrogation. As did his predecessors, he specified the location of the fire in his questions. Barrett simply agreed.

2308 (Mr. LEWIS) This is the bulkhead between sections 5 and 6?
Mr. BARRETT: Yes.

Question 2308 placed the fire into the starboard bunker at forward end of boiler room #5. A few questions later Lewis pointed out that the empty bunker was linked to the fireman's claim of ducking into a boiler room after the iceberg. Barrett was again told his location by the question. The stoker did not volunteer this critical detail from his own memory.

2310 (Mr. COTTER) You rushed through the emergency door into the next compartment, Number 5?
Mr. BARRETT: Yes.
2312 When you looked into the bunker you saw holes through the ship's side?
Mr. BARRETT: Yes.

To each of the above questions Barrett gave the same single word answer, "Yes." His tacit approval placed the bunker fire in boiler room #5. This was in keeping with the "big gash" version of the damage which doomed the ship to founder. Whether an honest mistake or a deliberate twisting of history, the Board of Trade inquiry thus helped Barrett create the myth that boiler room #6 suffered catastrophic flooding. This almost explosive flooding did not take place.

It was during the U.S. inquiry that Barrett first claimed ice crumpled the side of boiler room #6. He went on to day that water pouring into that compartment and forced him to scramble for his life into boiler room #5 where he discovered water tumbling into the fire-emptied bunker. He repeated essentially the same story he gave in London where his testimony sealed the fate of the mythical ship. Barrett's *Titanic* had its first four major compartments of the bow open to the sea and water coming into the fifth.

Harland & Wolff naval architect Edward Wilding helped design the ship. During the British inquiry demonstrated this much flooding doomed *Titanic* to founder. But, the flooding bunker was really in boiler room #6 and not #5 as he claimed. This means the length of damage on the hull was one full compartment shorter than conventional wisdom holds. Wilding's own calculations showed the ship should have been able to float with the real damage.

Writing a correct history of *Titanic* requires locating the burned-out bunker where Barrett noticed that open seam spewing water. He said this was the same bunker his men emptied on Saturday to put out the coal fire. It marked the apparent ending point of iceberg damage to the bow. If it ended in #5 as Barrett testified, then the ship was doomed to sink. However, if the open seam ended in #6, *Titanic* should have suffered happier fate. At the very least it should not have foundered before help could arrive. So, which bunker burned?

There were 28 bunkers in distributed among *Titanic*'s six boiler rooms. Two additional auxiliary bunker spaces were provided beneath hold #3, one on each side of the firemen's tunnel. Known as the "No.3 bunkers," they were intended to carry extra fuel for a few extra days of steaming on longer voyages.

The ship's Southampton clearance papers showed 5,800 tons of fuel were loaded for the maiden voyage. This was less than the 6,141 ton capacity of all 28 bunkers located within the six boiler rooms.[1-1]

The ullage was equal to the 341-ton capacity of boiler room #1's three bunkers. This explains why the five single-ended boilers located in #1 were never fired. There was no coal in those bunkers to feed their furnaces. For this reason, there was no need to store any coal in the auxiliary bunkers of hold #3 for the maiden voyage. All of the coal *Titanic* carried on its maiden voyage was easily contained in the ship's 25 in-boiler-room bunkers.

Harland & Wolff gave each bunker in *Titanic* a letter designation. Bunker "A" was located in boiler room #1 and bunker "Z" on the mezzanine level of boiler room #6. This identification system switched to lower-case letters for the remaining two. Bunker "a" was on the mezzanine level and "b" was below it. Both were located at the head end of boiler room #6 against bulkhead D. These letter identifications were apparently used only by the shipbuilder. The designations will also be used here to avoid confusion. (See page 31)

Ten of *Titanic*'s bunkers were paired back-to-back with a steel watertight bulkhead separating each pair. This pairing raised a problem. If one bunker of any pair caught fire, heat would transfer through the steel bulkhead and ignite coal in the adjoining bunker. This sort of excess heating of a bulkhead *was* observed during *Titanic*'s fire. Leading stoker Charles Hendrickson said the bulkhead of the blazing bunker became "red hot," indicating a color temperature of about 700° C (1,292° F). This is the minimum heat needed to turn steel "red hot" to a human eye in a dim 1912 ship's boiler room. Significantly, "red hot" is three times the ignition temperature of coal.

Hendrickson's recollections are important because heat travels so quickly by conduction through steel. If one side of a steel bulkhead was "red hot" (700° C), then the other side should have been equally as hot. Coal in the bunker on the other side of the bulkhead would have been exposed to heat above its combustion temperature as well.

Heat transfer underlies the theory and practice of shipboard fire fighting. The first step is always to cool steel bulkheads and decks exposed to flame. Simultaneously, flammable materials are removed from the hot area. Fire fighting rules taught to seamen are quite simple and direct:

Keep the fire from spreading...

A. ...begin cooling down the boundary bulkheads.... Even if the fire cannot be fought directly later on, the fire will not spread once boundaries have been set.

B. ...steel bulkheads surrounding the compartment on fire will get red hot as the fire burns on and any nearby combustible may be in danger of igniting.[1-2]

The dangerous mix of heat transfer through steel and the relatively low ignition temperature of coal eliminates any of the paired sets of bunkers as the location of the blaze. A fire in one bunker of the pair would have spread to the other. That did not happen. No other bunkers in *Titanic* burst into flames. Barrett said in London that the blazing bunker was the only one emptied as a result of the emergency.

2293. Were there any other coal bunkers empty forward?
Mr. BARRETT: No.
2294. Was this the only one empty?
Mr. BARRETT: Yes.

With these one-word answers Barrett ruled out the possibility of fire in any of the paired bunkers. It had to have been in an isolated bunker without coal stored on the other side of the bulkhead.

The Myth: The blazing bunker was located at the head of boiler room #5.

The Truth: The science of heat transfer and Barrett's own words rule out boiler room #5 as the location of the fire. It had to be somewhere else.

The task of the historian becomes finding a bunker in *Titanic* which meets the requirement of being free to burn for days without igniting coal or cargo stored on the other side of the bulkhead. An examination of all 30 bunkers shows only bunker "b" at the head of boiler room #6 meets this requirement. It was built against bulkhead D which separated the boiler room from hold #3. The forward side of bulkhead D was empty auxiliary bunker space. There was no coal in the bottom of hold #3 to ignite, so no fuel was in danger of ignition by heat transfer. Bunker "b" was also separated from direct contact with first and second class accommodations. Only cabins of the third class might have experienced discomfort from heat or smells from the fiery bunker.

Even so, there was still a chance that excess heat might transfer into the mixed cargo of flammable goods or threaten mail in the orlop storage room. Among the items on the cargo manifest were burlap, rubber, and *Factice.* This last was a flammable rubber-like compound made of vegetable oil vulcanized with sulfur. Preventing the fire from spreading into the cargo would have been part of extinguishing the blaze. Standard practice of fighting fires in steel ships required the crew to cool the steel separating burning bunker from hold #3.

Sure enough, Barrett confirmed just such efforts. "There was a hose going all of the time," Barrett said, confirming the effort to keep the fire from spreading through heat transfer (British question 2340). Of all the boiler room dividers, only bulkhead D at the head of boiler room #6 was exposed enough on one side for a hose to work properly. It should be noted that fire hoses in ships do not spray precious fresh water. Rather, they shoot salt water drawn directly from the ocean. This provides an unending supply of water without depleting the limited supply of drinking water.

Fire science may force the blaze into bunker "b," but there is still the problem of Barrett's testimony putting the fiery bunker at the head of boiler room #5. On Harland & Wolff documents this was bunker "W." It was paired across bulkhead E with bunker "Y" in boiler room #6. As noted, normal firefighting practice should have been to empty "Y" before tackling the burning bunker. Yet Barrett said that only one bunker was emptied and that was the bunker of the fire.

Many historians solve the one bunker problem by assuming the hose sprayed *into* the burning bunker. Not so and never so for several important reasons. First, it would have been difficult for enough of the cold water to reach bulkhead E. Lumps of fuel would have broken up the stream and blocked most of its cooling effect on the steel. The second reason for not wetting down the bunker was that damp coal was more likely to self-combust than dry. The importance of keeping coal dry was discussed in technical journals contemporary with *Titanic.*

> ...Any coal with conditions favorable to oxidation will be facilitated in that action by moisture...Without exception, in all of the series of tests, the wetting of the coal increased the activity as shown by the ultimate temperature.[1-3]

The final and most important reason for not wetting down burning coal with a fire hose was the corrosive effects of salty steam. Chlorine and other chemicals are liberated from coal that burns after being dampened with salt water. These corrosive chemicals would quickly damage vital furnace arches which are curved plates at the top of a firebox. The arches transfer heat from the fire to water inside the boiler. *Titanic*'s furnace arches were exposed to blazing coal on one side and 210 to 220 pounds of steam pressure on the other.

Life spans of arches were short at best. Engineers avoided exposing them to corrosive chlorine and other chemicals to prevent even more rapid failure. Replacing an arch was an expensive process during which the boiler was completely out of service. *Titanic*'s engineers would never willingly have considered serving their furnaces any coal wetted by salt water. Instead, the bulkhead could best have been cooled by spraying water on it from inside hold #3, which appears to have been done to exposing the arches to corrosive chemicals.

Why *Titanic*'s bunker fire was ignored from Tuesday until the following Wednesday is unexplainable. No one spoke on the record about this lack of concern. However, examination of Barrett's testimony has shown that standard fire-fighting tactics were employed after the ship sailed from Southampton. Even so, the fire never really put out. Instead, still-burning lumps of coal were shoveled straight from the bunker into the boiler furnaces. It was the most cost-effective method of getting rid of the problem. By Saturday evening *Titanic*'s bunker fire had been turned into steam to propel the ship.

This elegant solution to the bunker fire was only possible because it burned in bunker "b" of boiler room #6 and not, as Barrett claimed, bunker "W" in boiler room #5. No other location meets the historical requirements for the fire. If so, then Barrett's story about being in #6 at the time of impact and diving under a closing watertight door into boiler room #5 was flat wrong.

But, was it a lie?

During emergencies people become confused. Their confusion may translate into false testimony that is not really "perjury." Their memories may be wrong, but these people honestly believe what they say is true. Of course, "true" in terms of human memory is not necessarily the same as "fact." There is no reason to suspect Barrett intentionally lied. Nor has evidenced surfaced that he was "paid off" for his testimony. Like other survivors of traumatic events, Barrett simply suffered jumbled memories, one of which was critical to understanding events that transpired in *Titanic*'s boiler rooms.

After their return crossing of the Atlantic, the survivors of *Titanic*'s crew were forced to give depositions to the British inquiry before being reunited with their families. These depositions have been lost to history, so it is impossible to know what Barrett said while the accident was fresh in his mind. He probably told his now-familiar story of diving from flooding boiler room #6 into the safety of #5. Officials reading his transcript undoubtedly knew the man's story was confused. There was evidence from the other survivor of boiler room #6 that the compartment did not flood as Barrett described.

Of all the survivors, First Officer Charles H. Lightoller gave the most accurate description of the damage to the U.S. Senate inquiry. "I should judge the fore peak tank was pierced. I judge that (hold) number one, of which I have no proof, was pierced; and number two; and I should think number three." Senator Theodore Burton asked if "number four" was pierced. "There is no number four. Number four is number six stokehold. Burton asked if that compartment was pierced. "No, sir, I do not."

Barrett's story might have been discarded as fantasy except that it obscured many embarrassing details of the sinking Misplacing the burning bunker from boiler room #6 to #5 erased any possibility that *Titanic* sank because of any construction defects. It also eliminated discussion of damage control mistakes by the ship's engineers. Barrett's jumbled memories benefitted Harland & Wolff, the White Star Line, financier J. P. Morgan, and British interests on the high seas.

The manner in which Barrett's story first came to light remains suspicious a hundred years on. For never-revealed reasons the stoker was not called by the regular sessions of the U.S. inquiry. Instead, he was delivered in the nick o' time to Senator Smith's committee. Barrett arrived inside boiler room #6 of White Star Line's *Olympic*, the exact sistership to *Titanic*. The man was a gift to the American inquiry on the last possible day to take testimony. The senators had to go down to the dock to meet with him. Barrett did not leave the heat of *Olympic*'s boiler room to visit the U.S. hearing room. Back in London, the stoker limited his testimony about the location of the fire to only one word, "yes." He agreed with his questioner that he was in boiler room #5 when he saw water pouring into the burned-out bunker. And, he improperly counted stokeholds the one time he gave a location of ice damage.

> *...Water came pouring in two feet above the stokehold plate. The ship's side was torn* ***from the third stokehold to the forward end.*** [emphasis by author]
>
> Frederick Barrett
> Leading Stoker

Barrett said that he was talking with Junior Second Engineer Hesketh at the moment the ship struck. He never described the nature of their conversation. Most likely they spoke about fire-damaged bulkhead D. That cooling spray may have contained the fire, but it did not stop heat from warping the steel. Barrett and another leading stoker, Charles Hendrickson, agreed that the fire distorted the bulkhead. Hendrickson even claimed the metal had been "red hot."

> *...The bottom of the watertight compartment was dinged aft and the other part was dinged forward.*
>
> Frederick Barrett
> Leading Stoker

> *...Yes, you could see where* ***the bulkhead had been red hot****. ...All the paint and everything was off. It was dented a bit.* [emphasis by author]
>
> Charles Hendrickson
> Leading Stoker

After the metal cooled a protective coat of oil was applied to the damaged areas. This work had been completed earlier that Sunday. More than likely an inspection by shipbuilder Thomas Andrews of Harland and Wolff and Chief Engineer Joseph G. Bell would have been done Monday morning. Normal shipboard practice would have been for an engineer to make a pre-inspection of the work. Barrett had supervised the last part of the oiling, so he accompanied the engineer Hesketh inspecting the dinged metal. His concern would have been corrosion caused by heat and salt water on the forward side of bulkhead D. Looking for that damage required the two men to go into the empty auxiliary bunker of hold #3.

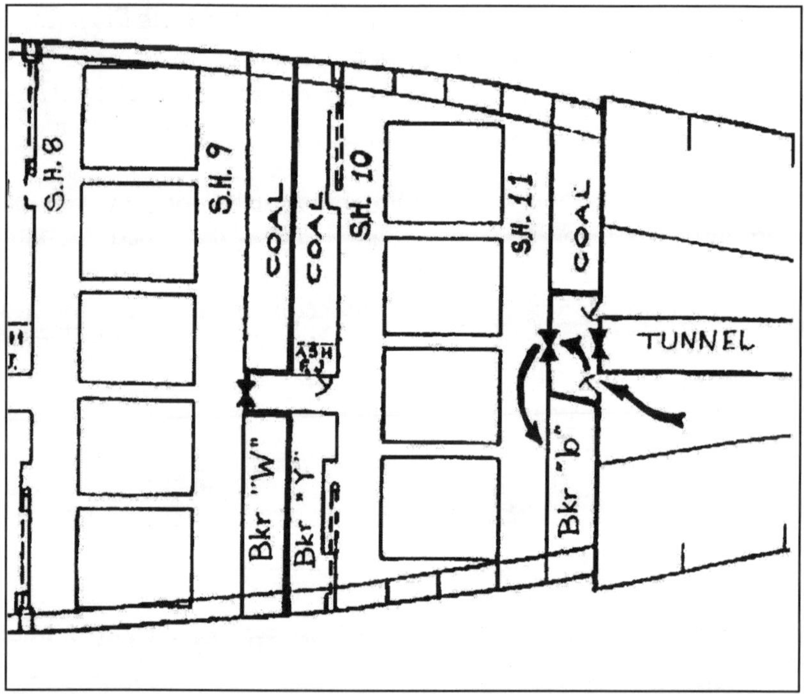

Figure 1-2 – Locating the fire in bunker "b" proves Barrett was in hold #3 when *Titanic* struck the iceberg. He ducked under a descending watertight door into boiler room #6 where he noticed an open seam admitting water into bunker "b."

Just then, *Titanic*'s side burst open and the sea poured in.

Barrett's story about the initial impact as pieced together from his testimony is quite simple. “Water came pouring in two feet above the stokehold plate,” Barrett said. “The ship’s side was torn...we sang out 'shut the doors' [indicating the ash doors to the furnaces] and there was a crash just as we sung out. Water came through the ship's side....Me and Mr. Hesketh jumped into this section and the watertight compartment closed up.”

The American record shows that he pointed to the boiler furnace doors when he said, "We sang out 'shut the doors.'" Barrett was correct in saying that the first thing done in boiler room #6 was to shut those doors (also referred to as "dampers"). Another man working in boiler room #6, George W. Beauchamp, was tending his furnaces of stokehold 10 at the after end of the compartment on the starboard side. He toiled in virtually in the same spot as where Barrett claimed to be standing when the ship opened to the sea.

Barrett: *I was in number 10 stokehold. The Starboard side.*

Beauchamp: *Number 10 (stokehold). The second one from the forward end.*

Both men claimed to be in exactly the same place when *Titanic* struck. One man said a torrent of water forced him to flee for his life. The other did not see the side being ripped open or water tumble into the compartment. Two men, two stories. Which man was correct about boiler room #6? The only way to answer this question is to compare their testimonies about a particular event that both men experienced and described in their testimonies. Each man recalled an order to close damper doors. Barrett yelled to shut the dampers and Beauchamp said he heard his leading stoker yell that order.

Barrett: *There is a clock rigged up in the stokehold and a red light goes up when the ship is supposed to stop... The red light came up. I am the man in charge of the watch, and I called out “Shut all the dampers.”*

> **Beauchamp:** *The telegraph went stop. The engineer and the leading stoker shouted together – they said, Shut the dampers."*

Titanic's steel bulkheads were secured by cast steel watertight doors. No human voice could not have penetrated from one boiler room to another. Beauchamp was in boiler room #6 at the moment of impact and did not leave for another 20 minutes until the furnaces were raked. Yet, he heard his leading stoker yell to shut the dampers. This proves Barrett was also in #6 when he shouted the damper order. Barrett did not duck into #5 to escape flooding in boiler room #6.

He was in #6 all along.

Barrett demonstrated his confusion in the second half of his answer to British inquiry question 1926. He stated that immediately after impact engineer Hesketh sent everyone to their stations. "My station was in the next boiler room," Barrett said, implying he was in #5 at the time. The stoker then recalled, "Mr. Shepherd and I went up an escape and down into the boiler room, but we could not get in. There were eight feet of water in it."

Nobody doubts that he and engineer John Shepherd went back to boiler room #6, but not until 30 minutes later. Those eight feet of water in boiler room #6 eventually became real, but they were not there when Barrett ordered Beauchamp to shut the dampers. If the leading stoker had been correct about #6 flooding almost instantly after the iceberg, then Beauchamp would have needed a snorkel to breathe as he raked down his furnaces. In reality, clearing coals out of the furnaces in boiler room #6 was completed without the hindrance of flooding.

Indisputable proof #6 stayed functionally dry came from steam screeching out of a pipe on the first funnel. This was steam from the four boilers of #6. It started to roar into the night air about 20 minutes after the iceberg. If water had been eight feet deep immediately after impact as Barrett suggested those boilers would have been as cold as the Atlantic Ocean. There would have been no steam in them to shoot out of the vent pipe. The booming steam was proof that 20 minutes were missing from Barrett's memory. That missing time was needed for Beauchamp to rake down his fires.

The cause of Barrett's confusion was most likely simple fright. He and Hesketh had been in the bunker below hold #3 when the ship struck. The scream of tortured metal filled their ears as they saw the hull rip open and water spurt through. In fear for their lives, the two men ducked beneath the closing watertight door into boiler room #6.

Safe from the iceberg in boiler room #6, Hesketh immediately ordered men there back to their stations. In his confusion Barrett mistakenly believed Hesketh was ordering men who escaped from boiler room #6 into #5 to go back to their work. In fact, it was the traditional first order of any officer facing an unexpected situation. Some stokers were undoubtedly enjoying a cool, dark spot away from their furnaces as a respite from the heat of the fires. Cooling off was permitted so long as the stoking and trimming was not neglected. Cooling was needed to prevent heat stroke. So, Hesketh called everyone back to their stations.

The stoking telegraphs went red and Beauchamp heard Barrett yell to close the dampers. These telegraphs helped control the firing of each boiler. This signal called for closing the dampers to reduce heat production and prevent building excess steam pressure while the engines were idle. Beauchamp then recalled a slight delay before the next action took place. "After the order was given to shut up, and order was given to draw fires. I could not say how many minutes, but the order was given to draw fires." Beauchamp's view was blocked by four huge boilers. He could not see the problem that caused this short delay.

Barrett came into the forward end of the boiler room where the empty bunker was located. He noticed water tumbling into the distorted metal storage area. "I went through this bunker here – it is a coal bunker – and then the water was rushing in. Pouring in the bunker," he said. Barrett shut the bunker door and reported the problem. Engineers took a few moments to survey his discovery.

Nothing was a bigger fear of shipboard engineers in 1912 than steam explosions. They decided to rake the hot coals out of the furnaces in boiler room #6 to end this nagging fear. It was a logical decision. *Titanic*'s system of bulkheads could be counted on to keep the flooding under control while steam was vented. Engineers undoubtedly expected to turn full attention to the rising water once the boilers were safe.

Eight stokers tended the 24 furnaces of the four boilers in #6. This was enough manpower under ordinary circumstances. However, with water rising beneath the stoker plates only eight men would have taken too long to rake out all those furnaces. Extra manpower was needed to speed up the process. Leading stoker Barrett appears to have been chosen to get a detail of men from the next boiler room aft, #5.

Boiler rooms #6 and #5 were "paired" to the #1 funnel. This pairing allowed the compartments to be joined by escape ladders and a metal grating walkway. Barrett could easily have gone up the ladder in boiler room #6, across the walkway over bulkhead E, and down into #5. After the sinking he confused his first errand with a second mission about 20 minutes later. Barrett and Shepherd were apparently sent back into #6 by engineers were beginning to work on the bilge pumps.

Some modern writers have theorized the bunker fire weakened the ship and caused it to sink. They base this supposition on distortion of the metal in the bulkhead. It came from thermal expansion of the hot steel, but was probably not critical to survival of the ship. “We calculate that the change in shape when heated would have been asymmetric diaphragm expansion,” says Dr. Timothy J. Foecke, a materials scientist in the metallurgy division of the National Institute of Standards and Technology (NIST). He has been studying large pieces recovered from *Titanic*’s hull and many of its rivets for nearly a decade.

“This would have expanded the wall by about 1/4-inch. It stressed the riveted junctions with the angle iron around the periphery, the horizontal rivets in shear and the vertical ones in tension.” Despite the heat, that small movement of the metal would not have caused failure of the bulkhead. Dr. Foecke is certain that *Titanic* did not sink because of the bunker fire. The ship did not sink because of the iceberg, either. Something else, something unthinkable went wrong. Before that could happen, however, a way had to be found to run over an iceberg.

Table 1-1
Location of Stokeholds Within Boiler Rooms

Bulkhead D
Boiler Room #6 Stokehold #11(fore) Stokehold #10 (aft)
Bulkhead E
Boiler Room #5 Stokehold #9 (fore) Stokehold #8 (aft)
Bulkhead F
Boiler Room #4 Stokehold #7 (fore) Stokehold #6 (aft)
Bulkhead G
Boiler Room #3 Stokehold #5 (fore) Stokehold #4 (aft)
Bulkhead H
Boiler Room #2 Stokehold #3 (fore) Stokehold #2 (aft)
Bulkhead J
Boiler Room #1 Stokehold #1 (fore)

Note: There was no bulkhead lettered "I" to avoid confusion with the numeral "1."

Right: This drawing of *Titanic*'s boiler rooms with bunkers identified by letters was contained in a reference notebook kept by the Harland & Wolff drawing office for quick reference. Obtained from the public archives of the New York Limitation of Liability hearings.

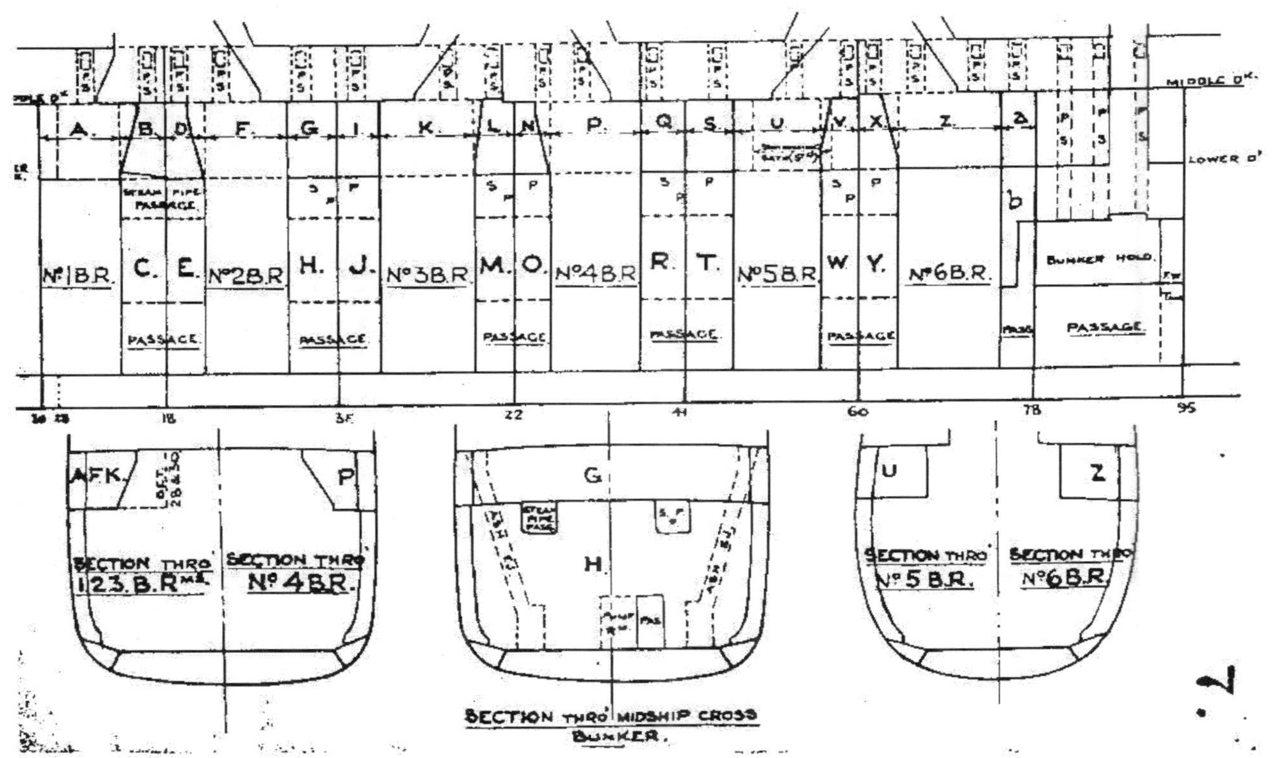
7.
MIDDLE D^K.
LOWER D^K.
N°1 B.R.
N°2 B.R.
N°3 B.R.
N°4 B.R.
N°5 B.R.
N°6 B.R.
STEAM PIPE PASSAGE
PASSAGE
BUNKER HOLD
SECTION THRO 1 2 3 B.R.^{ms}
SECTION THRO N° 4 B.R.
SECTION THRO' MIDSHIP CROSS BUNKER.
SECTION THRO' N° 5 B.R.
SECTION THRO N°6 B.R.

Table 1-2
Barrett's Actions Corrected

Running Time After Impact	Barrett's Location	Description of Barrett's Actions
(Before Impact)	Aux Bunker Hold #3	With engineer Hesketh examining oiling of fire-dinged bulkhead D
Impact	Hold #3 to Boiler Room #6	Barrett and Hesketh flee for their lives through firemen's tunnel vestibule and beneath closing W/T door into boiler room #6.
15 sec	Boiler Room #6	Hesketh sends men "back to your stations."Indicators go red. Engineer Shepherd shouts to close dampers. Barrett echoes this order and Beauchamp hears this command.
20 sec	Boiler Room #6	Barrett sees water entering bunker "b" and closes door. Reports situation to engineers.
2 min	Boiler Room #6	Engineers decide to rake down furnaces. Barrett sent to boiler room #5 for additional hands.
18 min	Boiler Room #6	Men finish raking furnaces. Water is coming over deck plates from bunker door.
18 min	Boat Deck	Steam from B.R. #6 begins to vent from funnel #1.
20 min	B.R. #6 to B.R. #5	Beauchamp and men abandon B.R. #6. Barrett goes to B.R. #5 with Hesketh & Shepherd.
22 min	From B.R. #5 to B.R. #6	Hesketh sends Shepherd and Barrett on errand to B.R. #6
23 min	B.R. #6 on ladder	Shepherd & Barrett find 8 feet of water in B.R. #6
25 min	B.R. #5	Shepherd & Barrett report flooding in B.R. #6

CHAPTER 2
DODGING ICE

The Big Myth: Captain Smith steamed blindly at high speed into an area of the Atlantic Known to contain dangerous ice and icebergs.

The Truth: Captain Smith carefully plotted ice warnings received by wireless and made at least two attempts to go around the ice on the night of the accident.

Ice concerned Captain Edward J. Smith most of the day and into the evening that fatal Sunday. He knew *Titanic* was approaching 50° West longitude where wireless reports from other ships were telling of field ice and icebergs. *Titanic*'s master dined with passengers, but excused himself early enough to be on the bridge before the ship got too near danger. Second officer Charles H. Lightoller recalled that after dinner Captain Smith asked about ice and the condition of the sea. It is probable Smith discussed the same issues with First Officer William M. Murdoch later when he took over from Lightoller. Unfortunately, both Smith and Murdoch died in the sinking so there is no record of what passed between them.

What we do know comes from Fourth Officer Joseph G. Boxhall who testified that Captain Smith requested help plotting the ship's position. "A near as I can remember I went to the chartroom with the Captain, but the Captain put down the star position when I gave it him, somewhere about 10 o'clock. He put the position on, and I was standing close to him, but I did not take that much notice whether any other positions were put on or not," recalled Boxhall. If those "other positions" existed, they could only have been the coordinates of ice contained in reports received from other ships by wireless. In the middle of the Atlantic ocean where *Titanic* steamed there are no islands, no unexpected shoals. There was nothing of importance to plot except ice.

Modern captains often draw their ship's track on a chart and place neat "X" marks at locations of reported dangers. It is relatively easy to compare a graphical representation of ship's track plotted against reported dangers. The human mind rebels against forming a mental picture based on a string of abstract latitude and longitude coordinates. Even so, graphical plotting was not standard practice during long, mid-ocean passages in 1912. In *Titanic*'s era latitude and longitude were calculated mathematically and the ship's position was normally plotted on a chart only once every four hours at the end of the watch.

"We do not use a chart," Fifth Officer Harold G. Lowe freely admitted when he described the 1912 practice of navigation to the U.S. Senate inquiry. "If we wish to place the position on a chart so that we may know the locality we may do so, because we have charts there. But, we work them out by tables and other things, books. We work out the positions." Until Captain Smith returned from dinner on that fateful Sunday evening, *Titanic* had been navigated "by the numbers" in the time-honored fashion described by Lowe.

The Myth: Captain Smith blindly ignored ice warnings received by wireless prior to the accident.

The Truth: Captain Smith was aware of the ice and demonstrated his concern by consulting about the danger with his boss, J. Bruce Ismay.

Captain Smith's occupation with ice warnings that Sunday was demonstrated by his handing of the famous ice message given to J. Bruce Ismay, managing director of the White Star Line. The shipping line executive showed this message to passengers throughout the day and evening until shortly before dinner. Twilight was ending as Captain Smith quietly sought out Ismay to request the return of the ice warning.

"I was sitting in the smoking room when Captain Smith happened to come into the room for some reason—what it was I do not know—and on his way back he happened to see me sitting there," recalled Ismay. Regardless of how innocent Ismay tried to make the captain's actions appear, the shipping line executive clearly recognized the reason for Smith's appearance in an enclave reserved for first class men. *Titanic*'s master came to the smoking room with the specific purpose of retrieving that ice warning so it could be posted on the bridge.

"By the way, sir," Smith asked of Ismay. "Have you got that telegram which I gave you this afternoon?"

"Yes," Ismay said reaching into his pocket. "Here it is." Smith nodded as he accepted the paper, telling Ismay, "I want to put it up in the officers chart room."

The Ismay ice warning affair has been wrongly elevated to mythical proof of Captain Smith's cavalier attitude toward ice warnings. Not so. In the social context of 1912 the exact opposite was more likely true. Smith would not have bothered his employer with trivial matters. By sharing the Marconigram ice warning with Ismay, the captain emphasized the danger. Ismay indicated he understood the importance of the message by returning it at the captain's request. In the end, this warning was posted in the ship's chartroom by 7:30 PM.

After dinner with passengers, Captain Smith returned to his bridge about half an hour before Second Officer Lightoller exchanged with First Officer William M. Murdoch. Change of watch for the senior officers was the best opportunity for Captain Smith to update himself about the existing situation and to discuss plans for navigating through the ice they expected to encounter.

"Not much wind," *Titanic*'s master said as he approached Second Officer Lightoller on the exposed bridge wing.

"No, it is a flat calm, as a matter of fact."

"A flat calm."

"Yes, quite flat. There is no wind. It's a pity we don't have a breeze while going through the ice," Lightoller said. Both men knew that without a breeze there would be no breaking waves against the bases of floating icebergs. The lack of foam from those breakers would make the dark bergs harder to spot.

"It seems quite clear."

"Yes, perfectly clear."

Smith must have felt the night chill all the more after the warm camaraderie of his dinner party. His comment about the freezing temperature brought a quick response from the second officer.

"Yes, it is very cold, sir," Lightoller agreed. "I've sent word down to the carpenter and rung up the engine room and told them it is freezing, or will be during the night."

The conversation on *Titanic*'s bridge as recalled by Lightoller seems lifeless by comparison to the dialogues in Hollywood films. However, anyone who has been there recognizes this as the sort of talk that really occurs on a darkened bridge. The men undoubtedly stood on the starboard bridge wing in keeping with tradition.

The starboard side had been reserved for officers ever since the 1860s when the *Rules of the Road* were promulgated to prevent collisions among steamships. Those *Rules* require steamships to give way to other power-driven vessels crossing from their starboard side. It became necessary for officers to have a clear view to their right. This resulted in the starboard side being reserved for officers while ordinary seamen were relegated to the port side as much as possible.[2-1]

Smith's last comment to Lightoller was that he would be "just inside" if needed. This remark has been twisted into a myth that claims the captain went inside to take a snooze. However, the myth makers have ignored that *Titanic*'s captain was supplied with a suite which included a bath, bedroom, sitting room, and a combination chartroom and office. His suite was entered directly through the master's private navigation office from the wheelhouse. The phrase "just inside" used by the captain quite obviously meant in the chartroom. According to Boxhall, Smith never got farther inside than his chart table that night.

The Myth: Captain Smith went into his cabin to snooze while *Titanic* raced toward its doom.

The Truth: Captain Smith went "just inside" to plot his ship's position against the reports of icebergs received by wireless.

On his way inside the captain grabbed Fourth Officer to assist at the chart table. "I saw the captain frequently during the watch," Boxhall said. "Up to the time of the accident. I was in the chart room working out positions, most of the evening, working navigation." A captain deeply concerned with navigation directly contradicts the popular myths that Smith either ignored ice warnings or dozed while Titanic raced toward disaster. The truth is that E.J. Smith was both wide awake and deeply involved with the safety of his ship. He did not succeed, but failure does not change the purpose of the work.

Titanic's officers might have spoken more freely about how and why their ship ran into the iceberg except for the threat of avaricious court proceedings. Fear of lawsuits was not as great in 1912 as today, but the ship's surviving officers (especially Fourth Officer Boxhall) were well aware that anything they said could have been used to obtain liability judgments against their employer, White Star Line.

First Officer Lightoller famously admitted in his autobiography that surviving officers applied "whitewash" during the two official inquiries into the sinking. Although he gave no additional details in public, he apparently spoke freely to his wife, Sylvia. In the fall of 2010 his granddaughter and novelist, Louise Patten, revealed family secrets. She claimed Lightoller believed the ship's quartermaster made a steering mistake that led to the accident. He also said that the iceberg had been spotted several minutes ahead of impact, not the 37 to 50 seconds of the conventional myth. And, he blamed the sinking on an order from Bruce Ismay to Captain Smith to start the wounded ship's engines and begin moving again.

In his "whitewash" comment Lightoller did not name the ship's fourth officer as one of the painters. However, Boxhall was the only officer who admitted lying under oath to the British inquiry. Boxhall first denied ever seeing a particular ice message. Later, he was forced to admit that not only did he see the memo, he actually wrote it with his own hand before posting it in the officers' chartroom.

The fourth officer was also less than candid in testimony about keeping track of the ship's position by updating the dead reckoning. Navigation was one of his primary duties as a junior officer. Even so, Boxhall said, "I cannot say that I had paid any particular attention to the ship's position that night." This was an astounding claim by a man whose primary job within the team of officers was to keep track of the ship's position. He might as well have claimed to not remember the name of Captain Smith. The fourth officer had the temerity to claim that his navigational duties got in the way of knowing the ship's position. “I had been too busy working it out, and I did not look it out on the chart.”

Truth is Boxhall did pay particular attention to the ship’s pre-accident position and he admitted as much under oath. “The 7:30 position,” he said referring to The second officer’s round of twilight star sights. “I had the 7:30 position in my work book. I had used that same position two or three times...between 10 o’clock and the time of the collision, for the purpose of working up stellar deviations...checking the compass error.”

Boxhall's perjury about the ship’s position allowed him to make the even more astounding claim that did not know *Titanic* was near ice mentioned in wireless reports. “I did not realize the ship was so near the region of the ice,” he said. Boxhall defended this amazing claim by saying he did not look at the pencil marks on the chart where Captain Smith plotted ice reports that night.

His argument implied he was unable to compare two sets of coordinates in his head. This would have been a disqualifying disability for any navigator in 1912. Remember, Lowe confirmed geographic coordinates were normally computed, not plotted. Officers did not routinely use charts. Boxhall’s self-proclaimed incompetent memory somehow escaped the attention of either the U.S. or British inquiry.

The Myth: Captain Smith’s failure to slow *Titanic*’s speed or post additional lookouts resulted in the fatal accident.

The Truth: Captain Smith intended to go around the ice at a wide margin, so more lookouts were not needed. Slowing the ship was also unnecessary.

The best legal defense against a charge of negligence is to prove the ship was following the ordinary practices of seaman at the time of the accident. If normal practice results in tens of thousands of safe voyages, then following it cannot be “negligent” even if one occasion results in an accident. Standard practice in 1912 was for high-speed Royal Mail Steamships to maintain maximum speed even after ice was spotted. Instead of slowing down, captains expected to steer safely around icebergs as they became visible. Although proven dangerous by

Titanic, this procedure was normal practice and, therefore, not negligent.

This 1912 approach to ice would be foolhardy today because we know *Titanic*'s sad outcome. On that April night, however, the ordinary practice of seamen had fallen behind technology. Radio communications were not yet factored into procedures for avoiding ice. Prior to wireless generations of captains had no useful knowledge about ice across their paths. The only available information came from other ships after they completed their voyages. Those pre-wireless ice position reports were days or even weeks out of date. They were of little or no value in planning a safe trip. The only practicable way to cross the Atlantic was to follow published steamer routes until ice was discovered. Then, after assessing the ice for themselves, captains chose an apparent safe course.

A favorite method employed to steer around ice was similar to one used by coastwise steamers to round a headland. Coastwise ships steered for the "point" where the beach disappeared over the horizon. As that "point" was really the horizon, it moved ahead with the speed of the ship. The result was that coastwise vessels maintained a set distance away from the shoreline.[2-2]

A similar technique would take a ship safely along the edge of a floating ice field until clear water was found. This may explain why Captain Smith did not slow *Titanic*'s speed or to post additional lookouts. He did not want to get close enough to require either action.

One shipmaster who defended Captain Smith after the accident was Bertram F. Hayes, master of White Star Line's *Oceanic.* "I take precautions according to the weather," Hays told the British inquiry. In doubtful weather he said, "We keep an ordinary look-out, which is always an excellent one. And I personally stay round. We proceed at the same rate of speed. No alteration."

Despite his brave words, Captain Hayes was not on the North Atlantic the night of *Titanic*'s mishap. His ship was one of many laid up for lack of fuel during Britain's recent coal strike. Hayes' lack of personal knowledge did not stop him from coming to conclusions about conditions faced by the ill-fated liner. "Ice does not make any difference to speed in clear weather. You can always see ice."

Shipmasters were not the only ones to be fooled by the dangers of ice. The official U.S. Government text on navigation gave the subject total neglect. The 1912 version of *H.O. Pub. 9, American Practical Navigator, Bowditch* discussed subjects from compass errors to weather. It gave detailed analysis of ocean currents. But, the premier American navigational text published for the year in which *Titanic* sank had not one word about ice, icebergs, or safe ice navigation.

Why necessary ice information was omitted from the premier American navigation text is unknown. It was common for ships to run afoul of ice prior to *Titanic*. Apparently, the danger was not perceived significant enough to warrant coverage. Everything changed after the *Titanic* tragedy when a new chapter, *Ice And Its Movement In The North Atlantic Ocean*, was added to later *Bowditch* editions. The first sentence expressed the change in attitude forced by the loss of *Titanic.*

> **546.** Vessels crossing the Atlantic Ocean between Europe and the ports of the United States and British America are liable to encounter icebergs or extensive fields of compact ice... (*Bowditch,* editions post-*Titanic*)

In April of 1912 these cautionary words not been written and Captain Smith undoubtedly shared the pre-*Titanic* of ice navigation expressed by Captain Hays. Smith intended to come only close enough to see the danger, then safely skirt around it. As will become obvious, Smith's avoidance technique consisted of a series of small course changes similar to those done when rounding a headland.

Second Officer Lightoller told the U.S. inquiry that the ice field should have become visible sometime after 11 PM. He changed his story after he got back home. Lightoller told the British inquiry that it was Sixth Officer James Moody who computed that the ship would be up to the ice after 11 PM Oddly, Lightoller told the London inquiry he thought the ship would first see ice before 9:30 PM. The 11 PM time becomes obvious if we assume Lightoller used April 14th ship's time and 50 west longitude for the eastern edge of the ice field.

Bowditch Table 6, "Distance of Visibility of Objects At Sea," indicates a 60-foot tall object)about the height of the fatal berg(should have been visible at 11:04 PM from the crow's nest and 11:08 PM from the officer's bridge. The distances given by the *Bowditch* table were for full daylight and clear air. Darkness and other factors affect "seeing conditions." They can significantly decrease the range at which an object could be seen. Standing on the footplate of the bridge wing, an officer would have been able to see a hazy horizon at a distance of about 9.5 miles.

After the disaster *Titanic*'s surviving officers were understandably reluctant to reveal much about events leading up to the accident. It is obvious they also did not relish lying under oath. Perjury brings penalties of fines and jail time. Rather than risk these penalties it appears surviving officers simply avoided talking about certain details of that night. Failing to volunteer information under oath is not perjury.

Chief among those avoided topics were Captain Smith's two course changes to avoid ice which have remained hidden from public knowledge until this book. Had they become known in 1912, Smith's reputation as a prudent mariner would have been preserved. Yet, his officers remained silent and their captain's reputation was ruined by charges that he dozed instead of taking action for the safety of his ship.

The surviving officers had reason not to divulge Smith's two attempts to dodge ice that night. In legal terms, the captain's first course change was *de facto* admission that he recognized the ice danger and took action to mitigate that danger. This recognition changed any subsequent iceberg accident from a random act of fate into human negligence.

When Captain Smith altered course for a second time, however, he changed simple negligence into what U.S. courts often call "gross negligence." The second course change indicated that he still recognized the ice danger, but was satisfied to continue using the same failed remedy of changing course. Using a proven failed maneuver raised the accident to that higher level of negligence which might have exposed White Star Line to economic penalties.

A full discussion of Captain Smith's ice avoidance maneuvers is found in Chapter 3. However, the proof of Smith's two ice-avoidance actions has been hidden in plain sight for a century within the records of radio transmissions from the sinking ship. *Titanic*'s cries for help contained not one, but two so-called "CQD positions." These were geographic coordinates sent to guide potential rescue ships to where *Titanic* lay sinking. "CQD" was a code used by wireless operators in 1912 to indicate distress.

Titanic's Two Sets Of CQD Distress Coordinates

Initial Set (Captain Smith)
41°44' N; 50°24' W (Sent at 10:25 PM NYT)

Second Set (Boxhall)
41°46' N; 50°14' W (Sent at 10:34 PM NYT)

As early as morning dawn after the sinking it was already known that both sets of latitude/longitude coordinates were considerably west of the actual spot where *Titanic* went down. Maritime historians incorrectly dismiss the CQD positions as "in error" and, therefore, useless in understanding of the accident. They overlook the critical juxtaposition of *Titanic*'s two sets of coordinates and instead focus only on Boxhall's famous 41° 46' North; 50° 14' West coordinates which are about 13 miles west of where *Titanic* sank. Thousands of words have been written to explain this discrepancy. Up to now, no explanations have been satisfactory because the relationship between the two sets of coordinates has been overlooked. Historians have unwittingly hidden from themselves what happened on the final leg *Titanic*'s disaster-shortened voyage.

That final leg began with a scheduled course change late Sunday afternoon prior to the accident. It came at an empty spot of ocean known to 1912 navigators "The Corner." No buoys marked the spot, but this was where the westbound shipping lanes from the British Isles changed from a great circle course to the rhumb line for New York City. This course change was technical in nature and of no real significance other than it gives a time and place to establish *Titanic*'s position. No proof exists that *Titanic* passed exactly through "The Corner." Even so, it is obvious that when the surviving officers testified about navigation they assumed their ship passed squarely through 42° North; 47° West – "The Corner."

Quartermaster Thomas Rowe sang out the time when "The Corner" was turned. This time would have been entered in the official log book. Rowe testified "The Corner" was turned at 5:45 PM, Boxhall said he used 5:50 PM in his dead reckoning. While reconstructing the fourth officer's work I discovered that an intermediate time of 5:48 PM fits quite well. This is easily explained by the need to compute the ship's position mathematically. Forty-five minutes, or 0.75 hours, is unhandy for mental computations. But, forty-eight minutes is 0.8 hours, an easier number for mental multiplication.

Boxhall and Third Officer Herbert Pitman both claimed the ship turned The Corner "late." Historians who accept the men's testimonies *verbatim* usually assume the turn came about 50 minutes late. That would make it a bit more than 18 miles past "The Corner" at 22 knots. However, there is no historical basis for choosing 50 minutes. In fact, Boxhall specifically ruled it out. "I did not say 50 minutes," he explained to the British inquiry. "I consider that the ship was away to the southward and to the westward of that 42 North, 47 West position when the course was altered."

Boxhall feigned incompetence as a navigator by stating flatly he did not how far past the corner the ship had steamed. "I do not remember what time it was but it was some considerable time; the difference I make between my time and the time that was given in the book – well there was such a big difference that I considered it worth mentioning to the senior officer of the watch," he said.

Conveniently for Boxhall, three of the ship's four senior officers (captain, chief officer, first officer and second officer) died in the sinking. Only the second officer remained alive. Since Boxhall did not say he informed Lightoller, it was impossible to cross-check the truth of his testimony.

The Myth: *Titanic* turned "The Corner" late, putting the ship south of the shipping track.

The Truth: *Titanic* should have arrived at "The Corner" at 5:45 PM. The turn was made exactly on time.

Understanding why *Titanic* ran over the berg requires knowledge of the rudiments of a navigation technique known as "dead reckoning." Boxhall used this method to calculate the location of the ship between fixes. A "fix" is an accurate position gained by observations of fixed objects or celestial bodies (sun, moon, and stars). The last accurate fix for *Titanic* was a 7:30 p.m. round of star sights. "I had a set of stars handed over to me that Lightoller had taken during the second dog watch," he told the BBC in 1962. [2-3]

Between fixes, navigators use time, speed, and direction to estimate their location through the process of "dead reckoning." For example, a ship making 22 knots will be 11 miles from its last fix in half an hour. It will be 44 miles away in two hours. In modern dead reckoning a fix is plotted on a chart and a line drawn from it representing the ship's course. Marks are made along this line to indicate the progress of the vessel over time.

In 1912, navigators preferred using "the sailings," a general term for mathematical methods of computing dead reckoning positions using time, speed, and direction information. This mathematical system had the advantage of yielding latitude and longitude directly. They must be measured off a chart when graphical plotting is done.

Simple dead reckoning indicates *Titanic* made "The Corner" on time. Titanic's noon position that Sunday was about 126 miles from "The Corner," which would have been about 5 hours 45 minutes of steaming at 22 knots. Boxhall said he used this speed for his calculations. This is in agreement with quartermaster Rowe's testimony that the "The Corner" was turned at 5:45 PM. These facts simply do not support Boxhall's later claim that the planned course alteration was made late. To the contrary, it appears "The Corner" was turned precisely on time.

Lightoller's star sights were taken at 7:30 PM. Boxhall's daily work required him to compute *Titanic*'s dead reckoning for 7:30 PM and then compare it with Lightoller's celestial fix. That comparison would have shown exactly how far the ship was south of its intended track. This knowledge would have allowed computation of the direction and speed of ocean currents in the area. So called "current triangles" are a normal part of every navigator's day's work. Boxhall's British testimony about the number of times he used Lightoller's fix implies he made this routine ocean current computation. "I had the 7:30 position in my workbook," he told the British inquiry. "I used it two or three times after giving it to the Captain."

It would seem the only thing Boxhall did not do with the 7:30 PM position was remember it. Perhaps there was reason for the fourth officer's selective amnesia. If he had he presented those coordinates, all confusion over the time of turning "The Corner" would have been resolved. It should have been obvious that if any "turn" was made too late to avoid disaster it was the second course change Captain Smith ordered just a minute before the accident. Had it been made two hours, an hour, or even a half hour earlier *Titanic* would not have struck on its iceberg and its maiden voyage would have ended significantly happier.

Scanty data about *Titanic*'s navigation makes it virtually impossible to know where the ship was actually located at any moment that Sunday evening. Instead, we are forced to reconstruct the work Boxhall apparently performed (and then conveniently forgot) during the hours leading up to the accident. It should be noted this reconstruction is primarily based on what little the fourth officer and other survivors passed along in testimony. Reliance on these survivor accounts is fraught with danger. The men involved had enough time aboard rescue ship Carpathia to sanitize and synchronize their stories about the ship's navigation.

Historically Verifiable *Titanic* Navigational Data:

1. "The Corner" 42° North; 47°West. Turned at 1745 per Rowe, or 1750 per Boxhall.
2. Ship's course to New York from "The Corner" — 266° True (Per Lightoller). [2-4]
3. Ship's Speed = 22 knots (Per Boxhall).
4. Boxhall CQD 41°46' North; 50°14' West.
5. Smith CQD 41°44' North; 50°24 West.
6. Wreck 41°44' North: 49°57' West (Boiler Field).

One piece of often-quoted information not included here is the reading of the taffrail log instrument reported by quartermaster Thomas Rowe. The taffrail log trailed a "spinner" through the water behind the ship. It twisted a length of cord connected to an odometer mounted on the port side of the docking bridge above the poop deck. This type of instrument measured only distance. Speed was found by dividing the distance run by the duration. The patent log was reset once each day at noon and the ship's "day's run" recorded.

During the 8-to-12 watch quartermaster Rowe was standing a lonely vigil on the poop deck when the accident took place. "I looked toward the starboard side of the ship and saw a mass of ice," he said. "It was so near...about eight or ten feet...that I thought it was going to strike the (docking) bridge. as soon as the berg was gone I looked at the log and it read 260 miles."

Based on Boxhall's 22 knots and a time underway of 12 hours 4 minutes (this duration is explained fully in Appendix B), *Titanic* should have covered 265.5 miles from noon to the accident. The taffrail log read only 260 miles, a discrepancy of about 2% low. This is well within the expected error rate of all taffrail logs.

The Taffrail Log

14. This is a mechanical contrivance for registering the distance actually run by a vessel through the water. ...

15. Though not a perfect instrument, the taffrail log affords a means of determining the vessel's speed through the water. It will usually be found that the indications of the log are in error by a constant percentage and the amount of this error should be determined by careful experiment and applied to all readings.[2-5]

"I never depend upon the patent log at all," Boxhall told the British inquiry. This statement disqualifies Rowe's log reading for inclusion in a reconstruction of Boxhall's dead reckoning. The fourth officer explained, "I thought the ship was doing 22 knots. It was an estimate that I had arrived at from the revolutions." This means he used the revolutions of the engines for the ship's speed. Then, Boxhall confused things again by saying, "I had no revolutions that watch." [2-6]

In this reconstruction of *Titanic*'s dead reckoning I accepted Boxhall's sworn testimony that *Titanic* turned "The Corner" at 5:50 PM, five minutes later than Rowe recalled. I also assumed the turn was made "dead nuts" in the center of "The Corner" even though such precision was unlikely.

From "The Corner," the I took Lightoller's testimony that the ship took a course of 266° toward Nantucket Lightship outside New York. This this track line does not cross either set of *Titanic*'s CQD coordinates, nor does it cross through the wreck site. All of those positions lie south of the 266° track line. Two interlocking inferences can be made from these observations, the first being:

1.) Captain Smith and Boxhall believed their ship was *not* on its proper 266 course to New York.

If *Titanic* had been steaming along its proper course, then at least one set of CQD coordinates or the wreck site would lie much closer to that track line. Neither does, or at least not close enough to be related to the track line. This leads to the conclusion that *Titanic* was not on its intended track when it struck the iceberg and sank. The second inference is an extension of the first:

2.) *Titanic* diverted from its 266° course at some point prior to the accident.

This 11:30 PM April 14th course change proves *Titanic* did not speed blindly to its doom. It shows the captain knew about the danger and intended to maintain a safe distance between his ship and the ice field. This hard navigational evidence puts "lie" to the myth that Captain Smith did nothing to avoid disaster that night. The truth is he altered course one point to the south of ice visible on the horizon across his ship's bow.

By definition, any line linking two geographic positions of the same vessel at two different times indicates its direction of travel (course) between those positions. The angular direction of a line linking Boxhall's CQD with Smith's coordinates works out to 255°. This is 11 degrees, effectively a one compass point different from the 266° course Lightoller said the ship should have been steering.

In 1912 steering instructions were often given to the quartermaster in "points" instead of degrees. In fact, the card used in Titanic's compasses was easier read in points than degrees. Cards marked only in degrees did not become common until after World War II. A compass point is one 32nd of a circle, or 11¼ degrees. *Titanic*'s instruments allowed accurate readings to within only one-half degree. Quarter degrees had to be disregarded as unreadable. This is why the difference between the 266° course and the 255° is an even 11 degrees.

The Myth: *Titanic* made no attempt to alter course in order to avoid the ice.

The Fact: The two CQD positions when combined with its course to Nantucket Lightship prove *Titanic* changed course to go south of the ice.

Both Captain Smith's and Boxhall's CQD coordinates were "off" by the same amount, 23 minutes. Their common mistake was most probably caused by the ship's dual Magneta clock system being not fully operational (see Chapter 9). Midnight starting April 15th became confused with the "midnight" of crew time used to regulate the change of watch. Later, scholars would doubly confuse things by assuming "midnight" referred to the end of April 14th, 12 hours after noon, April 14th. In fact, the end of Sunday should have come 12 hours and 47 minutes after noon to compensate for the ship's westward movement (also see Appendix B).

Changing course at 11:30 PM forced the fourth officer to re-compute the predicted midnight coordinates for the start of April 15th. The course change pulled the predicted midnight coordinates slightly to the east and south. If the ship had maintained its 266° course, the midnight longitude would have been close to 50°25' West. After the course change midnight moved to 50°24' West.

The difference between the two longitudes is slight, but significant. Captain Smith's initial CQD coordinates of 41°44' North, 50°24' West were nothing more than the new coordinates Boxhall computed for midnight. Smith must have known that *Titanic* never got to these midnight coordinates. So, he asked Boxhall to correct them.

Hands on the Magneta master clock in the chartroom pointed to 12 o'clock when Smith instructed Boxhall to update the CQD coordinates. Steam was now screeching from the vent pipe. Even inside the chartroom it was hard to hear another voice. Not surprisingly, the men misunderstood how each used the term "midnight." Smith knew he had the ship's predicted midnight location marking the start of April 15th. Boxhall as officer of the Starboard Watch assumed that when Smith said "midnight," he meant the 12:00 o'clock crew change of watch which happened to be showing on the Magneta clock dial.

Following the sinking, the fourth officer was extremely close-lipped about any instructions he received from the captain. However, his numbers tell the story. Boxhall's latitude and longitude are “backed up” exactly 20 minutes on the reciprocal of the new 255° course taken by *Titanic* after the course change. Smith’s coordinates were for true midnight marking the spot where April 15th would have started except for the accident. Therefore, Boxhall’s numbers were for the 11:40 o'clock preceding real midnight, 0000 hours of Monday. Because of this reason, both sets of the ship’s CQD coordinates were thus based on April 15th ship’s time which never existed for *Titanic*.

Boxhall probably did not realize his numbers were in error when he gave those famous 41°46' North, 50°14' West coordinates to the ship's Marconi radio officers. Later in life, he apparently became aware of the error. During a 1962 BBC interview he tried to explain it away by saying, “When the captain came up I showed her position on the chart and she was just over 20 miles ahead on her dead reckoning.”

A 20 mile error is highly unlikely as it represented almost an hour's steaming at 22 knots. But, claiming the ship was ahead of its dead reckoning put the ship very close to Boxhall's CQD coordinates. It gave a reason why they were so far west. At the time of the interview the location of the wreckage was unknown. Today, we know the exact postion of the ship on the bottom and it shows *Titanic* was not 20 miles ahead. Rather, the ship was very close to it's dead reckoning position as outlined in this chapter.

The accident took place during the period of time when *Titanic*'s clocks were being adjusted from April 14th to April 15th time. Due to the ship's westward movement, Sunday was to be 47 minutes longer than 24 hours. The Port and Starboard Watches of the crew were to split those extra minutes equally. At the time of the accident the on-duty Starboard Watch had already retarded its clock by 24 minutes. The extra 23 minutes of the Port Watch would have required a second setback of the clocks after the crew's "midnight" change of watch. An explanation of timekeeping in *Titanic* is found in Appendix B..

Smith's coordinates corresponded to 0000 hours April 15th, which corresponds to 2447 hours in April 14th time. Subtracting 20 minutes from that makes Boxhall’s time of the accident 2427 hours April 14th or 23 minutes after the actual event. Those 23 minutes represented the extra time not yet served by the off-duty port watch.

Time of Boxhall's CQD Coordinates

0000 April 15th - 20 min = -0040 April 15th

-0040 April 15th = 2404 April 14th

- 23 min Setback = 2340 Crew Time

2340 Crew Time = 11:40 PM Recorded Time of Accident

As will be demonstrated, 2404 hours (12:04 o'clock) April 14th was the correct time of the accident (see below and Appendix B). It was equivalent to 11:40 PM on crew clocks which were retarded by the 24 extra minutes already served by the men of the starboard watch. Both of these times are the same moment expressed in different notations. They were the equivalent of 0302 hours Greenwich Mean Time (GMT) by which the ship's log was kept.

12:04 PM April 14 = 11:40 PM Crew = 0302 hrs GMT

Knowing the time of the accident makes it possible to reconstruct the dead reckoning that Boxhall failed to provide to either inquiry. After turning "The Corner" at 5:50 PM *Titanic* took a course of 266°. At 11:30 PM in April 14th hours (11:06 PM for the crew) Captain Smith made a one point course alteration from its original 266° course to 255°. This alteration took place at 41°51.4' North; 49°47.5' West.

The duration from 11:30 PM in April 14 hours to 11:40 PM in crew time is 10 + 24 = 34 minutes. At 22 knots, *Titanic* would have steamed 12.47 miles. This allows the dead reckoning of the accident to be determined. If Fourth Officer Boxhall had done the calculations, he would have come up with these numbers for his CQD coordinates:

Dead Reckoning Of Accident

41°48' North; 50°04' West

This DR position should not be misconstrued as the actual location of the accident. Rather, it is only where the accident *should* have taken place if there were no winds or currents that night. Such natural causes would have retarded Titanic's forward progress. It is more likely that the ship struck the berg a few miles to the east, roughly on 50 West is confirmed by the wreck, which is usually accepted at 49°57' West.

CHAPTER 3

DANCING WITH DEATH

The Big Myth: The iceberg appeared in front of the ship less than a minute before impact.

The Truth: Lookouts Fleet and Lee spotted and reported the iceberg six minutes before impact.

It was a macabre dance with death. The fatal iceberg was in front of the ship when lookouts Frederick Fleet and Reginald Lee reported it by striking their bell three times. Just over six minutes later Titanic had changed course, but the deadly berg was still directly in front of the bow. Only now it was at terrifyingly close. Fleet found himself shouting those undying words directly into the bridge telephone, "Iceberg right ahead." Titanic rushed headlong into a cold pas de deux that ended in tragedy.

Popular myth has the iceberg "popping" into view without warning. But, truth is stranger than fiction. The lookouts first reported the deadly berg by ringing their warning bell at least six minutes before impact. During the ensuing minutes the lookouts watched the ship swing its bow away from the ice field only to see the same iceberg they had reported earlier was once again in the ship's path. For most of those minutes between first and second sightings Titanic was safe from harm. Death would have passed harmlessly a ship length or so off the port side, but something changed at the last minute. Death did not pass.

The "something" that changed was undoubtedly maritime history's most ironic twist of fate. A second course change ordered by Captain

Edward J. Smith for the safety of the ship proved Titanic's undoing. This fatal course alteration was performed innocently enough by Fourth Officer Joseph G. Boxhall. He was assisted by equally innocent quartermaster Robert Hichens. None of these men actually saw what was happening in front of the ship. The captain remained in his chartroom. Boxhall's view was blocked by the massive second funnel. Hichens was inside a closed and shuttered wheelhouse.

The only man who could see everything was First Officer William Murdoch, but he was odd man out. Nominally in charge of the ship as officer of the deck, he had no control over the captain's decision to change course. Nor did he control the exact moment when Boxhall would signal Hichens to turn the ship's bow to the left. All Murdoch could do was squint against the freezing ship's wind and wait for events outside his control to take place.

In myth Captain Smith snoozed while his ship ran headlong into danger. If only this myth were true! The captain's peaceful rest would have prevented Titanic from disaster. Had the captain snoozed, the course would not have been changed. Had the captain been snoring, Titanic would have avoided that berg. If the myth of the nodding captain were true Titanic might have sailed proudly into New York harbor and this book would not have been necessary.

Unfortunately, Captain Smith was a prudent mariner not taken to snoozing in the times of danger. He spent the 90 minutes before the accident plotting the reported positions of ice across the ship's path. He studied his chart to identify the best way around the danger ahead. When the faint line of ice finally became visible he twice took action to insure the safety of Titanic and its people.

Conventional versions of the accident are based on a short interval – approximately 37 to 45 seconds – between the three rings of the crow's nest warning bell and impact on the iceberg. This rapid-fire sequence of events was implied by lookout Frederick Fleet. when he told Senator William A. Smith. "I struck three bells and went to the telephone and rang them up on the bridge." Note that Fleet refused to give even a hint of the duration between ring the bell and telephoning the bridge.

The American senator understood amazingly little about the sea and seamen, but even he recognized the critical importance of the duration between warning bell and impact. So, he asked Fleet directly to estimate that length of time. The transcript of the discussion between Fleet and Senator Smith makes amusing reading. The lookout obviously struggled to avoid specifying the duration between warning bell and impact on the berg.

Senator SMITH: How long before the collision or accident did you report ice ahead?
Mr. Fleet: I have no idea.
Senator SMITH: Would you be willing to say that you reported the presence of this iceberg an hour before the collision?
Mr. Fleet: No, sir.
Senator SMITH: Forty-five minutes?
Mr. Fleet: No, sir.
Senator SMITH: A half hour before?
Mr. Fleet: No, sir.
Senator SMITH: Fifteen minutes before?
Mr. Fleet: No, sir.
Senator SMITH: Ten minutes before?
Mr. Fleet: No, sir.

The senator abruptly changed the subject of his questioning, a common courtroom technique intended to lull a witness into being caught off guard later. Senator Smith asked about the meaning of warning signals struck on the crow's nest bell and the location of the telephone in the nest. After a while, the questions abruptly switched back to the subject of duration. Senator Smith left no doubt about what he wanted to know. There was equally no doubt that Fleet was not off his guard. The lookout still chose being a fool rather than telling the senator the duration between warning bell and phone call.

Senator SMITH: Can you not indicate in any way the length of time that elapsed between the time that you first gave this information by telephone and by bell to the bridge officer and the time the boat struck the iceberg?
Mr. FLEET: I could not tell you, sir.
Senator SMITH: You can not say?

Mr. FLEET: No, sir.
Senator SMITH: You can not say whether it was five minutes or an hour?
Mr. FLEET: I could not say, sir.

Fleet presented himself as a dolt who could not tell the difference between a five minute interval and the duration of an hour. Such was not likely the case. Fleet looked foolish because of his obvious effort to avoid revealing the duration between warning bell and impact. Even so, his refusal to cooperate could not hide the truth. Seaman Joseph Scarrott, testified in London that Fleet's implied short duration was wrong. Scarrott said that from five to eight minutes passed between the bell warning and impact.

> *...it was round about half-past eleven...I could hardly recollect the time; but I should think it was—well, we shall say about five or eight minutes* [before impact]*; it seemed to me about that time.*[3-1]
>
> Joseph Scarrott
> Seaman, Titanic

Scarrott's simple and direct words destroy the myth that the iceberg suddenly "poped up" in front of the ship. Walter Lord got it as wrong in his 1955 classic book *A Night To Remember*. So did James Cameron 42 years later in his hugely successful 1997 movie, *Titanic*. Both men fell victim to the myth of the suddenly appearing iceberg. The truth is that the iceberg was not too close to avoid when it was originally spotted more than six minutes prior to the accident. History doggedly ignores Scarrott's estimate of five to eight minutes between Fleet's three bell strokes and the moment the real *Titanic* struck on the berg.

The Myth: The ship made a last-second emergency left turn (starboard helm in 1912) to dodge the iceberg.

The Truth: The ship turned left on starboard helm to avoid a field of ice, but resumed a straight course by the time of the accident.

Writers and film makers have also been fooled by another myth that goes hand-in-glove with the "pop up" iceberg. They put faith in a non-existent emergency left turn (starboard helm in 1912) because they think it was the best way to avoid the berg. Supporting testimony for this mythical emergency left turn from Fourth Officer Boxhall and quartermaster Hichens. Both men were adamant that a left turn (starboard helm) was done to avoid ice. The two men were deviously correct. Boxhall really did conduct a left turn and Hichens actually applied the starboard helm as they claimed. Titanic really did turn two points just prior to impact.

The devious part of their testimonies was making it seem the left turn was an emergency attempt to avoid the deadly iceberg. They did turn the ship to its left, but only as part of a second course change ordered by Captain Edward J. Smith to go south of the hazy ice field. Investigators and researchers with little or no experience maneuvering ships, but lots of time behind the steering wheels of cars, have swallowed whole the mythical "hard a-starboard" maneuver. A car or school bus could have sideswiped its front fender and then turned left to pull itself clear after that initial contact. By making a completely false analogy between wheeled vehicles and ships they have nourished an impossible tale told by Hichens and Boxhall.

One particular exchange during Hichens' appearance before the British inquiry illustrates how assumptions on the part of the researcher influence the interpretation of history. It came during the testimony of quartermaster Hichens. The conventional view of his words is that he put the wheel hard to starboard to steer around the iceberg.

955 The Attorney GENERAL: ... You had got an order, "Hard a-starboard"?

Mr. HICHENS: Yes.

956 You proceeded at once to put the wheel hard a-starboard?

Mr. HICHENS: immediately, yes.

957 Before the vessel struck had you time to get the wheel right over?

Mr. HICHENS: The wheel was over then, hard over.

Parsing questions #955, #956 and #957 shows the first two ask if the helm was put over immediately after the alleged “hard a-starboard” order. In response, Hichens properly replied it had. After all, he did turn the ship to the left by applying starboard helm in response to bell signals from Boxhall on the standard compass platform.

The bell system from the standard compass platform to the wheelhouse used to conduct course changes required Boxhall to signal when the ship was on its new heading. Upon hearing that signal Hichens would know what numbers on the steering compass to follow to make good the desired course. If the accident had occurred at that moment, Boxhall would still have been on the platform.

But, by the time the ship struck Boxhall testified he was already walking forward near the captain's quarters. The fourth officer's location is proof the course change had been completed and that the ship had resumed a straight course toward the iceberg. A straight-on approach to the berg is what lookout Fleet reported in his famous "Iceberg right ahead!" phone call.

It is curious that question #957 did not mention any helm order, port or starboard. This ambiguity allowed Hichens to say truthfully that the wheel was hard over at the time of the accident. In truth, after making the course change using starboard helm, Hichens steadied up from the left turn before applying port helm during the accident. The helm was hard over not to starboard, but to port.

The British inquiry helped twist the truth by linking this his agreement to the two previous questions about starboard helm. Subsequent historians have continued twisting the truth until it has been braided into the mythical emergency left turn of books and movies. However, careful reading of the testimonies reveals it has been historians and not Hichens who created the mythical hard a-starboard accident. The steering wheel in Hichens hand when the ship struck was hard over to port, not starboard.

Quartermaster Alfred Olliver was eyewitness to First Officer Murdoch's helm order as the ship rode onto the iceberg. He also observed what transpired in response to that order. "I heard hard a-port, and there was the man at the wheel and the officer...seeing it was carried out right."

Make no mistake, the two-point left turn described by Hichens (under starboard helm) was very real. He did not lie. Titanic did turn left two points to its left to avoid the ice field ahead. However, this real turn was not an emergency maneuver to dodge the fatal iceberg completed before the ship struck on the berg. And, Hichens was also correct in saying the helm was hard over during impact He had a hard a-port (right rudder) order from First Officer Murdoch.

The critical detail that Hichens and Boxhall deliberately kept hidden was that they completed the captain's second course change of two points about one minute before the ship struck. This non-emergency course change had been intended to turn the ship to its left, south of the hazy line of ice on the horizon. Instead, it was the direct cause of the accident. The emergency that became *Titanic's* iceberg accident was set in motion when this second course change was completed. To cover their roles in the disaster, The fourth officer and quartermaster used sailor's "sea story" license to transform Captain Smith's two-point left turn into the mythical "hard a-starboard" used in a desperate attempt to avoid the iceberg.

A half hour earlier they had obeyed Captain Smith's decision to alter course by one point (11 degrees) from 266° to 255°. That was done in conjunction with the 11:30 PM compass check.[3-2] Over the next 30 minutes it became apparent his first course change was not sufficient to go south of the ice field. So, the captain gave Boxhall instructions to make a second course change in conjunction with the next compass check scheduled for 12:00 o'clock in April 14th ship's time, or 11:36 PM in crew time.

The reason the two course changes were done a half hour apart is contained in the White Star line regulations. Compass checks were required every half hour. This meant they were to be done at least 48 times each day. Compass checks continued on their rigid 30 minute schedule even during the two hour period while the clocks were being adjusted to Titanic's anticipated noon longitude for Monday, April 15th.

As shown in Appendix B, the extra 47 minutes added to Sunday were to be divided evenly between the Starboard and Port Watches of the crew. This required crew clocks to be set back 24 minutes at 10 PM. An unintended consequence was that these checks no longer fell on the hour and half hour. The 11:30 PM compass check based on April 14th hours was done at 11:06 PM on crew clocks. The next schedule compass evolution was for 12 o'clock April 14th, or 11:36 PM on the crew clocks.

The Myth: Titanic turned left to avoid the iceberg.

The Truth: Titanic changed course to its left to avoid the ice and by doing so aimed itself directly at the fatal iceberg.

The irony of the accident is that it would not have taken place of Captain Smith had not ordered a second course change to avoid the ice field. This second diversion faced his ship at an iceberg that otherwise would have passed well of the port side. Hard as it is to imagine, Titanic was innocently, but deliberately steered to its destruction. This awful truth was what Boxhall and Hichens so carefully avoided mentioning in their testimonies. They did not want to reveal how they steered the ship to disaster.

As noted earlier, Boxhall and Hichens were not complete lairs. Both truthfully described Titanic's two-point left turn (using starboard helm in 1912 convention) before it struck on the iceberg. They simply omitted relevant details about it being an ordinary maneuver to go around the field of ice on the horizon. If they lied, it was by transforming this course change into a heroic but failed last-ditch effort to avoid the fatal iceberg. Boxhall and Hichens twisted the second course change into an emergency "hard a-starboard" iceberg evasion.

Titanic must have been on its new course when lookouts Fleet and Lee noticed their ship was making a straight-on approach to an iceberg. It was the very berg they reported a few minutes earlier. Obviously, the Boxhall/Hichens left turn and the Fleet/Lee straight approach to the berg could not have been the same event. A ship is either turning or it is steaming a straight course, but it can be doing both at the same time. The two-point left turn and the straight-on approach must have been two separate, discreet events taking place one before the other.

The mythical accident allows only 37 seconds for the ship to make a two-point left turn, steady up, and then go straight for the berg. This short duration between warning and impact is easily disproved by analysis of Olliver's situation. He heard the three strokes on the lookout's bell while on the compass platform. The ship did not strike on the berg until he returned to the bridge. The walk from platform to bridge would have taken Olliver at least 45 seconds and more likely a minute. His walk by itself rules out the 37 second duration. But, there is no reason to believe Olliver was coming off the platform when he heard the warning bell. He could equally well have been just starting to trim the oil lamps in preparation for a compass check. Either way, Olliver could not have gone from the compass platform to the bridge in only 37 seconds. It would just have been possible in 45 seconds, but that is neglecting the quartermaster's responsibilities of making a final check on the lamps and closing up the compass binnacle.

Scarrott recalled five to eight minutes passed between warning bell and impact. His estimate turns out to be reasonably accurate. Let's see how the time went. The series of events started with Boxhall coming out of the officers quarters door just as Fleet rang the bell. It took a minute for the fourth Officer to walk to the compass platform. Four minutes or so should have been sufficient for the compass check and course change.

After completing this work, the fourth officer took nearly another minute to walk forward almost to the bridge where he started down to B deck. Just as he started down the open companionway opposite the captain's cabin Boxhall heard three rings of the engine order telegraph. More seconds passed as Boxhall clambered down the stairway to B deck. While he was inside the stair enclosure he felt the ship strike on the iceberg. At a minimum more than six minutes must have ticked past between warning bell and the accident.

The iceberg spotted by the lookouts more than six minutes prior to impact was most likely the same berg on which the ship struck. If so, high school trigonometry shows that Titanic should have passed the killer berg with a safety margin equal to its own length. Boxhall claimed Titanic was making 22 knots at the time of the accident.

In 60 seconds between completion of the second left turn and impact Titanic covered 2,229 feet. Hichens told the British inquiry that the bowh had turned about two points, or 22 degrees before the accident. Trig functions allow us to approximate the berg was more than 800 feet (about the length of Titanic) to the left of the ship's center line when this two point turn was made.

$$\text{Sin } 22 \times 2229' = 835'$$

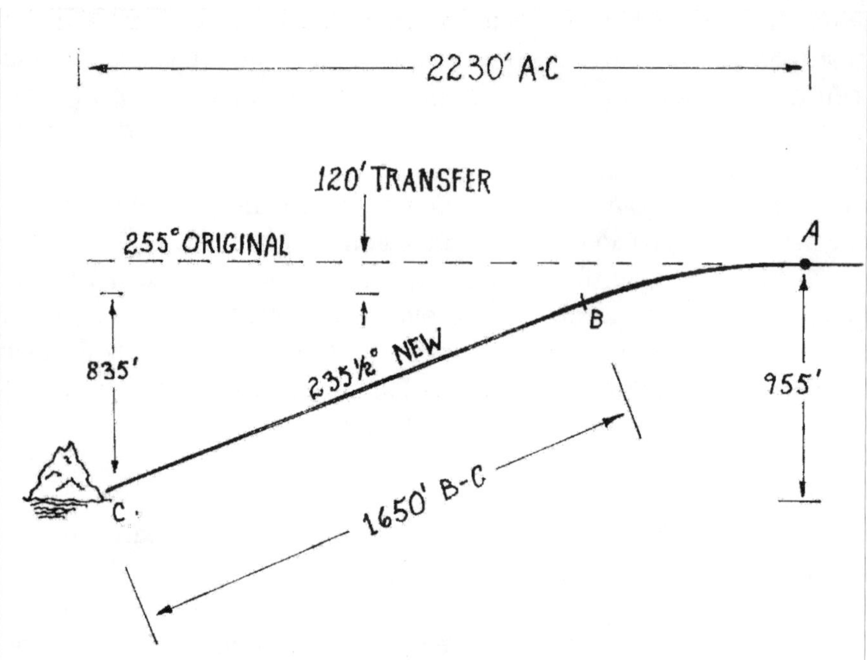

Figure 3-1 – A minute before impact *Titanic* was on course to pass the berg about 955 feet to port. A two-point (22.5 degree) left turn caused the ship to face the iceberg at a range of 1,650 feet. The berg was now "fine" on the starboard bow and unavoidable.

To the above 835 feet must be added the 120 feet of transfer obtained from Olympics maneuvering trials. This addition produces an estimate of how far the iceberg lay to the left of the ship's track.

835' + 120' = 955' left of ship's track

Titanic should have passed the iceberg safely to port had nothing else taken place after the lookouts first spotted their "black mass." If the berg lay 22 degrees to the left of the ship's original track at a range of 2,229 feet, the ice would have been 955 feet to port of the ship's original track line as Figure #3-1 shows.

This drawing also illustrates that except for the Boxhall/Hichens two-point turn the iceberg would have passed safely to port. There was absolutely no need to have turned either direction to avoid an accident. An experienced ship handler like First Officer William M. Murdoch would never have turned to the left for an iceberg more than 1/8th of a mile off his port side. Nor would Captain Smith have ordered his ship to point itself toward an iceberg. It is a reasonable assumption that Captain Smith, Murdoch, Boxhall, and Hichens all intended to take their ship safely around any ice that night.

Titanic became the victim of nothing more sinister than bad timing. Had the ship turned either 30 seconds earlier or a minute later, the accident would not have taken place. Unfortunately, Boxhall and Hichens performed the Captain's two point left turn (under starboard helm) at just the wrong moment. It was not their fault. None of the men involved in making that fatal turn could see any danger in front of the ship.

The Myth: The iceberg was only a few hundred yards away when it was first sighted by the lookouts.

The Truth: The iceberg was 2.3 nautical miles off the bow when the lookouts first reported it by ringing their bell.

Scarrott's minimum estimate of five minutes between the lookouts' alarm bell and impact put the berg almost two miles ahead of Titanic at 22-knots. The most likely duration of slightly more than six minutes pegs that distance at 2.3 miles.

Let us call Fleet's report of the silhouetted "black mass" as our "first observation" of the iceberg. To him it seemed to be directly in the ship's path, requiring a three stroke ring. What will be our "second observation" took place about 60 seconds prior to impact. This is when the ship turned two points (22°)to its left and steered straight for the iceberg. This second appearance of the berg caused lookout Fleet to make his famous phone call, "Iceberg right ahead."

Using these two "observations" and trigonometry it is possible to explain what happened. The ship's 255° track line effectively defines the adjacent side of two congruent right triangles. The larger triangle represents the first observation, while the shorter is the second. The adjacent side of the first observation triangle is 13,933 feet, or 6 minutes and 15 seconds minutes long at 22 knots. The adjacent side for the second observation is 60 seconds, or 2,229 feet.

In both of these triangles the side opposite is fixed at 955 feet, being the distance the fatal iceberg lay to the left of *Titanic*'s 255 track line. Titanic maintained a straight course between the first and second observations. Using the tangent function, it is easy to compute that the berg was about 3.9 degrees to the left of the bow at the first observation.

Tan = 955 / 13,933 = 3.9 degrees

An angle of four degrees off the bow would have been difficult for the lookouts nest to perceive at night. Darkness would have rendered the forestay cable invisible, depriving the lookouts of this handy reference for the ship's centerline. To them, an object 3.9 degrees to port at 13,933 feet distant would have seemed "dead ahead." The question becomes, "How far from the center of the ship's track would the iceberg have to have been for the lookouts not to have used the 3-strike "ahead" bell warning?"

Admittedly, any answer to this question is a personal judgment call. However, an assumption that one compass point, or about 11 degrees, either side of the bow represents "ahead" is reasonable. If so, then lookout Fleet sounded the correct warning. An object 3.9 degrees to port warranted 3 strokes on their bell.

Boxhall and Hichens said the ship turned left about two points (22.5°) before impact. They knew this first-hand because they conducted that maneuver. Trigonometry indicates the truth of their words. The second observation shows that when they made that two point turn, the berg lay at an angle off the bow of 23 degrees. Hichens steadied on the new course within sixty seconds of impact and Titanic started its rendezvous with death.

955 / 2229 = Tan 23.2

The math tells us that at about a minute prior to impact the lookouts would still have seen the iceberg 23 degrees off the port bow and passing clear of the ship. But, that is not what happened. Fleet did not see the berg passing to port. Instead, the deadly berg was once again in front of the ship at an embarrassingly close range. Fleet confirmed the new placement of the berg by reporting it as "right ahead" and not "off the port bow."

Myth: The iceberg was invisible because of the lack of moonlight and breaking waves at its base.

Truth: Sailors learn how to "see" dark objects at night by silhouetting them against a light background.

One nagging detail still needs explanation. The American navigational text *Bowditch* says it would have been impossible for the lookouts to have spotted an iceberg at a distance of more than two miles. The portion of text quoted earlier limited the expected visibility of icebergs to a quarter mile or less on a moonless night. Fleet and Lee should not have been able to see the berg at almost nine times that distance. How did they do it?

The answer is haze – a special haze visible to only two people: lookouts Fleet and Lee.

This special haze was not visible to Fourth Officer Joseph G. Boxhall from the compass platform. The air had the clarity of fine crystal. "Whenever I was on the deck or at the compass I never saw any haze whatever," said Boxhall. Third Officer Herbert J. Pitman agreed, noting, "The weather was very fine. From the time we left Southampton, perfect weather." Pitman could not remember any heavy seas the whole voyage, "None whatever. We had starlit sky. Yes, we had sky observations every night and every morning."

Despite this unusually fine weather the lookouts claimed their sight was hampered by haze. Or, Fleet and Lee saw something they later described as "haze" to the British Inquiry. Lee said it was "not so distinct" when he came on duty. "Not to be noticed, you did not really notice it then, not going on watch." Then, he added a caution. "But we had all our work cut out to pierce through it just after we started. My mate happened to pass the remark to me. He said, 'Well if we can see through that we will be lucky.' That was when we began to notice there was a haze on the water."

Atmospheric conditions that night were not capable of producing haze. None of the other survivors spoke of anything reducing the crystal-clear visibility. Claims by the lookouts of "haze" made John Charles Bigham, Lord Mersey, skeptical to disbelief. Mersey was the British wreck commissioner who investigated the Titanic disaster for the British Board of Trade. "The evidence before and after the accident is that the sky was perfectly clear," Lord Mersey remarked. "Therefore, if the evidence of the haze is to be accepted, it must have been some extraordinary natural phenomenon — something that sprang up quite suddenly, and then vanished."

Mersey's skepticism was valid. The night of April 14th was clear up until Titanic's accident. It remained clear during the sinking. The atmosphere continued to be clear afterward while Carpathia raced to the rescue. Meteorological "haze" obviously was not what the lookouts described when they employed that word. The Wreck Commissioner implied the word "haze" was a contrived defense by Fleet and Lee against charges they did not report the fatal berg in time. He was probably correct that the lookouts feared being blamed for the accident. However, Mersey was wrong about what the lookouts saw. There was a scientifically valid reason for their "hazy" horizon that night.

The night was moonless, but there was light. Clear air allowed a shower of light from the stars to fall on the North Atlantic. Starlight alone was not enough illuminate a distant iceberg, but it was sufficient to allow human eyes function at their minimal level. Color vision would have been virtually non-existent, so the men in the crow's nest could only have detected dangers using the more light-sensitive black-and-white receptors of their eyes. In the human eye these receptors provide peripheral vision. Sailors take advantage of the construction of human eyes by looking slightly above or below objects. This puts the images of those objects on the more sensitive black-and-white receptors in the eyes. Something invisible can become discernible by looking slightly to one side of it.

Fleet and Lee had been exposed to nothing brighter than starlight for more than two hours, so their peripheral vision would have been at peak sensitivity. They should have been able to perceive the dim loom of starlight reflected off of pack ice stretching across the ship's path. This phenomenon, called "ice blink," was documented by Royal Navy Captain William E. Parry as far back as 1821 during his expedition in search of a Northwest Passage from the Atlantic to Pacific oceans across northern Canada:

> BLINK.—A particular brightness in the atmosphere, often assuming an arch-like form, which is generally perceptible over ice or land covered with snow. The blink of land, as well

> as that over large quantities of ice, is usually of a yellowish cast.[3-3]

Titanic sailed 90 years after Parry, but navigational texts of 1912 such as *Bowditch* still discussed "ice blink" as a visual cue to the existence of ice at or beyond the horizon.

> 552. SIGNS OF THE PROXIMITY OF ICE.—The proximity of ice is indicated by the following-described signs:
>
> Before field ice is seen from the deck the ice blink will often indicate its presence. On a clear day over an ice field on the horizon the sky will be much paler or lighter in color and is easily distinguished from that overhead, so that a sharp lookout should be kept and changes in the color of the sky is noted.
>
> On clear nights, especially when the moon is up, the sky along the horizon in the direction of the ice is markedly lighter than the rest of the horizon. This effect can be noted before the ice is sighted.[3-4]

Ice blink is mostly a daylight phenomenon. Even so, Bowditch notes it can be seen on nights with a nearly-full moon. However, the navigation text does not tie the moon to night sightings of blink. Moonlight just helps. *Bowditch* also states blink can be seen "on clear nights" like that of April 14, 1912 which was as clear as any recorded on the North Atlantic. Full starlight was sufficient to produce a dim version of blink. This was most likely the "haze" mentioned by the lookouts. They did not lie about the hazy appearance of the horizon even though there was not a wisp of haze in meteorological terms.

Oddly, the lookouts testified they would not have sounded their warning bell if there had been meteorological haze on the horizon. "Certainly not," an indignant Lee told the British inquiry. "The officer of the watch would ask you what you meant by it," Lee explained. "He would ask you whether you were interfering with his duty or not."

It was the hazy appearance of the ice field that allowed Fleet and Lee to pick out the deadly iceberg at a distance of more than two miles. Bowditch was correct that the fatal ice was not visible by reflected light at distance greater than a quarter mile. Humans normally see objects in full color by the light they reflect. However, it was not necessary for the lookouts to see the ice directly in this manner to know it was there and to report its danger. All they needed was to catch its silhouette against the hazy background.

Sailors quickly learn another trick to detect objects at night. It allows them to spot dangers that are not illuminated by reflected light. A silhouette of a dark object can be seen for miles against a lighter background. Blink from an field ice across Titanic's path gave the necessary ghostly white appearance to the horizon. A dark iceberg silhouetted against such a horizon would have been detectable at a far greater range than the quarter mile specified in Bowditch. And, looking at the testimony from the lookouts we find that Lee described the classic situation of a lookout reporting an object in silhouette. "It was a dark mass that came through that haze and there was no white appearing until it was just close alongside the ship...," he testified in London.

An astute reader will note that *Titanic* may not have struck the same iceberg as first reported by the lookouts with three strikes on their bell. The two-point left turn could well have aimed the ship at a second and unsuspected berg lying about 900 to the left of the ship's original track. The result would have been the same in that this second berg would now have been dead ahead as Fleet reported in his phone call to the bridge. There is no way to know for certain whether there were two bergs or just one. I prefer a single iceberg simply because the sworn testimonies contain no hint of a second iceberg and trigonometry favors there being only one berg.

Lee saw the dark silhouette of an iceberg framed against the ghostly white blink from the ice field beyond. His use of the words "dark mass" to describe the berg is exactly how it would have appeared until about a minute before the accident. Fleet faced a problem. He had already warned the bridge of the looming berg. It would have been considered presumptuous on his part to ring the bell again. The telephone was reserved for officers to call the crow's nest with instructions. The lookout decided not to worry about embarrassing the officer of the watch. He would be presumptuous and violate protocol. Fleet picked up the telephone and seconds later uttered those famous words, "Iceberg, right ahead."

Reality Check

Hichens testimony about the accident does not follow the above analysis in specific detail. There is no doubt he intended the British Inquiry to believe that the "hard a-starboard" left turn was an emergency measure intended to dodge the iceberg. Here is the exact transcript of what he said in London:

943. Up to the time of the collision did she vary from her course at all?
Mr. HICHENS: Not that I am aware of, not more than a degree on either side.
944. Were there two clocks in the wheelhouse?
Mr. HICHENS: Yes.
945. Do you remember the vessel striking?
Mr. HICHENS: Yes.
946. Did you notice the time when she struck?
Mr. HICHENS: Yes.
947. What was it?
Mr. HICHENS: Twenty minutes to twelve.
948. Had you had any instructions before she struck? Had you been told to do anything with your helm before she struck?
Mr. HICHENS: Just as she struck I had the order "Hard-a-starboard" when she struck.
949. Just as she struck, is that what you said?
Mr. Hichens: Not immediately as she struck; the ship was swinging. We had the order, "Hard-a-starboard," and she just swung about two points when she struck.
950. You got the order, "Hard-a-starboard"?
Mr. HICHENS: Yes.
951. Had you time to get the helm hard a starboard before she struck?
Mr. HICHENS: No, she was crashing then.
952. Did you begin to get the helm over?
Mr. HICHENS: Yes, the helm was barely over when she struck. The ship had swung about two points.

953. She had swung two points?
Mr. HICHENS: Yes.
954. (The Commissioner.) Do let me understand; had she swung two points before the crash came?
Mr. HICHENS: Yes, my Lord.
955. (The Attorney-General.) I am not quite sure that I understand what you had done to the helm before this. You had got an order, "Hard-a-starboard"?
Mr. HICHENS: "Hard-a-starboard," yes.
956. You proceeded at once to put the wheel hard-a-starboard?
Mr. HICHENS: Immediately, yes.
957. Before the vessel struck had you had time to get the wheel right over?
Mr. HICHENS: The wheel was over then, hard over.
958. (The Commissioner.) Before she struck?
Mr. HICHENS: Oh yes, hard over before she struck.

There can be no argument against Hichens' contention that the ship was turned left on starboard helm prior to the accident. However, his assertion that *Titanic* was engaged in an ongoing left turn is indefensible because it would have created a totally different accident from the one which actually took place. As will be seen in the next chapter, the ship must have been steaming straight toward the iceberg at the moment of contact

CHAPTER 4
NOT A SCHOOL BUS

The Big Myth: *Titanic* might have avoided disaster entirely if the berg had been seen sooner. As it was, an emergency left turn almost pulled the ship away from danger.

The Truth: *Titanic* never wavered from course as it approachedhe iceberg. The only maneuvers came at impact and were designed to limit the amount of damage.

A heart-stopping moment in any darkened movie theater comes when the lurking iceberg finally reveals itself ahead of the speeding liner. The lookout rings the crow's nest bell, then telephones the bridge, "Iceberg right ahead!" The ship takes 37 seconds to make an emergency left turn which almost prevents the starboard bow from scraping against the iceberg. The continuing left turn then pulls *Titanic*'s starboard side away from the ice.

Exciting cinema to be sure, but all myth bordering on fairy tale. None of these familiar images took place because the familiar movie accident violates the laws of physics governing how ships maneuver. Science precludes the familiar sideswipe-and-pull-away myth. A school bus might steer around an iceberg like the cinematic *Titanic*, but not an 882-foot ship. Even so, the conventional myth prevails because portions are true and the majority of historians are automobile drivers with no shiphandling experience.

Ordinary people embrace the sideswipe accident because they are blinded by real-life experience driving automobiles. When they imagine the accident most researchers envision the way a school bus turns and handles on the road. Car drivers know to turn *away* from highway dangers. If a big yellow bus sideswipes its right front fender on a stationary object such as a utility pole, the driver turns left to avoid scraping the side of the bus on the pole as well. This "turn away" maneuver is based on the way a school bus steers with its front wheels. Turning the front wheels away from danger pulls the yellow sides of the bus out of contact with the pole and limits damage to the fender.

Alas, ships do not steer like school buses. Turning left while scraping its starboard bow against an iceberg would have been disastrous for *Titanic*. Understanding what happened starts with "unlearning" everything about driving on the highway.

A land vehicle points itself *toward* where it is going and everything else follows because it is steered by the front wheels. A ship steers by its rudder at the back end. This means a vessel rotates (sailors say it "kicks") its stern *away* from the destination. The ship's stern swings out at what is called a *drift angle.* This outward swing is never experienced in a car. Nor is the corresponding, if smaller, inward swing of the bow.

These inward and outward swings occur around the ship's *pivot point.* At slow speeds this point is located along the keel about one-third of the ship's length from the bow. As speed increases, the pivot point slides forward a bit. *Titanic*'s pivot point at 22 knots was probably just in front of the bridge. This location would have made the ship pivot almost below the feet of the officer of the deck. He would have had an easy time gauging the the hull's response to its rudder.

Like any large ship, *Titanic*'s size and weight prevented it from responding instantly to its rudder. Instead, the hull continued moving forward in the original direction even after the rudder was turned. This forward movement is called *advance.* Once the rudder took effect the hull began to pivot toward the new direction it would take after the turn was completed. The distance *Titanic* moved sideways in the new direction during a turn is called *transfer*.

While the ship is turning the pivot point describes the *maneuvering circle*. The size of this circle varies with speed and the amount of rudder angle applied. As the ship turns, its stern swings outside the maneuvering circle at an angle of between 5° and 10°. This is the *drift angle.* Because of drift angle, a ship can be thought of as skidding sideways as it turns.

The Myth: *Titanic*'s emergency left turn pulled its hull away from danger, limiting iceberg damage to the bow.

The Truth: They mythical emergency left turn would have forced *Titanic* to ride against the iceberg, causing damage along the whole side. The laws of physics do not allow the mythical left turn during impact.

The location of the pivot point forces the bow to swing inside the maneuvering circle while the stern is swung outside. This concept, that the bow swings inside and the stern outside is key to understanding why the mythical left turn during impact was impossible. If the ship had been under hard-over left rudder ("hard a-starboard" helm in 1912 parlance) the forefoot of the bow would have swung far enough inside the maneuvering circle to have escaped damage. Impact on the berg would have begun farther aft, probably in way of hold #2. From then on, outward swing of the drift angle would have forced the starboard side into ever-tighter contact. The iceberg would have crashed and bumped its way along the full length of *Titanic*'s hull.

That is not what happened. Actual ice damage done to *Titanic*'s bow was almost exactly the opposite. Survivors said the peak tank under the point of the bow crumpled enough to flood rapidly. Flooding from ice damage was also noted in all of the forward holds. But, uncontrollable ingress ended abruptly below the face of the bridge at the after end of hold #3. This real pattern of damage to the bow was exactly opposite to that of the mythical "hard a-starboard" left turn. The real pattern of damage is proof that at moment of impact the *Titanic* absolutely was not turning left to avoid the iceberg. The ship was not a school bus.

Although the mythical accident was impossible, it does contain an element of truth. The "hard a-starboard" (left turn) of myth would most definitely have produced impact. Several years ago Captain Charles S. Weeks and I performed nearly two-dozen computerized iceberg avoidance maneuvers. These electronic maneuvers were done on the full-size ship's bridge simulator at the Maine Maritime Academy. They took place over a period of two years with a variety of different people taking the roles of the real officers and crew. All but one of our simulations resulted in the ship running into the iceberg.

Upon the sound of three strikes on a ship's bell our would-be *Titanic* officers attempted to maneuver around an electronic iceberg located dead ahead at a range of 40 to 45 seconds.[4-1] Time and again the students smashed into the electronic iceberg of the simulator. Some of our would-be Murdoch's were briefed on the conventional story. They did marginally better than those who approached the problem "cold." One pair of students managed to avoid the berg on their first try, but could not repeat their success on subsequent attempts. In the end our simulator experiments proved the obvious – that a ship of *Titanic*'s size and maneuvering characteristics almost certainly could not have avoided an iceberg that unexpectedly "popped up" dead ahead 45 seconds before impact.[4-2]

Our simulations also showed the mythical accident would have produced nasty interaction between ship and iceberg. Even so, there was a major problem with our results. The simulation stopped the instant the electronic ship touched anything that in real life would be hard enough to cause damage. This includes the ocean floor, a seawall, or a floating iceberg. So, our experiments could only confirm that the mythical accident would have ended in contact between ship and ice. That much of the myth is true.

The computer was unable to produce data on the nature of impact or the damage done to our electronic ship. Fortunately, the simulator could print a second-by-second display of how the ship's course, drift angle, and other data. From these printouts we determined that the forepeak tank and even hold #1 should have escaped contact each time. First impact always took place farther aft in the area of holds #2 and #3. This is the "bluff of the bow" where Fourth Officer Joseph Boxhall accurately reported seeing the berg during Titanic's real encounter.

Understanding *Titanic* requires more than just un-learning automotive habits. It is also necessary to discard all conventional wisdom that is at odds with the real accident. The facts must be examined fresh to develop an explanation of events that matches eyewitness accounts of events. This explanation must account for how the ship approached the berg. And, this scenario must predict a pattern of damage in the same locations where it was actually located on *Titanic*'s hull.

The Myth: *Titanic* was turning to its lcft and had rotatcd about two points (22½°) when it sideswiped the iceberg.

The Concurrent Myth: *Titanic* just started to turn left when it struck on the iceberg.

The Truth: *Titanic* approached the iceberg straight on. The bow yawed to the left as the ship felt Newtonian pressure from the ice.

In Chapter 3 we learned how Fourth Officer Joseph Boxhall and quartermaster Robert Hichens created the "hard a-starboard" emergency left turn. From that grew a second myth that First Officer William M. Murdoch actually attempted to drive around the iceberg. An odd quirk about this myth is its internal contradiction. It claims *Titanic* simultaneously managed to do three opposed actions as it closed with the berg: 1.) it just started to turn to its left [Fleet and Lee]; 2.) it was rotating to its left after having turned left about two points [quartermaster Hichens]; and, 3.) it made a straight approach to the iceberg [Fleet and Lee].

All three of these opposing conditions could not have occurred simultaneously. Either the ship was just starting to turn, or it had turned two points. Alternatively, *Titanic* could not have been turning if it approached the iceberg straight-on. Each of these three options excludes the other two. These paradoxes disappear when the lookouts' overall description of how the ship approached the berg is accepted as fact and the starboard helm (left) turn is put into perspective.

Both men in the crow's nest would certainly have noticed *Titanic*'s bow turning left for 37 seconds before the accident. But they saw just the opposite. "We were making straight for it." Fleet testified before the U.S. Senate inquiry. He told Ohio Senator Theodore E. Burton that *Titanic* went straight toward its doom despite his three rings on the crow's nest alarm bell to warn the bridge. "you notice how quickly they turned the course of the boat after you sounded the gongs?" the senator asked. Fleet's answer was unequivocal. "No, sir. They did not do it until I went to the telephone. While I was at the telephone the ship started to move," the lookout said.

The phone Fleet used was a direct line to the wheelhouse on the bridge. Sixth Officer James Moody answered and Fleet uttered the three most famous words spoken on *Titanic,* "Iceberg right ahead!" His choice of words certainly did not describe an object that he perceived to be moving off to the starboard side because the bow was turning left. "Right ahead" meant the bow was neither rotating left or right, but rather pointing straight at the looming iceberg. In sailor terminology, the ship was maintaining a constant bearing relative to the danger while the range (distance) decreased.

It's axiomatic that a constant relative bearing combined with decreasing range means risk of collision. Sailors even call this situation a "danger bearing." An understanding of the importance of a constant bearing combined with decreasing range is so critical to safety that it is specifically mentioned in the Rules of the Road designed to prevent collision between ships.

International Rules Of The Road

Rule 7 Risk of Collision (i) such risk shall be deemed to exist if the compass bearing of an approaching vessel does not appreciably change...

Fleet exactly described a danger bearing as defined by the Rules. *Titanic* never wavered while the distance between the ship and iceberg decreased rapidly. Fleet's eyewitness account totally discounts the mythical emergency left turn to avoid the iceberg. There was no "hard a-starboard" maneuver.

...we were making straight for it..."

and,

"Iceberg right ahead."

Frederick Fleet
Lookout, *Titanic*

The visual pattern of ship and iceberg the lookout described — constant bearing and decreasing range – would have been completely impossible under the Boxhall/Hichens version of events which has thc ship turning left on "hard a-starboard" helm as it approached the berg. If the myth were true, lookouts Fleet and Lee would have seen *Titanic* slewing its starboard bow toward the berg for the half a minute before contact. The berg would have been well to port as the ship turned left to make contact. Yet, Fleet said without any hesitation, "we were making straight for it."

A ship can't be turning and going straight at the same time. What really happened? To find out we have to look beyond just what the participants said in testimony. Damage inflicted on the bow was indicative of the straight-on approach described by the lookouts. If the ship had been turning as Hichens implied, the small triangular void space known as the "peak tank" would have rotated inward and away from danger. But, it was damaged by contact with the ice. This tells us that in reality the peak tank rolled across an underwater outcropping of the berg and it broke open with a resulting loss of watertight integrity.

Note that there was no damage or water ingress above the tank in the forepeak compartment. This is telling evidence that the initial impact was not the mythical sideswipe. The accident was more like *Titanic* ran aground, only in this case the "ground" was the underwater portion of the berg.

Experienced ship handlers also recognize that an abrupt end to iceberg damage would have been a natural result of the ship turning to its right ("port helm" in 1912), or *toward* the iceberg and not left, away from it. No school bus driver would deliberately turn his yellow vehicle toward danger, but this was exactly what First Officer Murdoch had to do to protect both *Titanic*'s starboard side and its vulnerable wing propeller. Turning right, *toward the berg,* was his only hope to limit the damage by swinging the stern out of danger and carrying the hull away from the ice.

Isaac Newton wrote the classical physical laws that explain why the mythical accident never took place. Newton said an object at rest tends to remain at rest. Compared to *Titanic*'s 22 knot speed, the slowly drifting iceberg was "at rest." It takes a great deal of force to accelerate a mass that large. Despite its speed and more than 50,000-ton deadweight, *Titanic* simply did not have the muscle necessary get the iceberg moving. So, in accordance with Newton's third law, the iceberg "remained at rest" and instead "pushed back" against the ship's starboard bow with a force "equal and opposite" to what *Titanic* used to impact the ice. With contact on the starboard side, the ship's smaller mass deflected to its left. From the crow's nest this appeared the same as if the ship was turning left under its own rudder.

In myth the ship was under left rudder (starboard helm) when it struck. Newton's "equal and opposite" force would have caused a rapid swerve to the left called a *yaw*. It would have sent *Titanic* staggering somewhat violently (for such a large vessel) to port. Think of an eight ball caroming off the cushion of a pool table. Nobody reported a violent yaw because of actions taken by First Officer William M. Murdoch. He may not have been able to quote Newton, but hard experience taught him that a Newtonian yaw would swing the stern outward to the right, forcing the starboard side into tighter contact with the iceberg.

Even though Murdoch acted corrcctly to mitigate damage from this yaw, people who witnessed the accident still observed Newton at work during the acciedent. In accordance with his third law the lookouts watched *Titanic*'s bow appear to turn left while Fleet was speaking into the telephone. They thought they saw the result of an avoidance maneuver caused by the ship's rudder. "Well, she started to go to port while I was on the telephone," Fleet testified.

Note the Newtonian yaw started only after the ship began to feel the ice. Until that time *Titanic* steamed straight toward the berg. The yaw caused the bluff of the bow to rotate into hard contact with the topside of the berg. Boxhall saw it happen. And, he reported the ice that tumbled into the well deck from this contact.

As the ship approached the iceberg First Officer Murdoch contemplated what was coming. With under a minute to go to impact it was possible to see the iceberg was not dead center of the ship's track. Rather, it was now slightly off to starboard, "fine on the starboard bow" in sailor jargon. He did not have enough distance to steer around the berg. Some interaction with the iceberg was inevitable. His job now was not to prevent it, but to minimize the unavoidable damage.

Murdoch expected the bow to yaw off to port when ship and ice came into contact. And, he knew this would expose the vulnerable side and starboard wing propeller to damage. There was only one way to mitigate this damage. He had to do the unthinkable in a school bus. Murdoch had to turn *Titanic*'s bow to its right, *toward* the danger. He had to bury the bow into the berg even though this would increase damage in that portion of the hull. Crumpling the bow was preferable to opening the starboard side and wrecking the starboard propeller.

Myth: Murdoch reversed both engines. Instead of stopping in time, the resulting reverse thrust prevented the rudder from steering *Titanic* around the iceberg.

Fact: Murdoch *did not* reverse both engines. He reversed only the starboard engine in an attempt to protect that propeller from damage.

The enduring cinematic cliché of Titanic's two giant steam engines pounding in reverse is false. Murdoch never attempted to stop the ship as a way of preventing the accident. Do not blame Hollywood script writers. They did not come up with the idea that both engines raced in reverse. Rather, the myth that Murdoch tried to stop Titanic by reversing its huge triple-expansion steam engines originated during the British inquiry during summer, 1912. It came from Fourth Officer Boxhall who testified, "Full speed astern, ***both***." *[emphasis by author]*

Titanic sped toward the iceberg at 37 feet per second and Murdoch's mind raced with it. He needed to find a combination of helm and engine orders that would minimize the damage that was sure to result from impacting the berg. A familiar maneuver came to mind. It would protect the liner's starboard propeller and also warn the engine room that an emergency was occurring. In a flash of intuitive ship handling the first officer reversed *only* the starboard engine.

Murdoch's daring plan was not invented on the spot. He copied an ordinary maneuver used to get the 882-foot bulk of *Titanic* and its sistership, *Olympic*, through The Solent when entering or departing Southampton. One twist of that channel was too sharp for the super-liners to negotiate steering with their rudders alone. To get around the buoy the ships routinely reversed one engine while simultaneously putting the helm hard over. *Titanic* had done this split engine maneuver at a speed of 19 knots four days earlier at the start of its maiden voyage.

The ship had three propellers. Two giant 4-cylinder, triple-expansion reciprocating engines drove the port and starboard wing propellers. The center shaft was powered by a technologically advanced steam turbine. Both reciprocating engines were equipped with Brown reversing machinery. Instead of shifting an automotive stye transmission into reverse, *Titanic*'s engines were brought to a stop and then re-started in the opposite rotation. The center turbine only operated in forward, so was normally secured in harbors or other crowded waters.

Fourth Officer Boxhall had no reason to doubt he was accurate when he used the plural, "engines." He heard telegraph bells clang three times when Murdoch "double rang" to emphasize the importance of his order. Even so, as an old seaman in 1962 he told the BBC that Murdoch reported, "I'm going full speed astern on the port engine." Of course, in Chapter 3 we learned Boxhall was not on the bridge to hear Murdoch report anything. So, while the truthfulness of this radio interview comment is highly suspect, it does indicate that contrary to his 1912 testimony, the fourth officer knew for certain that only one of the reciprocating engines had been reversed.

Mechanical telegraphs like those in *Titanic* sounded only when the handles were moved to send an order down to the engine room. A telegraph had a dial with "sectors" each named for a particular action. Commands such as *Ahead Full*, *Astern Slow*, or *All Stop* were sent by moving the handles so a pointer window covered the correct sector. A bell rang only when the handle was in motion. "Double ringing" resulted in more attention-getting clangs because the handles were moved several times for a single order. Starting from Ahead Full, this was Murdoch's double ring sequence:

Ring One – from Ahead Full to Astern Full;

Ring Two – from Astern Full to Ahead Full;

Ring Three – from Ahead Full to Astern Full.

Titanic's telegraphs had two handles, one for each reciprocating steam engine. The same mechanical bell would have sounded whether Murdoch operated both handles or just one handle for the starboard engine alone. As shall be seen, Murdoch called only for reversing the engine and propeller in danger on the starboard side.

While maneuvering under engines, *Titanic* handled like a twin-screw vessel. In theory it was possible for the ship to pivot in its own water by reversing one reciprocating engine and going forward on the other (the ship's narrow beam would have made this a difficult maneuver). At speed, slowing either engine would cause the hull to slew off course. If the starboard engine were slowed or stopped, *Titanic* would slew to starboard. This was at the heart of Murdoch's plan. By reversing the starboard engine, Murdoch expected to slew the bow toward the iceberg and, consequently, swing the stern out of danger.

When the ship departed Southampton there had been a full crew of engineers on duty. Tonight, only a handful of *Titanic*'s engineers were standing sea watch. This smaller number of men was sufficient to make routine checks the two giant reciprocating steam engines and the other steam-powered pumps and equipment. With about a thousand miles to go to New York the smaller group of on-duty engineers was not expecting orders to come down from the bridge.

The first officer knew his unexpected order to reverse the starboard engine would catch the engineers off guard. To a great extent it did not matter whether they succeeded in reversing the starboard engine or not. Just slowing the speed of its propeller would have accomplished much of his goal. Anticipating some lag time, Murdoch issued his innovative engine order before any others in conjunction with the iceberg. He even operated the engine telegraph before closing the watertight doors.

Relief quartermaster Olliver returned to the bridge just as Murdoch was operating the switch that released the steel doors. In the movies it is attached to a board showing the outline of the hull and lights indicating whether each door is open or closed. No such board existed on the real *Titanic*. The real switch was located on the forward wall of the wheelhouse. Its location forced Murdoch to turn and face aft, away from the iceberg, just when his full concentration should have been on what was taking place in front of the ship.

Olliver was about to enter the wheelhouse when he felt *Titanic* to take the ice and First Officer Murdoch yelled the command needed to turn the bow toward the berg. "What I knew about the helm is, hard a-port," Olliver testified to the U.S. inquiry. "I know the orders I heard when I was on the bridge was after we had struck the iceberg. I heard hard a-port, and there was the man at the wheel and the officer. The officer was seeing it was carried out right."

In 1912 nautical parlance, "hard a-port" meant to turn the ship to the right. Put simply, Murdoch deliberately ordered *Titanic*'s bow to make hard contact. Despite his intentions. Newton and not the rudder was steering the ship. *Titanic* was bulling through "calf ice" that invariably surrounds icebergs as they break apart in 42 North latitude. The port bow tossed this ice aside like a plow clearing snow from a highway. On the starboard side, however, the calf ice became trapped between the ship and what was for practical purposes an immoveable iceberg. In accordance with Newton's laws of physics *Titanic* began yawing to its left.

"While I was at the telephone the ship started to move," Fleet recalled. His statement implied that the turn away from the berg came as the result of his phone call. Fleet's partner, Reginald Lee, was more specific, "As soon as the reply came back, 'Thank you,' the helm must have been put either hard a-starboard or very close to it, because she veered to port, and it seemed almost as if she might clear it."

The speed of response described by the lookouts was impossible for a vessel the size of *Titanic*. Even if the steering wheel had been turned at the start of Fleet's call, the ship would have taken several seconds to begin to turn. It took time for the steering system to react and for the rudder to pivot. There would have been additional delay while the force of the rudder overcame the straight-line inertia of the ship. To someone in the crow's nest there would have been considerable delay between the phone call and the rotation of the bow. But, they saw the bow rotate during the call. Some force must have been at work other than the ship's rudder.

The lookouts may have felt relief when the bow began to turn away from the berg, but quartermaster Robert Hichens in the wheelhouse was vexed by Newton steering the ship. Hichens' job was to keep *Titanic* on course no matter what. He had to correct this unexpected port yaw if he wanted to avoid a rebuke from the officers. That required application of right rudder which in 1912 was known as "port helm." Any good quartermaster would have begun moving the wheel by instinct, without being ordered to do so.

Up in the crow's nest lookout Lee had no knowledge of what Hichens was doing down in the wheelhouse. After speculating about why the bow appeared to rotate to the left, Lee added something that was not a guess. "I suppose there was ice under water," he said as an afterthought. With that statement he became the first person to correctly describe the accident as a grounding rather than a sideswipe.

Lee gained his first-hand experience about under water ice when the ship rode onto the berg. A strange motion surged up the mast and into the crow's nest. It was not the side-to-side whipping that would have resulted from a sideswipe of the iceberg. Rather, Lee felt the ship's starboard side start to rise up and the mast tilt to port. These motions were caused by the bilge riding over the underwater portion of the berg. "The ship seemed to heel slightly over to port as she struck the berg," Lee said. "Very slightly over to port as she struck along the starboard side. There was a rending of metal. You could hear that from where we were."

Contrary to long-standing myth, we saw in Chapter 1 that boiler room #5 received no ice damage and remained dry for at least an hour after impact. The dry condition of #5 proves false another myth about *Titanic*. The ship did not sink because water flowed over top of its bulkheads. If it had, #5 would have flooded to the top before any water appeared in #4 behind it. The opposite occurred. Boiler room #5 remained dry even while water was rising slowly in boiler room #4.

The most likely explanation for ingress in boiler room #4 is overlooked ice damage. Several anecdotal accounts support this supposition. Trimmer George Cavelle's story is most compelling. He was working in a coal bunker of #4 during the accident. "I felt a shock," he said. It started a small avalanche. "It did not have time to knock me over," he told the British inquiry. "The coal surrounded me before I knew where I was."

Passenger Hugh Woolner in the first class smoking room probably experienced that same bump. "We felt a sort of, not exactly a shock," he said later. "We sort of felt a rip that gave a sort of a slight twist to the whole room." Veteran U.S. Army Colonel Archibald Gracie was sleeping in his first class stateroom on the starboard side of C deck. "I was aroused by a sudden shock. I jumped from my bed," he said.

There are other anecdotes about water and chips of ice being sprayed onto the upper decks as far aft as the *a la carte* restaurant. Some passengers even reported small pieces of ice tumbling into port holes. George Harder and his wife were in bed as the iceberg passed down the starboard side. "We were not asleep yet, and I heard this thump," he recalled. "It was not a loud thump, just a dull thump. Then I could feel the boat quiver and could feel a sort of rumbling scraping noise along the side of the boat. When I went to the porthole I saw this iceberg go by."

Despite ice chips and water sprayed on deck from the passing berg, Murdoch's attempt to limit damage to the bow was largely successful. There is no doubt his actions protected the vital starboard wing propeller from the ice. His "hard a-port" helm order played a critical role in mitigating damage, but it was most likely his split engine command — forward on port and astern on starboard — that was most successful. This did not go unnoticed during the 1912 London inquiry. On day 12 of the British proceedings Second Officer Charles H. Lightoller was interrogated about a split engine maneuver by Thomas Scanlan, counsel for the National Sailors' and Firemen's Union.

14511 (Mr. SCANLAN)...Have you any way of changing the course of a ship than by the rudder, by the helm?
Mr. LIGHTOLLER: By the engines.
14512 Taking the ship going at full speed, or at a speed of 21 knots, in what distance could you turn her, if you put one propeller at full speed ahead and the other propeller at full speed or three-quarter speed astern.
Mr. LIGHTOLLER: No actual trials have been made to my knowledge with a ship traveling at her speed.

Lightoller was correct. Slamming one engine into reverse while maintaining full forward on the other was not a common maneuver in mid-ocean. It was normally an emergency maneuver reserved for situations like Murdoch faced. The one glaring exception to this rule was when *Olympic* or *Titanic* entered or departed Southampton. Lightoller never mentioned the routine maneuver of slamming one engine into reverse helped the ships round a tight curve in that channel.

For his part, Scanlan never hinted how he came up with the idea of putting one engine into full reverse while the other continued to turning full speed forward. He may have been privy to information obtained privately from crew members. Or, Scanlan may simply have made a lucky guess. Either way, he continued to probe the operation with one reciprocating engine in forward and the other in reverse.

14513 Was any trial made as to what you could do with the ship by putting the two propellers in opposition to one another?
Mr. LIGHTOLLER: Yes, I believe so.

Lightoller was not to be pinned down. *Titanic*'s second officer politely tried to take the discussion away from steering with opposed engine thrust. He switched to talking about a maneuver in which the engines were both in forward and the rudder alone was used to turn the ship's head.

14514 Did you as an Officer responsible from time to time for the navigation of this great ship know what could be done by reversing one propeller and sending the other ahead?
Mr. LIGHTOLLER: Do you mean the actual distance she would turn a circle in?
14515 Yes?
Mr. LIGHTOLLER: With the helm over I think she could turn in about three times her length.
14516 Does that mean with the helm hard over and one propeller directed full speed ahead and the other propeller astern?
Mr. LIGHTOLLER: No. I think that is with the ship going ahead and both engines going ahead.

Scanlan was not to be deterred. He came back to the subject of maneuvering using opposed thrust on the two reciprocating engines.

14517 Was it not important to find out how her course could be changed by reversing one propeller?
Mr. LIGHTOLLER: Quite so; it was done.
14518 It was done?
Mr. LIGHTOLLER: Yes.

The doggedness of Scanlan raised the ire of Wreck Commissioner Lord Mersey. Lightoller never got a chance to answer the next question. Mersey disrupted the discussion with meaningless questions about maneuvering circles.

14519 And, apart from the action of the helm, in what distance, by changing the propeller and putting one astern, could her course be changed?
The COMMISSIONER: Course be changed?
Mr. SCANLAN: I mean could she be changed in a circle.
The COMMISSIONER: You mean turned right round?
Mr. SCANLAN: Yes.
The COMMISSIONER: Do you mean turning half round or wholly round. Do you know which you mean?
Mr. SCANLAN: I do my Lord; I mean both.

Lord Mersey's pointless questions about whether "turned round" meant a half or a full circle were an obvious digression intended to change the line of questioning. When his tactic did not work, the head of the British inquiry revealed his true motive for interrupting Scanlan. Mersey did not want to pursue the subject of reversing only one of the ship's two reciprocating engines. Lightoller was slow to take Mersey's hint, so the Wreck Commissioner bluntly told him to "drop it," not once but twice.

14520 Mr. SCANLAN (To Witness): To turn her completely round on her axis so to speak, in her length, could she be turned on her axis by reversing one propeller?
Mr. LIGHTOLLER: You mean completing the circle?
14521 No, a half circle.
Mr. LIGHTOLLER: Sixteen points?
14522 Well, take it at sixteen points.
*The COMMISSIONER: I think I would **drop this at present**.*
Mr. LIGHTOLLER: I do not quite understand.
*The COMMISSIONER: **Drop it at present**....* [emphasis by author]

Mersey attempted to smooth over his interruption by saying there would be, "somebody else who will be able to tell us far better." His underlying intentions were not obscured by this verbal camouflage. The wreck commissioner simply did not want split engine orders discussed in his hearing room. He proved that by failing to call to the stand any experts with actual on-water ship handling experience to testify about a split engine maneuver. By forcibly ending discussion on the subject, Lord Mersey excised Murdoch's creative split-engine maneuver from the official *Titanic* record. The myth of both engines pounding in reverse became the accepted version despite being dead wrong.

Even so, the testimony of greaser Frederick Scott seems to lend credence to the myth that all of the engines were stopped prior to impact. "I noticed 'Stop' first," he told the British inquiry, speaking of the engine telegraphs. He went on to say that this "Stop" order came "after the shock" of impact on the iceberg. Scott was in the turbine engine room at the time. "I felt the shock and thought it was something in the main engine room that had gone wrong."

Scott's location was near the watertight door connecting the turbine and reciprocating (main) engine rooms. Still, he was not in the best of positions to see everything that happened. In fact, it became impossible once the watertight doors closed. He then left the turbine room to go aft to release a man trapped in the shaft tunnels. Returning to the turbine room he claimed that he heard the bridge ring down "Slow Ahead." This latter statement is doubtful since the engine telegraphs rang in the main engine room, not the turbine room where Scott was located. And, at the time the watertight doors were still closed.

As a greaser, Scott was not a highly skilled member of the engine department. It is probable that he confused the stopping of the turbine which powered the ship's center screw with the main reciprocating engines. This possibility is borne out by testimony from another greaser, Thomas Scott. He was on the electrical platform overlooking the turbine engine and, "about two minutes afterwards (after impact) we saw the turbine engine was stopped. There are two arms that come up as the engine turbine stops."

One man intimately involved in the accident never saw the iceberg that sank *Titanic*. Quartermaster Hichens at *Titanic*'s wheel was blinded by those shutters on the wheelhouse windows. Afterward, he seems to have harbored thoughts that the ship struck because of the port helm (right rudder) he applied in response to Newtonian yawing. He may have worried about being blamed for the 1,500 deaths which followed. Self doubt, if not guilt seem obvious motivations behind his odd behavior in a lifeboat later that night. Hichens shouted to other boats asking the name of the officer of the watch at the time of the accident.

Canadian Major Arthur G. Peuchen survived in the same lifeboat as Hichens. The major gave insight into Hichens' apparently guilty conscience. "The quartermaster was asking them who was on the bridge and they were calling over and they did not know which officer was on the bridge, and the quartermaster called out to another boat, to the quartermaster or who ever was in charge of the other boat. He said, 'You know one officer was on duty on the bridge at the time we struck.' So far as I could gather, the officer was in command of the other boat. He did not know."

Hichens apparently needed to reassurance that he correctly followed Murdoch's helm orders. He may also thought Murdoch's "hard a-port" order was a rebuke for not acting fast enough in counteracting the yaw just before contact on the berg. Either way, his fears were groundless. The quartermaster's instinctive reaction played a small role in confining damage to the bow. Had Hichens acted less instinctively, ice damage may have extended farther aft. We can only speculate, but it is certain Hichens was blameless for the ship sinking.

CHAPTER 5
KILLER GRAVITY

The Big Myth: The iceberg sliced a 240-foot gash in *Titanic*'s starboard bow, sealing the ship's fate. Water rose over the bulkheads until the ship sank.

The Truth: Water pouring over the bulkheads did not sink *Titanic*. Water did not rise over any bulk-head until after human error sealed the fate of the ship.

Titanic was not be burned up; nor did its boilers blow up. It was brought down by the force of gravity. It was the pull of gravity, not an iceberg, that created the damage in the hull. Gravity drove water through those holes to fill the ship. But, this flooding alone was not enough to sink *Titanic*. Gravity had to take advantage of human errors operating bilge pump valves to send a rush of water into boiler room #5. Then, as the hull lost buoyancy, the familiar force of gravity pulled *Titanic* beneath the waves.

Gravity was the killer. The iceberg and water were only accomplices.

Over the years people have come up with theories of how the holes in the hull could have been plugged to keep water out. Although well-intentioned, these theories ignore the reality that it is gravity and not water than sinks ships. It is not necessary for damage control efforts to focus only on keeping water out. A ship will float as long as its deadweight (the weight of the steel, engines, etc.) is less than its buoyancy.

Titanic's damage was confined near the bottom of the hull. This meant that water entered under a 33 to 35-foot head pressure. Water spurting into the ship under that much pressure is usually terrifying to anyone caught deep below the waterline. Fireman Frederick Barrett's confusion over where he saw the ship's side open up is fully understandable.

That first rush of water can also demoralize a crew's damage control efforts. At the beginning the ingress often exceeds the ability of the ship's pumps to remove it and sailors begin to believe nothing can prevent the ship from sinking Abandoning their ship appears to be the only alternative. Patience is advised. The more water pours into a hull, the slower the ingress becomes. Eventually the pumps may be able to save the vessel from foundering.

Afirst the incoming water meets the resistance only of air inside the compartment. Air is easily displaced. Over time the incoming water is slowed by water already inside the ship. The weight of the water inside begins to counter the head pressure of water outside. After the water level inside the ship rises to the outside level, any pressure differential disappears and water ceases to flow into the hull.

This is why even though the initial ingress may be greater than the capacity of the ship's pumps, the condition is not necessarily permanent. At some point the inward flow slows to match the capacity of the pumps to remove it. From then on, the water will not rise inside the damaged compartment as long as the pumps can be kept working. If enough buoyancy is stll retained, the ship will "float on its pumps."

The deaths of all members of *Titanic*'s engineering staff deprived history of first hand knowledge of attempts to pump water out of the ship. Only a few tantalizing hints are contained in the testimonies of men like Barrett. Yet, the true story of how and why the ship sank cannot be told without studying both the nature of the damage control efforts and any efforts the crew made to dewater the hull.

Titanic was not sliced open by the iceberg. The century-old nonsense of a 240-foot long "big gash" needs to be put to rest. Nothing remotely resembling a knife cut opened the side of the ship. A stiletto of ice (if such a thing could exist) could never have sliced open the ship because steel is stronger and more durable than ice. If this were not so, there would be no icebreakers and no winter cargo service around the globe. Yet, from Russia and Scandinavia to Canada and the Great Lakes ships deliberately throw themselves against ice that is every bit as cold and hard *Titanic*'s berg. Their success delivering the goods illustrates the strength of steel against frozen water.

Harland & Wolff naval architect Edward Wilding understood. "In New York, to which these ships run, it is no uncommon occurrence in winter to have to force your way through ice," he told the London inquiry. Even though what he said was true, the ship designer was disingenuous in suggesting ice "three or four inches thick" was the equivalent of an iceberg. However, Wilding was not discussing strength of materials. His goal was to show that Harland & Wolff considered ice operations in designing Olympic-Class ships like *Titanic*. However, sometimes things do go wrong. The great liner was badly injured by its encounter with an iceberg.

The Great Lakes are a good place to see the kinds of damage ice can do because ships routinely push through ice during spring and fall. The straight-deck bulk freighter *SS James M. Schoonmaker* was built and launched concurrently with *Titanic* in 1911. It was the world's largest bulk freighter at 617 feet in length and a then-astounding capacity of 15,000 tons of iron ore. The ship remained in service until the 1980s when it became a museum in Toledo, Ohio. U.S. and British ship construction techniques were virtually identical in 1911 when the *Schoonmaker* and *Titanic* were knocked together. There was one difference. The *Schoonmaker* was made of 1.125-inch steel plate an eighth of an inch thicker than *Titanic*'s hull plating. The extra thickness of the freighter's skin was needed to carry 15,000 tons of iron ore. A passenger ship never carries such a concentrated load of cargo.

Underwater rivets on both ships were set with their heads inside and the "pins" or "tails" on the outside. When bashed up tight, this riveting practice made the outside of the hull nearly smooth to reduce drag through the water. However, putting the heads inside the hull also made the tails vulnerable to ice pressure. Only a small amount of metal had to be dislodged to force the tails into the ship.

In the 1960s the *Schoonmaker* crunched through what was thought to be thin spring ice in Duluth, Minnesota. The ice proved thicker than expected. The result was sprung seams in the bow which had to be repaired before the ship could resume its normal service. In 2003 a former crew member visited "his" ship while I was also aboard. He related how after the ship pushed through spring ice men sent to inspect the forepeak found rivets pushed inward. Some were even pushed out of their holes in the bow plating. The damaged seams leaked, but the hull plating was not bent and remains in place today.

More recently, the present-day largest freighter on the Great Lakes suffered serious ice damage during its first trip of the 2008 season. The *Paul R. Tregurtha* is a 1,000 foot ship capable of carrying 68,000 tons of bulk cargo. Coming out of Sturgeon Bay, Wisconsin, the ship expected to meet less than 15 inches of March ice on Lake Michigan's Green Bay. Instead it ran into floes more than 20 inches thick near Sherwood Point. Captain Timothy Dayton tried to back and fill using hard right rudder. The effort was futile. Eventually an icebreaker was sent to open a path for the ship.

No one noticed the *Tregurtha*'s bow lift. There was no ominous rumbling and no sounds of metal cracking. The deck did not heave or twist underfoot. Even so, the crew discovered water spurting out of the ship at the forward end of number one ballast tank. The ship proceeded to Superior Wisconsin where the damage was inspected. From the outside it appeared to be no more than a broken weld in a seam. Inside the inspectors found a different story. A 10 by 56-foot hull plate was cracked and at least 7 frames were bent or cracked.

The experiences of ships like the *Tregurtha* and *Schoonmaker* indicate that when *Titanic* struck on its iceberg there was a high probability of damage to the seams where the ship's steel plates joined together. The shell plates of both Great Lakes ships stood up to ice. It was almost certainly the same with *Titanic.* The ship's side was not sliced open. The 240-foot long "big gash" was a complete myth.

The Myth: *Titanic* was opened by sideswiping the iceberg.

The Truth: *Titanic* did not sideswipe the iceberg. The damage was caused by "grounding" on an underwater shelf of ice.

Chapter 4 explained how *Titanic* approached the iceberg head-on and then turned to the right once contact was made. The truth is completely opposite to conventional myth which has the ship turning left as it sideswiped the iceberg. Even so, the sideswipe myth was universally accepted by summer of 1912 when the British inquiry began. Naval architect Wilding was asked if a ship of *Titanic*'s size could be built strong enough to withstand hitting an iceberg at 22 knots.

"It depends," Wilding said truthfully, "on the severity of the contact. This contact seems to have been a particularly light one ...because we have heard the evidence that lots of people scarcely felt it." He was then asked what would have happened if the ship had struck the berg a "fair blow," meaning head-on. "I think we should have heard a great deal more about the severity of it, and probably the ship would have come into harbor...instead of going to the bottom. I am quite sure she would have (survived). I am afraid she would have killed every firemen down in the firemen's quarters, but I feel sure the ship would have come in."

Two aspects of Wilding's comments are significant. First, his explanation of what would have happened in a head-on impact definitely does not describe *Titanic*'s accident. Even so, lookout Frederick Fleet was adamant, "We were making straight for it." His testimony was backed up by fellow lookout Reginald Fleet. Their words created an apparent paradox of a straight-on approach that did not end in crumpling of the bow and killing firemen sleeping there. Part of the solution of this paradox is that the bow was not pointed at the center of the berg as it approached. Rather, the iceberg was slightly off to starboard. In sailor's jargon it was "fine on the starboard bow."

Second, Wilding's description of light contact match the nature of a grounding of the hull on the underwater portion of the iceberg. Trying to imagine a 50,000 ton ship going aground on millions of tons of floating ice is not easy. The bow can be thought of as cone-shaped with its apex forward. But, what about the iceberg? We have no idea about the shape of the invisible ice beneath the water because it melted long ago. The berg's underwater configuration cannot be examined, but we were given a hint as to its shape by the lookouts who experienced the accident from the crow's nest.

Recall that Reginald Lee said, "There was a rending of metal," He added, "It seemed to be running right along the starboard side. The ship seemed to heel slightly over to port as she struck the berg. Very slightly to port, as she struck along the starboard side. You could hear a rending of metal right away. It seemed to be running right along the starboard side."

His partner Fleet was less eloquent, "I know when we got up to it, it struck our bow – a little of our bow just about in front of the foremast. She listed to port right afterward, a slight list. Just afterwards." Senator Duncan U. Fletcher asked if the "blow" came from beneath the surface of the water and caused the slight list. "Yes, sir," Fleet answered.

Steel is stronger than ice. *Titanic's* knife-like bow must have cleaved into the berg like a maul splitting wood. Splinters and broken chunks of ice must have been sent flying as the ship tried to carve its way through the frozen shelf. Some ice resisted and the ship began to ride up and over the underwater portion of the berg. Fleet commented that the list to port came "just after" the ship struck on the ice. A check of *Titanic*'s underwater shape reveals he was correct. The lifting would not have been noticeable during the early seconds. Only as the berg passed the foremast was enough grounding pressure generated to create the slight lean to port both lookouts described.

The forward portion of the keel angled upward until at the knuckle of the stem the bow drew about 15 feet less water than rest of the hull. The average draft of this rising portion of the keel beneath hold #1 and the forepeak tank was about 27 feet just forward of bulkhead A, the ship's collision bulkhead which divided the peak tank from hold #1. Both compartments were opened by contact on the ice, so 27 feet can be considered as the approximate depth of water over the underwater shelf or ridge of ice on which *Titanic* struck. If the ice had been farther below the surface the peak tank would not have suffered any damage.

A steel hull is surprisingly fragile. It can be easily damaged by unfair lifting of a small section of hull. This is demonstrated every time a large vessel is drydocked for inspection or repair. While afloat, the total weight of the vessel is supported by upward pressure of the water. This pressure is distributed uniformly over the entire bottom.

However, when a vessel is drydocked it rests on wooden blocks which focus the total upward pressure on small portions of the bottom. Textbooks on the subject warn mariners that considerable damage can be done if those blocks are not placed properly:

> The dockmaster must first obtain a docking blueprint or docking plan of the vessel. this plan tells him how to set up the keel and bilge blocks to support the vessel. The major weight is supported by keel blocks along the keel.[5-2]

> When a vessel is dry-docked...the total weight of the vessel may have to be borne by small portions of the ship's bottom. ...special cribs are placed at strategic locations, such

> as under longitudinals and under transverse bulkheads to take the load... ...most insurance companies do not permit the dockmaster to load the blocking over 15 tons to the square foot of supporting materials.[5-3]
>
> ...the dockmaster or docking officer first refers to the ships docking plan. This furnishes necessary information concerning the underwater hull for docking purposes. ...every ship should carry its own docking plan. During the period when the ship is in dock, no change of any kind in her weights should be made... Improper changes in weights may cause the ship to do serious damage to herself. [5-4]

Titanic did not sideswipe the iceberg. The accident is properly described as a "bottom swipe" which explains how contact was in Wilding's words "slight" while at the same time destructive. The difference between the 27-foot draft of the forefoot and *Titanic*'s draft of the keel beneath the forward holds was about 6 feet. That is the theoretical vertical distance the starboard side of the hull had to rise up to pass over the iceberg. Such a huge lift obviously did not happen. Lee said the ship leaned only slightly to port. He did not describe the wild swing of the crow's nest which would have resulted from lifting the starboard side by six feet.

The nest was about 90 feet above the keel. If the side had lifted several feet, the lookouts would have swung back and forth through a dizzying arc. Neither man described motion anywhere near that violent. If the side did not lift the full amount, a couple of other things must have happened to reduce the lifting.

The relatively small mass of the ship compared to the much larger iceberg would have held any tipping of the ice to a minimum if the berg was evenly balanced like a ship. Such fine balance is seldom the case in the real world. Bergs can be so precariously balanced that the addition of very little weight can cause one to tip over. In the 19th century whaling sailors went aboard icebergs to cut ice to melt for drinking water. Sometimes they found their body weight was enough to cause bergs to become unstable and even capsize. Post-*Titanic* editions of the navigation text *Bowditch* point out this instability. "Often bergs are so nicely balanced that the slightest melting of their surfaces causes a shifting of the center of gravity," the text cautioned, "and a consequent turning over of the mass into a new position."

It is probable that *Titanic*'s berg was "nicely balanced" so that the additional weight of the ship aided the instability of the berg and allowed it to tip faster than would otherwise have happened. Evidence for tipping of the berg came from the chunks of ice it deposited into the well deck. These must have come from contact between the ship's topsides and the upper portions of the iceberg. Due to the sloping sides of the spires and peaks typical of North Atlantic bergs, topside contace could not have occurred unless it tipped toward the ship.

The ice shelf underneath the ship was crushed and broken as *Titanic*'s hull rode forward across it. This also reduced the lifting of the starboard well deck, but not enough to prevent damage. The narrow shape of the ice concentrated the “grounding pressure” onto a very small portion of the structure and rivets, seams, plates, girders, and frames began to fail. The ship’s forward motion worsened the situation by introducing rolling shear. The area tortured by excessive grounding pressure moved or "rolled" aft because of the ship's forward motion during the almost seven seconds of contact. The result was that a new portion of the bow was lifted as the previous section dropped back into its original position.

This rolling lift of *Titanic*'s starboard side by the iceberg had the same effect on the hull as improper blocking in a drydock. Weight is a manifestation of gravity. Too much of *Titanic*'s weight was supported by too little of the shell plating and underlying framework. Gravity did the dirty work that probably included ripped plates and sheared rivets.

If it could have been seen from alongside, this lifting and dropping would have appeared like a “hill” moving along the starboard side. First the forecastle deck would have lifted. It would have dropped back as the well deck came up, and so on until the ship broke free of the ice. The moving “hill” was something like a stadium wave done by sports fans. People in the crowd raise and lower their arms in turn so that a wave of motion seems to sweep across the seats even though each fan stays in his or her place.

Rivets in the joint where *Titanic*'s sides met the bottom were undoubtedly the first failures in what became a chain of structural failures. Steel plates must have buckled and some may even have cracked under the pressure. The methods of failure and resulting damage will be long debated. But, where failure took place is easy to pinpoint – the joint where the sides met the bottom. Although the turn of the bilge was rounded on the outside, structurally the sides met the ship's double bottom in a right-angle joint. This angle was what is called a "stress riser" because it served to concentrate the stress caused by the flexing of the bottom as the ship rode over the ice. It was here that the bottom released the stress by disconnecting at random points from the stiff vertical side.

One man experienced this happen first-hand. "Water came pouring in," leading stoker Frederick Barrett recalled. "The starboard side...about two feet from where I was standing." He also said it came in about two feet above the "stokehold plate" on which men stood when tending boiler furnaces. As noted earlier, Barrett was incorrect about being in boiler room #6 at the time of the accident. As demonstrated in Chapter 1, he was in hold #3 when the water came pouring into the ship forcing him to jump into the forward boiler room, #6.

The sudden ingress of cold seawater caught Barrett just below his waist."The water came through the ship's side about two feet above the floor plates, starboard side. A large volume of water came pouring in," he said.

Myth: Titanic was fatally wounded by the iceberg and nothing could have kept it afloat for more than a few hours.

Truth: Although the wounds were serious and the ship may have foundered anyway, *Titanic* should have been kept afloat to "act as its own lifeboat" until rescue vessels could come to take its people off.

In Chapter 1 we properly located the fire in bunker "b" at the head of boiler room #6. This means the water stoker Barrett saw coming into the fire-emptied bunker was actually in #6 and not in boiler room #5 as myth claims. The majority of iceberg damage occurred in the forward three holds. The importance of the location and number of flooded compartments was explained by naval architect Wilding who helped design the ship at Harland & Wolff. Using diagrams he explained to the British inquiry that *Titanic* could float with forward holds flooded. It could even float precariously if boiler room #6 were also flooded.

"On the plan I have handed in to my Lord there are three elevations shown. In the first one, which was the evidence we had in the earliest stages, number 1 hold, number 3 hold, and number 6 boiler room...was flooded," he testified. "As your Lordship will see, the water did not then reach the top of the bulkheads."

Wilding testified in London without access to all of the materials needed to compute the effects of flooding. He depended upon his staff at the Harland & Wolff shipyard in Belfast to make the tedious calculations necessary. "I then told them at Belfast by wire to flood number 2 compartment, also the forepeak, and see what happened. The water is still at that time below the level of the top of the bulkheads which run to the E deck." The margin of safety was narrow, but on paper Wilding's calculations showed *Titanic* should have floated with all three forward holds, the forepeak, and boiler room #6 flooded.

Myth: Titanic could float with three of its largest compartments in the bow flooded. It would sink if four were flooded.

Truth: Not a myth at all. *Titanic* would have floated "as its own lifeboat" with the forward three holds flooded. It became dicey if boiler room #6 flooded, and any more flooding doomed the ship.

The stunning truth is that the actual damage inflicted on *Titanic*'s bow was most likely survivable. This is not the author's opinion, but what the ship's designer said. Even so, *Titanic* eventually lost buoyancy and gravity pulled it to the bottom. Wilding had to come up with a logical explanation for this unfortunate turn of events. "I then flooded number 5 boiler room in identically the same way as I had previously flooded number 6 ... and I got the black line which, as you will notice, puts the forecastle entirely under water."

Wilding had just created the now-legendary scenario of water overtopping the bulkheads one by one. He neglected to mention that in terms of water pouring over bulkheads of a sinking ship *Titanic* was in no way unique. It is exactly what happens when every multi-compartment ship sinks. Water overtops the bulkheads and fills the undamaged watertight compartments. This overtopping process takes some time. "Assuming the extent of the damage in this particular case, it would take, I should think, an hour to an hour and a quarter, as well as I could estimate," the naval architect said of *Titanic*.

Wilding never claimed the ship was wounded from the stem all the way aft to the head of boiler room #5. He simply performed calculations of the ship's ability to float with ever-increasing amounts of flooding. It was the popular press that took one of his calculations out of context and used them to manufactured the mythical "big gash." Wilding knew better. His numbers showed *Titanic* should have remained afloat with its peak tank and all three forward holds flooded. It would only sink if boiler room #6 was open to the sea and then #5 also flooded.

Wilding's assessment means that the real damage inflicted on the bow put the ship on the cusp of floating or sinking. Had there been a successful effort to stem the rising water in #6 and had #5 been kept dry there should have been no sinking and no deaths on that April night. Wilding's math showed *Titanic* could float so long as the engineers kept the level in #6 below the top of bulkhead E. *Titanic* could and should have served as "its own lifeboat" as intended.

There is a flaw in Wilding's conclusion about water overtopping the bulkheads. Boiler room #5 was not damaged by the iceberg. Nor did it flood from water overtopping any bulkhead. Comparing the havoc the iceberg actually created to Wilding's assessment of the ship's ability to sustain damage, we cannot escape the conclusion that flooding in *Titanic*'s was not fatal. *Titanic* should have been able to "serve as its own lifeboat" as intended. More than 1,200 people should not have died that night on the Atlantic Ocean.

Without meaning to dishonor the ship's engineers we must still find out what they did wrong after the iceberg disappeared astern. Why did their ship sink if the iceberg wounds do not appear to have been fatal?

It turns out the ship's engineers faced a more complicated situation than Wilding envisioned in the quiet dignity of the British hearing room. There was more damage to the hull than he included in his calculations. History continues to overlook the importance of this additional ingress even though Wilding went on to say, "We had evidence that as far aft as number 4 boiler room the water was found rising above the stokehold plates." Lord Mersey asked if this water came through some "external means," apparently referring to iceberg damage. "Yes," was Wilding's simple answer.

Evidence of *Titanic*'s second encounter with the iceberg has languished in the official record for a hundred years. The avalanche of coal around trimmer George Cavelle as well as first class passenger Hugh Woolner's "slight twist" to the smoking lounge were likely the result of the hull bumping the massive iceberg one last time. Naval architect Wilding realized this and explained how it happened. "It seemed very probable, he said, "that after the ship finished tearing herself at the forward end...she would tend to push herself against the iceberg a little, or push herself up the iceberg, and there would be a certain tendency, as the stern came round to aft under the helm, to bang against the iceberg again further aft."

Support for Wilding's assessment is found in reports of water rising in boiler room #4 later that night. It was seen coming over plates on which the stokers stood while they raked coals out of their furnaces. "The water started coming over her stokehold plates. It came gradually. About a foot," Cavelle recalled of the situation.

Wilding cited efforts by the ship's engineers to rig extra suction pipes. "We know from the evidence that they were doing their best to pump out No. 4. We have had evidence that they took pipes along. The inference that I drew was that an attempt was being made to pump out this water which the engineers found coming in. That was the reason why they sent aft. They had only one pump in No. 4 boiler room, and the reason they sent aft for those additional pumps was to get additional pumping power on to No. 4 boiler room with a view to keeping it down," Wilding conjectured.

The naval architect's comments about pumping water out of boiler room #4 should have raised questions about the overall plan to dewater the ship. Nothing more was said on this subject. The official record is devoid of information about damage control efforts by Chief Engineer Joseph Bell and his men. Reverence for the engineers may have kept the 1912 inquiries from searching too diligently for the truth. *Titanic*'s engineers perished to a man as they kept the lights burning brightly so that others might live. There was little interest in tarnishing their image by exposing any errors or omissions they may have committed. However, even the efforts of heroes must be scrutinized in a rigorous search for the truth.

Fighting water rising in boiler room #4 was a life-or-death

struggle even though that was apparently not obvious to men in that compartment. Water in #4 was robbing the ship of the buoyancy it needed to prevent water from overtopping bulkhead E between boiler rooms #5 and #6. The ship had enough bilge pump capacity to get the job done, but the evidence is that the pump in #4 was out of service due to lack of steam. A suction hose was brought forward from farther aft where the boilers had not been robbed of their fires.

Chief Engineer Bell did not simply overlook the pumps which might have saved the ship. He and his senior engineers appear to have made a conscious decision not to use them. The reason for this decision was rooted in commonplace events of 1912. Steam boiler explosions occurred all too often in factories, on railroads, and aboard ships. They were the number one fear of steam operators. The scotch boilers in *Titanic* should not have exploded even if struck by freezing cold salt water. But, rational or not, fears of explosions obviously drove events in boiler rooms #4 and #6. Rather than starting the pumps located in those compartments, engineers chose to rake down the furnaces and release the steam needed by the pumps in those compartments of their sources of power.

Cold ocean water spouted into boiler rooms #4 and #6 even before the iceberg passed astern. The greatest ingress, however, was in #6 near the bow. Leading fireman Frederick Barrett described the flow into burned-out bunker "b" as equal to a "fire hose." If so, it should have been within the capacity of the bilge pump located in an alcove at the after end of the compartment. Normally, this pump mixed clinkers and ash from the furnaces with ocean water and pumping the resulting slurry overboard. It was arranged to double as a bilge pump for boiler room #6 in an emergency.

Scant attention was paid to the ship sinking during the early minutes after impact. Commands were issued to rake down the fires in #6 so the boilers would cool and not explode. Raking hot coals out of the fireboxes took about 15 minutes with the work being completed about 20 minutes after the accident. Men in boiler room #6 then stood around awaiting new instructions. Proof that the bilge pump was not working came when water started flowing over the stoker plates on which the men stood.

"Everything was shut down and an order was given. Someone shouted, 'that will do,' when everything was safe, when everything was shut down. ... and so I went up the escape ladder," stoker George Beauchamp recalled. He clambered up the escape ladder to join other stokers and trimmers milling around in Scotland Road on E deck.

No one suspected that abandoning boiler room #6 was a major link in what became a chain of damage control mistakes. The first link was the silent and unused bilge pump which should have been working to remove water spurting through the open seam in bunker "b." Instead, steam to operate it was screeching into the cold night air. Lawrence Beesley remembered the sound in his book about the sinking. "There were now more evidences of the coming catastrophe," he wrote. "One was the roar and hiss of escaping steam from the boilers. A harsh, deafening boom that made conversation difficult." [5-5]

By now Captain Edward J. Smith was conferring with the man who oversaw *Titanic*'s construction, Thomas Andrews. Both men arrived in the engine room almost simultaneously for what became a three-way meeting with Chief Engineer Joseph Bell. What they decided during this meeting led directly to Captain Smith's decision to launch the lifeboats. It also affected the way Chief Engineer Bell divided his efforts between controlling the flooding and keeping the electric lights burning. Unfortunately for history, none of the three men survived to remember their conversation.

Stokers and trimmers climbed out of boiler room #6 to the apparent safety of E deck. Engineers Hesketh and Shepherd and leading stoker Barrett followed them up the escape ladder, but then crossed over bulkhead E to another ladder descending into boiler room #5. They were hardly at work in their new compartment when a phone call came through from the engineering control station in the main engine room. "They rang through from the engine room to send all the stokers up," recalled Barrett.

Only one man had authority to issue this order. He was Chief Engineer Bell. Unfortunately, his humanitarian concern for the safety of the black gang came without full knowledge of its consequences. The resulting lack of manpower in boiler room #5 allowed a life-threatening situation to develop.

The ship's engineers in boiler room #5 returned to the problem of pumping out the now-flooded boiler room #6. Builder Andrews undoubtedly explained to Chief Engineer Bell the dire consequences of flooding in that compartment. Whatever their reason, men began to work on valves in boiler room #5 that apparently connected to the suctions in #6. Engineer Shepherd grabbed stoker Barrett to go back into their abandoned compartment in conjunction with this work. The pair started back over bulkhead E and into #6.

"It was not a quarter of an hour, just on ten minutes. My station was in the next boiler room, and Mr. Shepherd and I went up an escape and down to the boiler room," Barrett recalled. No one had an inkling of what Shepherd and Barrett would find. At worst, they probably expected knee-deep water. The truth was sobering. "We could not get in," Barrett said. "There were eight feet of water in it."

The two frustrated men climbed back over bulkhead E before descending down into boiler room #5. They reported high water in #6 to two disappointed engineers. "Mr. Harvey and Mr. Wilson, they are engineers, second assistant engineers, attending the pumps," Barrett said. The implication of this meeting is that Harvey and Wilson were waiting on Shepherd and Barrett to adjust the something in boiler room #6 so that the large pump in #5 could be put to work. The depth of water in #6 meant those plans would have to be changed.

In myth, *Titanic*'s electric lights blazed brightly until the end, and for the passengers that was true. Lights in cabins, public rooms, and on the boat deck did glow right up until the end. The opposite was true for electric lights in the boiler rooms where men worked to both prevent boiler explosions and pump water out of the damaged hull. These tasks were hardly begun when all six boiler rooms plunged into darkness. Men in the stokeholds had only the reddish glow of the furnaces to illuminate their hot, dangerous work. Portable lights were needed.

"Mr. Harvey sent me up for some lamps," fireman Barrett remembered. "I went to the top of the escape and sent two firemen. They fetched 12 to 15 (lamps) back."

Titanic boasted 10,000 electric lights sprinkled throughout its 882-foot length. Oil lamps like those in a cow barn may seem anachronistic, but technology does not progress evenly. Although hard-wired electric lighting was nearly fully developed in 1912, battery-powered portable "torches" ("flashlights" in the U.S.) were little more than curiosities. The only reliable light came from time-tested oil lanterns.

Off-duty leading stoker Charles Hendrickson did not notice the boiler room lights go out from his bunk in the forepeak. A "mate" came by with news that water was pouring into a spiral staircase used by stokers to go to the boiler rooms. This staircase led to a watertight tunnel through holds #2 and #3. Tonight, it was blocked by automatic watertight doors closed by First Officer William Murdoch during the accident. Many of the off-duty men did not realize this door was shut. At the midnight change of watch some of them found water rolling forward on the deck. Hendrickson went to see for himself.

"I saw water rushing in. I saw water running out of the fore part of the pipe tunnel right down at the bottom of the stairs. That is the tunnel we go through from our quarters to go into the stokehold. There are two staircases, one up and one down, but there is only one our side. I was looking down the one on the port side, not down the staircase, but at the side of the staircase. It came from the ship's side I am telling you, the starboard side at the bottom of the tunnel," Hendrickson said.

The British inquiry took it for granted that the tunnel began to flood immediately from iceberg damage. Naval Architect Wilding was asked how far into the ship the ice must have penetrated to damage the watertight structure of the firemen's tunnel. "I think it scales about 3 feet 3 inches from the corner horizontally to the shell of the ship," he answered. Unfortunately for this myth, ice is not strong enough to jab more than three feet into the hull.

If ice had jabbed into the tunnel during impact, there would have been immediate flooding. But, the tunnel was dry for nearly 20 minutes after impact. Water was not discovered there until the crew's midnight change of watch. Even then, flooding was confined to the deck on the starboard side. It did not fill the tunnel. The timing and limited amount of this water rules out iceberg damage which would have filled it within moments of impact. This leads to another sobering conclusion. The most probable cause of water in the tunnel was human error. Somebody appears to have opened a valve to let water from a flooding hold into the formerly dry firemen's passage.

Barrett described engineers working on the pumps in boiler room #5 just when the lights went out. Those men were apparently connecting bilge suctions in the flooded bow to high-capacity pumps in the engine room. This was taking place at the same time as water began to fill the tunnel. All of the ship's pumps connected to a complex system of valves and pipes that allowed suction to be directed to specific areas of flooding. Ominously, these pipes and valves could also connect flooding compartments with dry spaces in the hull.

Opening a wrong valve would have allowed water to gravitate into the firemen's tunnel through the ship's bilge piping. The force of gravity causes water to seek its own level. This flow from a full space to an empty one will even occur through the bilge pipes meant to take water out of the hull. If an engineer opened valves to pump water out of the tunnel without realizing that it was still dry, then water from a flooding hold would have flowed, or "gravitated," into the passageway. Due to the ship's slight list to starboard, this water would have flowed in a stream along the starboard wall of the tunnel exactly as Hendrickson described.

Human error of this type was possible because *operating rods controlling the valves led upward to "the lower deck above the load line."* This information about the bilge suction arrangements was contained in Wilding's report to the British inquiry. The intention of the arrangement of rods and valves was to allow someone to operate them even if the compartment was flooded.

> The valves in connection with the forward bilge and ballast suctions were placed in the firemens passage, the watertight pipe tunnel extending from No. 6 boiler room to the after end of No. 1 hold. In this tunnel, in addition to two 3 in. bilge suctions, one at each end, there was a special 3 ½ in. suction with valve rod led up to the lower deck above the load line, so as always to have been accessible should the tunnel be flooded accidentally.
>
> *"Pumping Arrangements"*
> *Board of Trade Report*
> *On the Loss of the "Titanic"*
> *July, 1912*

Wilding's report did not mention that anyone operating the remote valves did not have had direct sight of his work. Similar situations exist on modern ships, but hand-held radios allow direct communications with assistants who can see what is happening. There was no way for an innocent operator in *Titanic*'s crew to get this sort of feedback, especially if he operated the wrong valve during an emergency.

An undamaged watertight tunnel would not have begun to flood for no reason. The most likely possibility was that the drain (or "suction") in the tunnel was opened into the bilge pump system. At the same time, another suction was open in a flooded compartment such as one of the holds. The result would have been water gravitating into the tunnel from that flooded compartment. The possibility that a mistake flooded the tunnel is supported by what happened when Hendrickson went aft to report the flooding. He found Second Engineer John H. Hesketh in Scotland Road on the port side of E deck where valves were located. "I met Mr. Hesketh, the second engineer, and reported to him," Hendrickson said.

The engineer reacted to news of this additional flooding as if he already knew it was happening. Instead of pressing for more details, Hesketh sent Hendrickson on an errand to find oil lamps for the boiler rooms. The engineer's nonplus makes sense only if he already knew the cause of the tunnel flooding and was not concerned by it.

As the boiler room blackout continued neither the ship's sleepy passengers nor its struggling engineers were aware that darkness concealed a burgeoning threat to their lives. A potential bomb was ticking in boiler room #5 where fires still burned in the furnaces. Those fires had to be overlooked in the darkness of the boiler room blackout until oil lamps eventually arrived from the main engine room. “When I got down there I met Mr. Shepherd. He said to me, ‘you have got the lamps, have not you?’ I said, ‘Yes, sir.’ He said, ‘That is right, light them, and put them up by the water gauges of the boilers.’ So I lit them up,” Hendrickson recalled.

Oil lamps were being placed when the electric lights in all six boiler rooms flashed back to life. Leading stoker Barrett quickly checked the boiler water gauges and discovered the frightening situation. “I looked at the water. There was no water in the boilers. With the ship blowing off, it had blown out,” he explained. Steam venting up pipes attached to funnel #1 carried with it vital feed water. The boilers in boiler room #5 went “dry” and were now true threats of explosion. If someone unwittingly sent feed water into any of those boilers, that water would have flashed into more steam pressure than the boiler could handle.

This potentially disastrous situation grew worse every minute because fires still burned in the furnaces beneath the dry boilers. Barrett and Hendrickson were sent to gather men to come back down and rake down the furnaces. Although critical to the survival of the ship, the work of making the boilers safe diverted attention away from keeping the ship afloat. While they raked and shoveled the flooding continued unabated in boiler room #6 and water continued to rise slowly in #4. Naval architect Wilding's prediction of foundering was coming true.

Fifty minutes had now passed since the iceberg did its mischief. Boiler room #6 had been abandoned for nearly 30 minutes. By now the water level must have been ominously close to the top of bulkhead E.

With that in mind engineer Herbert Harvey resumed improvising a way to pump water out of the bow. "He asked me to lift the manhole plate off," said fireman Barrett who was working in the still-dry boiler room #5. "It is something you lift up to get at the valves. I do not know what valves it is. It is just like a hole in a table. You lift it off to get to the valves to turn on the pumps or something." The logical reason for engineer Harvey's request would have been to connect the 250-ton pump in #5 to suction pipes in #6.

Lifting of that manhole is additional proof that boiler room #5 was fully dry almost an hour after the accident. Had there been ingress, the space between the stoker plates and the tank top would have been filled with icy water. Work on valves in that space would have been difficult or impossible. There would have been little use in lifting the manhole. But, Barrett pulled up the plate. He did not report any flooding beneath the stoker plates at that moment. The manhole was hardly open when another engineer hurrying across the boiler room failed to notice the result of Barrett's work.

"All the water which had been thrown on the furnaces when they were pulled out was making the stokehold thick with steam. Mr. Shepherd was walking across in a hurry to do something," recalled fireman Barrett. Screaming both in fright and from pain John Shepherd disappeared into that open steel mantrap. "He fell down the hole and broke his leg. We lifted him up and carried him into the pump room, me and Mr. Harvey."

An injured man inevitably draws attention away from the task at hand. In this case, Shepherd's broken leg may also have taken a key man out of the damage control team. Operating the correct valves in the open manhole required someone with intimate knowledge of *Titanic*'s plumbing. Shepherd was probably not that man. The key man whose attention was diverted was probably Harvey who rushed to tend Shepherd's injuries.

Once again, the design of the ship's bilge pipe system allowed human error to become a factor in the sinking. The pumps could be cross-connected in a variety of ways. As with the tunnel, control rods on the valves were taken to the "bulkhead deck" which was also known as E deck. As with the firemen's tunnel, a man working one of these valves would have had no contact with events going on down on the tank top level more than 20 feet below him.

The next major event in boiler room #5 had all the hallmarks of a human error made by someone of little knowledge trying to carry on while his boss was occupied elsewhere. "A rush of water came through the pass, the forward end. It is a space between the boilers where we walk through," Barrett said. "From the forward end."

This sudden, almost explosive appearance of water had no precursor. There was no groaning and weeping typical of a bulkhead about to give way under the weight of water it was holding back. There were no reports of pipes spurting water just before their joints let go. Boiler room #5 which had been dry throughout the emergency suddenly flooded, apparently without any of the usual warning signals.

How did that happen?

Barrett described a gush of water that would have followed someone opening the wrong valve on one of the 10-inch suction mains. This would have allowed water to shoot into the compartment under more than 30 feet of head pressure. The result would have been a "rush" of water sufficient to scare Barrett into scrambling up the escape ladder. Killer gravity now had control over *Titanic*'s future.

Wisely, Barrett escaped on deck. "I never stopped to look," he said. "I went up the ladder. Mr. Harvey told me to go up. All the men who remained behind were lost.

The rush of water in boiler room #5 has often been attributed to flood water pouring down from E deck above. Barrett was positive that did not happen. "I do not see how it could come over the top, no," he told the British inquiry. "The water was coming down the alleyway from forward. Just a little." [5-6]

CHAPTER 6

FINAL DESTINATION

The Big Myth: After striking the iceberg *Titanic* came to a stop and sat quietly awaiting its fate.

The Truth: After striking the iceberg *Titanic* resumed steaming for a new destination. Instead of New York, the ship headed for Nova Scotia where two passenger trains would be waiting to take passengers to New York.

Darkness cloaked promenade suite B-52 as *Titanic* bore down on its iceberg. One of two so-called "millionaire's suites," it had been intended for men like American financier J.P. Morgan and their families. Morgan's money paid for construction of the ship even though *Titanic* sailed under British colours with a British crew. White Star Line was owned by Morgan's thoroughly American company, International Mercantile Marine.

Morgan was not aboard this night. His place in the master bedroom was occupied by J. Bruce Ismay, managing director of White Star. Ismay expected his slumber to be as undisturbed as if he were sleeping in a hotel ashore. However, he was about to be awakened by an inconvenient iceberg.

Ismay's suite was located almost directly above boiler room #4 where trimmer George Cavelle was moving coal. Neither man was bothered when the bow began sliding over the iceberg. It was a second impact with the iceberg that caught both men's attention. A hard thump of ice against steel caused coal to avalanche down onto the hapless Cavelle. It also brought Ismay back to consciousness.

"I presume the impact awakened me," Ismay told the U.S. Senate inquiry. "I lay in bed for a moment or two afterwards, not realizing, probably, what had happened."

Murdoch's Astern Full command on the starboard engine came about a half minute before impact. Circumstantial evidence shows the engineers actually managed to slow the massive 4-cylinder engine nearly to a stop by the time the ship struck on the berg. This meant the starboard wing propeller was dragging through the water like a spinning sea anchor. Sometime during the seven seconds of impact it may even have begun revolving in reverse.

Titanic came off the berg moving forward at more than 20 knots, but with one propeller trying to go the opposite direction. The resulting turbulence created ever-increasing sound and vibration from the stern. Several members of the hotel staff (stewards, etc.) had been aboard the sister ship *Olympic* when it lost a propeller blade. These vibrations seemed all too familiar.

> *About 11:40 there was a kind of shaking of the ship and a little impact, from which I thought one of the propellers had broken off.*
>
> George F. Crowe
> Saloon Steward

> *I thought at first it was the propeller gone.*
>
> William Ward
> Saloon Steward
>
> *I did not feel much because we thought she had lost her wheel or something, and somebody passed the remark, "Another Belfast trip."*
>
> James Johnson
> Saloon Steward

Titanic snubbed its bow on the iceberg. There was never any doubt about that. Yet, these three experienced stewards placed the problem at the other end of the ship. They had been to sea before, and should have known the bow from the stern, so they did not confuse front with back.

What they felt and heard was not the rumble of the steel forefoot on the ice. It came from beneath their feet more than 400 feet from the bow. Their location in the first class galley was directly over the reciprocating engines. Noise and vibration of disturbed water from *Titanic* dragging its starboard propeller through the water is what drew their attention.

Ismay was still struggling to wake himself while a flurry of activity took place two decks above on the ship's bridge. Captain Edward J. Smith rushed out of the chartroom and through the wheelhouse. By now the starboard engine was beginning to reverse and First Officer William M. Murdoch was moving toward one of the engine order telegraphs. The captain realized what was about to happen and went to another telegraph. Both men rang down "All Stop" to the engine room on different telegraph systems.

Greaser Frederick Scott was in the engine room. "I noticed Stop first on the main engines," he told the British inquiry. The orders came down on both the main engine order telegraph and on what Scott described as an "emergency" set. According to him, "All four went together, Stop. Two greasers at the bottom rang back. They were feeding the engines and were close handy at the time," Scott said.

Engineers began shutting the throttles. The low rumble of reciprocating pistons that had filled the hull day and night since the ship left Queenstown (now Cobh) faded away. With it went the vibration at the stern. *Titanic* continued moving, but now it was "shooting" forward under its own momentum and not by thrust from its propellers. Bruce Ismay threw off his covers and stood up. "Eventually, I got up and walked along the passageway and met one of the stewards and said, 'What has happened?'" Ismay told the U.S. inquiry" "And, he said, 'I do not know, sir.'"

The quiet B deck corridor outside the promenade suite held no answers as to the strange motion of the ship followed by the even stranger silence. Ismay returned to his room for his overcoat. He knew it would be cold on the bridge where Captain Smith was sure to be found. "After I put on my coat I went up to the bridge," he said later. "I should think it might have been ten minutes after the accident." Meanwhile, Captain Smith had taken personal charge of the emergency. His first order sent quartermaster Alfred Olliver to rouse out the ship's carpenter to sound the bilges for flooding.

Next, the captain asked his first officer what had taken place. Bits and pieces of their conversation were heard by quartermaster Robert Hichens in the wheelhouse. Sixth Officer Moody was taking advantage of the dim electric light inside the wheelhouse to make notes in his scrap log. The lowest-ranking officer on duty, it was Moody's job to keep notes for the ships formal logbook. He must also have overheard what Murdoch had to say, but did not survive to report it to either inquiry. Fourth Officer Joseph G. Boxhall was forward checking on the status of third class passengers (see Appendix A).

Ismay took this moment to burst onto the bridge in his odd costume of pajamas and overcoat. Murdoch and Smith did not survive to record their impressions of Ismay's visit. The only survivor of the conversation was a tight-lipped Ismay. In the aftermath of disaster all he would say about his meeting with the captain was that Smith admitted "we had struck ice" and the situation was "serious."

Subsequent events often echo what was said in lost conversations. Ideas presented by U.S. President Abraham Lincoln in a meeting with Generals Grant and Sherman toward the end of the American Civil War were not recorded. However, both generals later faced the task of writing surrender terms ending that bloody conflict. Documents penned separately by the two generals are filled with the same reconciliation and hope that Lincoln expressed in his Gettysburg Address. It is easy to catch Lincoln's thoughts in documents written later by his generals.

Ironically. Lincoln and his generals spoke aboard a river steamboat. Just as their words were lost to history, the conversation between Ismay and Captain Smith on *Titanic*'s bridge a half century later is equally unknown. Ismay's demands were not recorded. But, the captain's first action following the conversation was so bizarre that it continues to confound maritime researchers and historians. What he did was not in keeping with a prudent master, but has the hallmarks Ismay's management style. Captain Smith ordered his damaged ship's engines to roll once again. *Titanic* pointed toward a new and final destination.

A lesser man than E.J. Smith might have passed responsibility for restarting the engines to one of his officers. That would have placed some of the blame for moving the damaged ship on another man's shoulders. Instead, the captain did it himself. Loyalty was a two-way street for E.J. Smith. He expected it from those below him in his command and he gave the same in return. By operating the telegraph himself the captain protected his officers from recriminations for what might follow.

There was a witness to Smith's actions. Quartermaster Olliver returned to the bridge from his errand to the ship's carpenter just as the captain operated the telegraph. The rating "knew his place" as a member of the working class in Edwardian society. Olliver would never have admitted overhearing a conversation between his captain and the head of White Star. But, Olliver was free to talk about the almost unbelievable event he witnessed after Ismay was gone.

Senator BURTON: Was she backed?
Mr. OLLIVER: Not whilst I was on the bridge. But, whilst on the bridge she went ahead, after she struck. She went half speed ahead.
Senator BURTON: The engines went half speed ahead, or the ship?
Mr. OLLIVER: Half speed ahead, after she hit the ice.
Senator BURTON: Who gave the order?
Mr. OLLIVER: The captain telegraphed half speed ahead.

The import of Olliver's American testimony was not lost on the British inquiry. His lucid account of Captain Smith ordering the wounded vessel to resume steaming opened White Star Line to unlimited liability damages. The connection to Ismay was as obvious then as now. By just visiting the bridge the shipping line executive gained "privity and knowledge" of events that led to the loss of the ship and more than 1,500 lives. "Privity and knowledge" is a key legal phrase in Admiralty Law. Shipping companies enjoy protection of liability from actions of their ships and crews because normally company executives cannot exercise day-to-day control over them. Once executives gain "privity and knowledge" of events on any of their ships, that knowledge becomes legal grounds for piercing liability protection.

In 1912 naval officers knew that moving a ship with a damaged bow under its own power was dangerous. Captain Smith held reserve commissions in the Royal Navy. He would have been familiar with the events of June 22, 1893 (19 years before Titanic) when the British battleship *HMS Victoria* was rammed by HMS *Camperdown* in the Mediterranean off Tripoli. An ill-conceived attempt to drive the mortally wounded *Victoria* onto the beach turned embarrassment into tragedy. The warship to capsized and foundered. *Victoria* was gone in only 13 minutes with the stunning loss of more than 800 sailors, including Admiral Tryon. Most observers concluded the ship's forward motion drove the bow under too fast for the crew to escape.

Fifteen years before *Victoria* and 34 years prior to *Titanic*, naval architect Robert E. Froude conducted tests on a model of *HMS Invincible.* His goal was to learn what would happen if that ship were driven forward with a damaged bow. Froude was the son of William Froude, one of the founders of the science of naval architecture.[6-1] The younger Froude built a scale model of HMS *Invincible* with bow damage. When his model was driven forward in a test tank, the forecastle was pushed under exactly in the manner of HMS *Victoria.*

Captain Smith's *Titanic* now had similar bow damage to that which Froude's experiment anticipated. Smith should have known of the results, and he certainly knew of the loss of HMS *Victoria*. He knew the risk he took by starting the *Titanic*'s engines once again. Even so, Olliver saw Smith's own hand send orders down to the engine room. The wounded *Titanic* began to move northwest.

During the short time while *Titanic*'s engines were stopped greaser Scott found himself groaning to lift a watertight door. Another man had been trapped in the propeller shaft tunnels when Murdoch closed the watertight doors in anticipation of the accident. Scott and another stoker managed to heave up the door enough for the unwilling prisoner to crawl out. They had just finished when Scott heard a bell ring. It alerted men working around the reciprocating engines that the cranks and rods were going to begin moving again.

5565 Did you hear any signal given to the bridge?
Mr. SCOTT: From the engine room?
5566 Yes?
Mr. SCOTT: Yes.
5567 What?
Mr. SCOTT: When they rang the stand-by. Is that what you mean?

5568 Yes?
Mr. SCOTT: That is all I heard, and then they rang down, "Slow Ahead."

Trimmer Thomas P. Dillon was also in the engine room. He thought the engines stopped and then went astern for about two minutes after the accident. He actually witnessed the engineers reversing the starboard engine in accordance with Murdoch's instructions. Then, he saw both engines stop for a short time before they started up again.

3726 And did they stop again?
Mr. DILLON: Yes.
3727 And did they go on again after that?
Mr. DILLON: They went ahead again.

Moments later Dillon heard someone yell, "Keep up the steam." This order was in response to the captain's desire to move the ship under its own power again. Dampers on the fireboxes had been closed when the ship first came to a stop to prevent excess buildup of steam. With the two 4-cylinder triple-expansion engines rolling again the dampers had to be opened to maintain full steam pressure.

It is impossible to prove that Ismay influenced Captain Smith's decision to re-start the engines. Smith may not have needed any prodding from his boss. Although unlikely, the master may have decided to move the ship into clear water away from any ice that might interfere with launching the lifeboats. Whatever Smith's reason, *Titanic*'s engines began their familiar beat and a bow wave once again curled around the cutwater.

Passenger Lawrence Beesley was traveling second class. In a book published immediately after the disaster he described the reassurance that came from the ship moving again, "*...The ship had now resumed her course, moving very slowly through the water with a little white line of foam on each side. I think we were all glad to see this.*"[6-2]

Beesley was not the only passenger to notice the ship moving again. New York businessman Charles E. Stengel was awake at the time of impact. He noted the engines come to a stop and then after a short pause resume their reassuring beat.

Senator SMITH: How long after the impact was it before the engines stopped?
Mr. STENGEL: A very few minutes.
Senator SMITH: Give the number of minutes, if you can. You are accustomed to machinery and matters of that kind.
Mr. STENGEL: I should say two or three minutes, and then they started again just slightly; just started to move again. I do not know why; whether they were backing off, or not. I do not know. I hardly thought they were backing off, because there was not much vibration of the ship.

It is not possible to pin down the exact minute when Captain Smith ordered his vessel to begin moving again. A good guess would be 9 minutes after impact and close upon the heels of Boxhall's positive report that he found no injured passengers or visible damage in third class quarters. In defense of the captain, he was not yet aware of the full extent of the damage. This put Smith at a disadvantage in arguing against his boss, Ismay. There was no reason to doubt the watertight bulkheads would keep the injured ship afloat. *Titanic* seemed as solid as a church planted on the glass-smooth North Atlantic.

A chart of the North Atlantic shows why Ismay most likely instructed Captain Smith to steam for Halifax, Nova Scotia. Just prior to the accident *Titanic* had turned left about two points in an unsuccessful effort to get around the hazy line of ice. As a result, it was heading southwest when the accident took place. With Murdoch's "hard a-port" right rudder and dragging starboard screw, the ship' path curved toward the north after passing the iceberg. Purely by chance *Titanic* was headed west-northwest, almost directly at the Canadian port when it first slid to a stop.

Not only was Halifax the closest harbor, but it also belonged to the British Empire and had water deep enough to accommodate *Titanic*. Using this Canadian port would allow landing passengers in North America without coming under the jurisdiction of U.S. maritime law. The iceberg incident could be kept a tight-lipped British family affair.

Captain Smith's second unusual action after Ismay's visit was to depart his bridge altogether. It is the practice for shipmasters to remain at their vessel's command centers during emergencies. Smith broke this time-honored tradition by walking aft to the small suite of rooms occupied by the ship's Marconi equipment. Inside, he found senior operator John "Jack" Phillips hunched over the telegraph key. Assistant operator Harold Bride was asleep in the next room.

Bride would later claim that Smith visited the Marconi office to alert the operators to the *possibility* that a distress message might be sent. It was a charming story, but it does not fit the way real captains commanded their ships in 1912 or, for that matter, today. Smith would never have departed his bridge just to be polite to the radio operators. There was no need to warn them of anything. In an emergency Smith would simply have demanded the operators stop all commercial traffic and begin sending distress signals. No warning would have been expected by the operators or given by the captain.

During his appearance before the U.S. Senate inquiry Bride's description of the captain's visit was somewhat subdued by comparison to his quotes in the newspapers. The radio operator said he retired just after 8 PM. "I was in bed," he told Senator William A. Smith. "I woke up of my own accord about five minutes to twelve. I had promised to relieve Mr. Phillips earlier than usual. I went out to speak to him before I dressed. I only had pajamas on. I asked him how he was getting on," Bride testified. The radioman then added a quotation from Phillips which indicated the true reason for Captain Smith's odd visit to the Marconi office. "He (Phillips) told me he thought she had got damaged in some way and that he expected that we should have to go back to Harland & Wolff's."

Phillips knew the ship was injured from the contents of a message Captain Smith apparently dictated to company headquarters in Liverpool. Phillips had sent that message by his own hand, letter-by-letter in Morse code while his partner, Bride, was still asleep. Motivation for Smith to dictate that message is contained in IMM/White Star policy. The company rule book required Captain Smith to report *Titanic*'s injuries to the closest company office. This rule book was specific about reporting accidents, especially when a ship diverted to a port other than its original destination.

> *111.* ***Accident, Collision or Salvage.***—*(b) In case of accident to the vessel requiring her to proceed to a port of refuge, a report should be at once telegraphed to the*

Management and to the nearest Company's office, giving particulars of accident and damage.

Chief radio operator Phillips almost certainly sent such a message to White Star headquarters in plain language. This is surprising because the use of private "secret codes" was common in 1912. Passengers knew they were charged by the word. So, many invented their own ciphers that saved money by reducing the number of words in a message. Captain Arthur Rostron of the rescue ship *Carpathia* used a substitution cipher for messages about survivors sent to Cunard's New York headquarters. However, it appears that anyone listening to radio signals crackling over the Atlantic that night could have learned in plain English that *Titanic* had struck an iceberg; that everyone aboard was still safe; and that it was steaming for Halifax.

Myth: The only wireless messages from *Titanic* concerning the iceberg accident were the ship's cries for help as it was sinking.

Truth: Several radio messages from *Titanic* apparently contained the cheery message that everyone aboard was safe and the ship was steaming for Halifax.

By Monday morning *Titanic* was front page news on both sides of the Atlantic. Naturally, the imperfect wireless technology of 1912 meant details were scarce. Long-distance radio communication was a nighttime phenomenon with range cut short during daylight. Ships in mid-ocean were mostly out of range of shore stations after the sun rose over *Titanic*'s watery grave. Under these circumstances it was not surprising that newspapers largely got the story wrong. Or, so it seemed. On April 16th, a day after the sinking, the *Daily Mirror* of London blamed communications for the apparently erroneous reporting that occurred during the aftermath of the tragedy.

...her fate and that of the thousands on board remained in doubt on both sides of the Atlantic for many hours. It was at length known that every soul was safe, and that the vessel

> *itself was proceeding to Halifax, either under her own steam or towed by the Allan liner* Virginian.
>
> *Daily Mirror*
> London
> April 16, 1912

North American newspapers on the Monday morning of the tragedy published stories similar to a dispatch from the *Montreal Star*. This news came out of Canada at 9:43 am New York Time, nine hours after *Titanic* foundered.

> *...the* Montreal Star *to-day says that unofficial dispatch from Halifax stated that word had been received there that the* Titanic *was still afloat and was making her way slowly toward Halifax.*
>
> Dow Jones News Service
> Montreal
> April 15, 1912

Maurice L. Farrell, managing editor of the Dow Jones News Service, followed the developing story with keen interest. Later, he read a copy of one of his agency's dispatches from Montreal into the U.S. Senate inquiry record.

> *Dispatch from Montreal received by White Star officials says* Titanic *was afloat at 8.30 and that women and children had not yet been taken off, though lifeboats were ready in case of emergency.*
>
> *The steamship is heading in direction of Halifax, from which the Virginian is approaching. It is thought that bulkheads will prevent ship from sinking. Titanic is moving under her own engines.*

Historians traditionally place the *Titanic*/Halifax connection in the category of a "misunderstanding" over another ship in the vicinity that was also in trouble. The oil tanker *Deutschland* had run out of fuel and was drifting without power. This hapless ship was later towed to safety by *Virginian*. The claim was made in 1912 that emergency traffic regarding *Deutschland* and *Virginian* became intertwined the *Titanic* emergency radio traffic. This is a possibility loses its believability in light of a cheerful message delivered to the parents of operator Jack

Phillips who lived in Godalming, Surrey.

> Making slowly for Halifax. *Virginian* standing by. Try not to worry.[6-3]

British newspapers said this message was delivered on Monday evening the day the ship sank. Phillips' family received it hours after the world knew the grim truth. The family's reaction when they received this cheery reassurance can only be imagined. Then, the story took an even more bizarre twist. The heroic radio operator's brother stepped forward to say that he sent a bogus wireless message in Jack's name. The brother said it was an attempt to calm their mother's fears. His outlandish claim fails the test of logic. If true, he apparently thought he could dupe his family into believing that *Titanic* was afloat hours after everyone else knew it had foundered with great loss of life.

> It was stated yesterday that the message received by Mr. and Mrs. Phillips, of Godalming, the parents of Mr. J.G. Phillips, the wireless operator...was not from the liner, but from another son in London. [6-4]
>
> Daily Sketch
> London
> April 17, 1912

It is virtually impossible to believe that the "try not to worry" message was a brother's attempt to calm their mother. If there was a hoax, it was more likely the brother's absurd claim of authorship. However, newspapers were not inclined to investigate the origin of the mysterious message. Instead, they seized on it to explain why they had been so wrong about the ship being safe and steaming for Halifax.

> *Some of the London newspapers went to press this morning in the belief that all aboard the* Titanic *were safe and the vessel was proceeding for Halifax....Later dispatches recording the sinking of the* Titanic, *with loss of life, appear only in the latest editions.* [6-5]
>
> *New York Tribune*
> April 16, 1912

The Halifax story was reported by newspapers on both sides of the Atlantic on that Monday. All reports contained two critical details. First, that the ship was steaming for Halifax; and second, that *Virginian* was "standing by." It is highly unlikely that a message from Phillips' brother could or would have contained both of these items. The writer even used wireless telegraph jargon that was misunderstood by editors in 1912 and continues to be misunderstood by historians ever since. The use of the term "standing by" strongly indicates the message originated in a wireless office and not a brother's imagination.

To Jack Phillips and other Marconi operators, "standing by" did not mean *Virginian* was along side the stricken liner or even coming to the aid of *Titanic*. Rather, it meant only that *Virginian*'s operator was staying near his equipment ready to receive or relay messages from *Titanic*. Radio operators knew that "standing by" did not carry any indication of proximity between the two stations.

News bureaus in 1912 hired freelance radio operators to listen to the traffic between ships. Rich and famous passengers not yet savvy to electronic eavesdropping and often sent messages containing private details of their lives. David Sarnoff was one of those operators. He later developed the concept of entertainment radio broadcasting, but on the morning following the sinking he was ensconced in a small room atop the Wanamaker Building listening to signals from the Atlantic. "I was on duty...and got the first message from the *Olympic*, 1,400 miles out at sea, that the *Titanic* had gone down," Sarnoff recalled.[6-6] He remained at his post for three days catching messages from *Carpathia* that listed the names of survivors.

The story of the ship striking an iceberg and steaming for Halifax broke simultaneously in newspapers on both sides of the Atlantic. Relatively primitive radio and expensive transoceanic telegraph cable communications of 1912 made it difficult for the same news to appear on both sides of the ocean at the same time. For this to occur required a single news source located somewhere on the North Atlantic within radio range of both America and Europe. Only a ship could send a message that could be heard on both sides of the ocean simultaneously. The only place that news could have originated was the wireless of R.M.S. *Titanic* which reportedly had the strongest radio signal afloat.

When the facts are known, newspaper headlines proclaiming the wounded ship was steaming for Halifax with "all safe" *were correct* for at least ten minutes or longer after the accident. *Titanic* was still floating and functional as a ship. And, it had resumed steaming. Most important, at the moment Captain Smith dictated his message there had been no known casualties and all aboard were safe. Thanks to their electronic eavesdroppers the newspapers got the story right, but events overtook the speed of news dissemination. By the time their headlines hit the streets, the ship had foundered. It was an embarrassing affair for editors who quickly explained it away rather than investigate what appeared to be their own blunder.

The Marconi company denied any connection to the message received by Phillips' parents. A man identified as "Mr. Turnbull of the Marconi Wireless Telegraphic Company" told the London Daily Sketch that several of the unfounded statements could not be traced to any wireless operator. "For example," Turnbull said, "we are accused of stating that all passengers had been saved, and that the Titanic was proceeding under her own steam to Halifax. This report was not issued by any wireless operator, but was the result of a telegram sent from London by the brother of the Titanic's senior operator." [6-7]

Turnbull's words were courageous, but they do not stand up to events which emerged on the other side of the Atlantic. The truth was told by a steam locomotive and its train of passenger cars coupled together near Boston. They were part of two boat trains contracted for by Phillip A.S. Franklin, the American vice president of International Mercantile Marine and parent company of White Star. It would have been mandatory to notify Franklin if *Titanic* changed its destination to Halifax because his job would have been to move the injured ship's passengers from there to New York.

Franklin ordered the necessary trains. That's a fact which the railroad later confirmed. Even so, he also claimed that no message about *Titanic* steaming for Halifax came to him from Captain Smith. "We never had the slightest communication of any kind from the Captain of the *Titanic*," he told Senator Smith. Franklin told the truth in both cases. Any "steaming for Halifax" message he received would have come via trans-Atlantic cable from White Star's home office in Liverpool and not by wireless from *Titanic*.

Ismay's office was in the company's Liverpool headquarters. He undoubtedly asked the captain to informed his office of *Titanic*'s situation. Smith's message about the accident would then have been transcribed in Liverpool and re-transmitted via undersea cable to Franklin in New York. So, as Franklin truthfully testified, he did not receive any message directly from Captain Smith.

There is no proof of any cable about Halifax either coming or not coming from Liverpool. The truth must be imputed from the actions that Franklin took on the Monday of the sinking. Just before noon New York time he ordered two special trains dispatched to Halifax to pick up *Titanic*'s passengers. Ordering those special trains was expensive. Cost alone would have prevented Franklin from taking such an action on a guess or personal whim. Franklin's actions must have been the result of instructions from his corporate headquarters based on the "all safe" message from *Titanic*.

Myth: The entire story of *Titanic* played out on the cold waters of the North Atlantic while people ashore did nothing but wait for news of the ship's fate.

Truth: White Star Line's office in New York City ordered two passenger trains to Halifax to pick up *Titanic*'s passengers after they arrived in that Canadian port.

In any event, a railroad locomotive and coaches to carry more than 700 people were physical proof that Franklin believed *Titanic* was still afloat on Monday. Two special trains were arranged at his personal request. One of them actually started north from Boston bound for Halifax. So, despite his denials, Franklin acted precisely as if he had received word from *Titanic* that it was steaming for the Canadian port city.

> *...P.A.S. Franklin, vice president International Mercantile Marine, says arrangements have been made with the New Haven Road to send a special train to Halifax to meet passengers of the* Titanic. *Train will consist of 11 sleepers, 2 diners, and coaches sufficient for 710 people.* [6-8]

Dow Jones News Service
3:01 PM NYT
April 15, 1912

News of the Halifax-bound train broke in mid-afternoon on Monday of the sinking. However, to get that train rolling north it had been necessary for Franklin to call the New Haven Railroad earlier that morning. The railroad needed time to make up a crew off the "extra board," fire the locomotives, and couple together the needed passenger coaches. One of the two trains was actually assembled. This first *Titanic* boat train was confirmed by Benjamin Campbell, vice president of the New York, New Haven and Hartford Railroad Company.

"Mr. Franklin called me on the telephone between 11 and 11:30 o'clock AM. Monday the 15th asking if we would arrange to send sufficient equipment to Halifax to take Titanic's passengers to New York," Campbell said. "At 1:10 o'clock I called up Mr. Franklin on the telephone. I told him...trains would be ready to leave Boston at 5 or 6 o'clock that evening.

In the meantime confusion over the fate of *Titanic* continued in White Star's New York office. Daylight ended reliable long-distance wireless communications. New information became scanty. Reports that trickled in from the Atlantic were often conflicting. Franklin tried not to be fooled by the wild news stories. His handling of the situation continued to be based on trustworthy company messages like the one he received from *Olympic* shortly before 1 PM.

> *Parisian* reports *Carpathia* in attendance and picked up 20 boats of passengers and *Baltic* returning to give assistance. Position not given.

Olympic's message said nothing about the fate of the ship. Franklin and his New York staff still presumed was afloat. However, Franklin was becoming worried. Within an hour he sent an urgent request to *Olympic*'s Captain Herbert J. Haddock.

> To HADDOCK, *Olympic*: April 15, 1912.
> *Thanks your message. We have received nothing from Titanic, but rumored here that she proceeding slowly Halifax, but we can not confirm this. We expect Virginian alongside Titanic; try and communicate her.*
>
> Franklin

While awaiting Haddock's reply, Franklin continued to prepare for

Titanic's arrival in Halifax. The first of the two special trains was highballing north of Boston at 6:16 PM New York time when Captain Haddock sent a message from *Olympic* that ended all hope. Dots and dashes spelled out the epitaph of the world's largest ship.

> *Carpathia* reached *Titanic*'s position at daybreak. Found boats and wreckage only. *Titanic* had foundered about 2.20 am. in 41.16 north 50.14 west. All her boats accounted for. About 675 souls saved, crew and passengers, latter nearly all women and children. Leyland Line S.S. *Californian* remaining and searching position of disaster. *Carpathia* returning to New York with survivors; please inform Cunard.
>
> Haddock

"I have often been asked what were my emotions at that moment," radio eavesdropper Sarnoff remembered. "I doubt if I felt at all during the seventy-two hours after the news came. I gave the information to the press associations and newspapers at once and it was as if bedlam had been let loose." That bedlam was not confined to Sarnoff's radio shack. It seems to have affected White Star's New York office. Not everyone there seems to have gotten the tragic news. More than two hours later at 8:27 PM a telegram went from the New York office to a Mr. J.A. Hughes in Huntington, West Virginia.

> *Titanic* proceeding to Halifax. Passengers will probably land there Wednesday. All safe.
>
> White Star Line

Franklin never denied this message was sent by his office. He only claimed not to know who was responsible for sending it. "We have had our entire staff in No. 9 Broadway asked," he told Senator Smith. "We can not find out who sent that message. The office was very crowded on Monday morning, and a good many of the juniors were answering communications....it might be, possibly, that the telegram was sent by one of these juniors."

A sad phone call to the railroad recalled the train from its pointless run. There would be no passengers arriving in Halifax. *Titanic* was gone. Now the question turned to the survivors. Who would arrive in New York? "I sat for hours listening," Sarnoff said. "Now we began to get the names of some of those who were known to have gone down. This was worse than the other list had been -- heartbreaking in its finality -- a death knell to hope." [6-9]

Unheard by Sarnoff at his receiver and unseen by survivors aboard Carpathia out on the trackless Atlantic there was a new mythical ship rising. In time it would become the *Titanic* books, movies and television documentaries. The real ship remains on the bottom of the Atlantic where it rusts silently a little more with each passing year. In time the steel of history's most famous shipwreck will be gone and what remains will be myth.

CHAPTER 7

DEATH OF A TITAN

The Big Myth: *Titanic*'s bulkheads were not tall enough, so water simply poured over top of them and sank the ship.

The Truth: *Titanic*'s bulkheads were sufficient to keep the ship afloat, but only if the engineers operated the bilge pumps properly. In the end, a human mistake sent the ship to the bottom.

That fateful evening on the calm Atlantic *Titanic*'s captain, Edward J. Smith, expected the worst from the very beginning. Or, that's the tale told by his actions after the ship stopped for the final time. He knew water was rising in the bow, but that was to be expected after contact with an iceberg. And, water in the bilge did not mean his ship was sinking or even in imminent danger. After all, *Titanic*'s system of bulkheads and watertight doors was designed to deal with this situation. Even so, Captain Smith was taking no chances. He would survey the damage for himself and talk directly with the ship's Chief Engineer, Joseph Bell, and builder, Thomas Andrews. Before that, however, he made another stop in the Marconi office. The message this time left no doubt about the captain's thoughts. "Send for help," he told the operators.

Considering the captain still did not know *Titanic* was sinking as he spoke to the radio operators, his decision to send distress signals was an act of courage. Ship captains traditionally take care of their own problems and admit they need help only as a final resort. Smith did the opposite. He first sent for help and only then went to determine whether or not his ship was sinking.

A few minutes later Captain smith returned from the engine room with gut-wrenching knowledge of what was to come. He had suspected *Titanic*'s trouble on his way below when he told the Marconi operators to send for help. Now, on his way back he had to deal with unthinkable reality. The engineers might keep Titanic floating longer than the two hours Andrews predicted. But, there was no getting around the unthinkable – *Titanic* was fighting for its life.

The captain's thoughts as he climbed back to the bridge can only be imagined. *Titanic* could float, but if anything went wrong it would founder rapidly. Did that mean he should begin putting people into lifeboats? Launching loaded boats would be risky during the dark of night. Frigid ocean water would quickly incapacitate and ultimately kill anyone dumped overboard while launching the lifeboats.

Captain Smith was more worried now than he had been when he sent his first wireless calls for help. Those came even before he knew his ship was sinking and indicated the way the man approached his duty. Smith's lifeboat decision was made before he returned to the ship's bridge. He would not worry about personal embarrassment or the dangers of handling davit tackles in the dark. The captain's first act after returning to the bridge was to order Chief Officer Henry T. Wilde to begin loading passengers into boats.

Then, *Titanic*'s master sought out his navigation officer to check that the ship's coordinates had been updated. Fourth Officer Joseph G. Boxhall recalled, "I encountered him when reporting something to him, or something. I said, 'Is it really serious?' He said, 'Mr. Andrews tells me he gives her from an hour to an hour and a half."

Boxhall may have known the truth, but *Titanic* still concealed its condition from most passengers and crew. Continuing confidence in the ship was demonstrated by the difficulty the crew had in getting people to enter the lifeboats. The first boats generally carried about half their rated capacity of persons.

> *They called for the women and children to board the boats first. Both women and men, however, hesitated, and did*

> *not feel inclined to get into the small boats, thinking the larger boat was the safer.*
>
> --James R. McGough
> First Class Passenger [7-1]

> *...I considered that the lifeboats were merely a precaution and upon my wife's suggestion...we then proceeded immediately upward, my wife being rather alarmed...but for her I should have remained in bed, reading.*
>
> --Norman C. Chambers
> First Class Passenger [7-2]

> *...we dressed fully and went up on deck, and there we saw quite a number of people talking; and nobody seemed to think anything serious had happened. There were such remarks as "Oh, it will only be a few hours before we will be on the way again."*
>
> --George A. Harder
> First Class Passenger [7-3]

Water poured into the hull for 45 minutes with little visible effect to passengers. Negligible tipping of the bow allowed passengers and crew to reassure each other that the ship might settle a bit, but it would surely remain afloat. Charles M. Hayes, president of Grand Trunk Railroad, told fellow Canadian, Major Arthur G. Peuchen, "Oh, I don't know, you cannot sink this boat. No matter what we have struck, she is good for eight or ten hours." Hayes was just restating the "float as its own lifeboat" claim made by the designers of the giant liner.

Titanic did not act like a sinking ship because, technically it was not yet foundering. Even as the first lifeboats were lowered it was still possible for the engineers to pull of a miracle. They should have been able to keep the waterlogged ship afloat until help arrived. Unfortunately, a simple mistake prevented them from pulling off that miracle. As will be seen, that mistake caused *Titanic*'s premature death.

Failure did not come from a lack of will or inadequate skill. In 1912, Chief Engineer Bell and his men were too early on the damage control "learning curve" for big, multi-compartment ships. If the accident had taken place in 1918 after four years of World War I, the same men facing an identical situation would have done far better. The first "battle of the Atlantic" against German U-boats gave British sailors invaluable experience surviving damage worse than that infliced on *Titanic*.

But, the accident took place during the innocent days of 1912. With the ship not yet foundering, *Titanic*'s decks remained steady and the electric lights burned brightly. The band played for the first class. And, it was warm inside the public rooms where passengers gathered wearing uncomfortable white canvas lifevests. People chatted in small groups as they ignored the first lifeboats to be loaded and launched.

"My husband cautioned us all to keep together, and we went up to A deck, where we found quite a group of people we knew," first class passenger Emily Ryerson recalled. "Everyone had on a life belt, and they all were very quiet and self-possessed. We stood around there for quite a long time. My maid ran down to the cabin and got some of my clothes. Then we went to the boat deck."

At first U.S. Army (Ret) Colonel Archibald Gracie was among those who were not worried. "I saw Mr. Ismay with one of the officers," he told Senator Smith. "He looked very self-contained. That gave encouragement to my thought that perhaps the disaster was not anything particularly serious." Despite the apparent normalcy of the ship, Gracie's military training told him to pack three bags. "I thought if we were going to be removed to some other ship it would be easy for the steward to get my luggage out." Once on deck, he accepted a life vest from a steward before stopping to reassure a group of women.

Steward John Hardy initially believed the ship would survive. "Everybody had full confidence that the ship would float up to the time my boat left," he told the U.S. inquiry. He expressed his confidence to First Officer William Murdoch whose response came as a rude shock. "I was walking along the deck forward with him and he said, 'I believe she is gone, Hardy.' And, that is the only time I thought she might sink, when he said that."

Far below them in the boiler rooms a party of men worked its way forward from the engine room opening the automatic watertight doors as they went. Behind them a hose pipe was being dragged forward. Coal trimmer Thomas P. Dillon was among those men. "The next order we got was to get out of the engine room and into the stokehold and open the doors, the watertight doors," he said. "One leading from the engine room to the stokehold was lifted up high enough by hand to let us get underneath. I assisted to open them as far as we could forward."

Dillon's party was told to open the doors by Chief Engineer Bell, "to allow the engineers to get forward to their duties, the valves and the pumps." It appears engineers extended a suction hose forward as part of efforts to dewater the ship. This was an odd activity considering *Titanic* equipped with 10-inch pipes connecting the engine room pumps to any of the ship's sixteen watertight compartments. The use of a flexible hose indicates something was wrong with the ship's built-in bilge eduction system. Did it become blocked somewhere? Was it never completed before the maiden voyage? Questions raised by the use of the hose can never be answered because all of the engineers died in the sinking.

The men opened watertight door between boiler rooms #3 and #4 and then started to move forward to open the next door into boiler room #5. An engineer unexpectedly ordered them to halt. Dillon and the others stood around waiting additional orders. While he was waiting Dillon noticed something odd in boiler room #4. "There was water coming in forward. Coming from underneath the forward part. Small quantities," he recalled.

Trimmer George Cavelle was working in boiler room #4 raking down the furnaces. Although it was not his regular job, this was an emergency. The raking was partly done when he noticed something odd. "The water started coming up over her stokehold plates," he told the British inquiry.[7-4] He said it was about a foot deep and men were working almost to their knees in the cold salt water. "It came gradually," Cavelle said, "and then I thought to myself it was time I went for the escape ladder."

No water should have been rising in boiler room #4 at that time unless that last "kiss" between ship and iceberg was more forceful than thought. Ice damage was the only logical cause of flooding in this compartment. Dillon specifically noted the water he saw did not come through the side of the ship. Rather, it came up from "underneath." Those unfamiliar with ships have sometimes interpreted this to mean that water was coming up *through* the tank top deck. This was virtually impossible because the tank top was solid steel caulked watertight. Located two feet beneath the stoker plates on which Dillon walked. The tank top was *Titanic*'s inner shell intended to keep the ship afloat if the outside plating of the bottom should become damaged.

Dillon's story mirrored that of fellow trimmer Cavell. Both men saw water rising in #4 that did not come through the side of the ship. The source of the slow flooding in boiler room #4 remains unknown even though the British inquiry entertained the idea of undiscovered damage to that compartment. Naval architect Edward Wilding favored this concept. Wilding helped design the ship for the Harland & Wolff shipyard. Unfortunately, his scenario required nothing less than a minor miracle. He proposed that a piece of ice broken from the berg plugged a hole in the side of boiler room #4. It kept water out until either melting or washing away. This "ice plug" was a flight of Wilding's fancy. He had no hard evidence to back it up.

Explorers of the wreck have found no visible damage on the bow section of the hull to corroborate damage as far aft as boiler room #4. Still, this compartment was directly below where Col. Archibald Gracie was awakened by impact on the iceberg. It is also where iceberg impact started a coal avalanche on Cavell. So, the possibility that contact between the ship and iceberg opened a seam cannot be discounted.

Water rising a foot above the stoker plates at the front of boiler room #4 is additional evidence that some sort of ice damage was inflicted there. It is significant that it rose prior to any flooding of boiler room #5 just forward. Water did not overtop the bulkhead because the compartment from which it would have come, boiler room #5, was still bone dry.

By now, even passengers with little knowledge of ships were beginning to sense impending doom. Some third class men had already had absolute proof the end was coming. They had been forced out of their cabins by stinging cold sea water. No such problems bedeviled life in first class where the attitude was becoming less jovial, more somber. "In the hallway I met a great many people, ladies and gentlemen with their life belts on. The ladies were crying, most of them. It was a very serious sight, and I commenced to realize how serious matters were," said Canadian Maj. Arthur Peuchen.

Second Officer Lightoller initially did not see the importance of loading boats to their capacity. "I had no idea it was urgent. I would have taken more risks. I should not have considered it wise to put more in (people in the boats), but I might have taken risks," he admitted. "I took chances afterwards." Eventually, the growing slant of the deck made the truth obvious to all. The percentage of fill in the lifeboats began to increase. Toward the last, some boats were sent away with more people than their official rated capacity.

Launching *Titanic*'s 16 regular lifeboats was confounded by more than just reluctant passengers. Manpower was the real controlling factor. *Titanic* carried hundreds of stewards, cooks, scullions, and hotel staff, but only had 48 true seaman in its crew. Two seamen were required as skilled crew in each boat, accounting for 32 sailors. The remaining 16 were needed on deck to handle the davit tackles lowering the boats. The line handlers could be divided among four sets of davits, allowing two lifeboats to be lowered simultaneously from either side.

Conventional wisdom claims *Titanic* did not have enough lifeboats. This ignores the 1912 approach to lifesaving apparatus. Although they were called "lifeboats," these craft were really little more than rowboats with no weather protection. No sailor imagined that anyone could or would survive for any length of time on the sea in one of those craft. Instead, their intended purpose was only to taxi *Titanic*'s passengers and crew to a rescue ship in an emergency.

Modern historians are unaware that the boats were not 16 separate pieces of lifesaving apparatus, but only individual parts of a much larger lifesaving system. The key element in this system was the ship itself. *Titanic* was not designed to be "unsinkable." Rather, the bulkheads and watertight compartments were intended to control flooding and prolong the life of the vessel. The ship was to "be its own lifeboat" long enough for rescue vessels to arrive. Only then would the mis-named "lifeboats" transfer people by rowing them to rescue ships.

The logistics of coordinating sixteen boats simultaneously in a ferry operation would be staggering. Additional boats would have done little more than complicate the process. Second Officer Charles H. Lightoller explained this situation to Senator William A. Smith during the American inquiry.

> *Senator SMITH: Were they* [the lifeboats] *gotten out with their full complement of oarsmen?*
> *Mr. LIGHTOLLER: We were not undertaking a boat drill then, sir. We were saving life, and we were using the men to the best of my knowledge and ability.*
> *Senator SMITH: How many men?*

> *Mr. LIGHTOLLER: As a rule, I put about two seamen in a boat. There is no use in sending too many men away and then finding yourself short. The idea was--*

Senator Smith unexpectedly interrupted the second officer in mid sentence with a meaningless question about the number of lifeboats carried by *Titanic*. The senator did not understand the underlying concept of the ship's lifesaving system. Fortunately, on the night of the sinking the trained seamen working on the slanting decks of the ship did understand. They worked "handsomely" in sailor talk, meaning as fast as the job could be done without things getting out of hand and no faster. By not rushing, all 16 regular lifeboats were lowered safely.

One sailor unselfishly jumped out of lifeboat #6 to help with the davit tackles. He knew that trained hands were needed on those tackles to prevent dumping a boatload of passengers into the freezing water. This selfless act of heroism resulted in a lifeboat with insufficient trained crew. A second act of heroism ended this deficiency. This time one of the male passengers stepped forward.

> *Mr. LIGHTOLLER* (continued)*...I was calling for seamen, and one of the seamen jumped out of the boat and started to lowering away. The boat was about half way down when the women called out and said that there was only one man in the boat. I had only two seamen and could not part with them...when a passenger called out and said, "If you like, I will go."*

The agile Canadian who called out from the shadows of *Titanic*'s boat deck was Major Arthur G. Peuchen. He left behind a ship populated with people still timid about getting into the lifeboats. Seaman Frank Osman noted that he was not alone in thinking that launching lifeboats was only a precaution. "I never heard anything amongst the passengers as to whether she would sink," Osman said. "The only thing I heard was one passenger was saying he was going in the boat, and stand by the ship."

It took courage for women wearing the fashions of 1912 to leave the ship. Boarding a lifeboat meant approaching the edge of a 60-foot steel cliff and then stepping over the abyss into a fragile wooden craft swaying on creaking manila ropes. “The decks were lighted, and as you went through the window it was as if you stepped out into the dark,” recalled Mrs. Emily B. Ryerson. “We were flung into the boats. I fell on top of the women who were already in the boat.” Mrs. Ryerson was lowered in lifeboat #4 from the port side. She was accompanied by her two grown daughters and 13-year-old son.

Titanic's baker, Charles Joughin, distributed bread to most of the lifeboats. On his way below again he noted the ship was listing and so decided to throw a small pile of deck chairs overboard on the chance someone might need a makeshift raft when the ship sank. Back in his room he decided to have a "drop of liquor" even though it was against company regulations. About then Joughin noted water puddling in his room. "If it had been higher, I should have thought something about it," he said later. "But under the circumstances I though it might have been a pipe burst because there was a pipe burst on the *Olympic*...and we got the same water. It might have been the same thing."

Joughin was wrong. Water was flooding aft along the working alleyway known to the crew as "Scotland Road." It was an ominous sign. Water was bleeding deeply into the ship.

On the slanting boat deck Fourth Officer Boxhall was helping Chief Officer Wilde clear and load lifeboat #2, the emergency cutter on the starboard side. Captain Smith came over to stand beside the young officer. “He told me I had to get into that boat and go away,” Boxhall recalled of the captain’s final order to him. New manila rope creaking through blocks accompanied jerking of the boat. As the tackles paid out the faces of those left behind grew smaller. The captain and fourth officer were first feet and then yards apart. Eventually, the distance between the living and the dead grew into hours, days, and then years. Years later the old sailor could still conjure up memories of those faces growing small in the darkness.

Only two of *Titanic*'s 16 conventional lifeboats and all four of the collapsible boats remained. A pair of collapsibles were stored quite logically on the boat deck adjacent to the davits for the emergency cutters. These were eventually erected and launched properly. The two remaining collapsibles had to be wrestled down from the top of the officers quarters. Tackles to attach to the #1 funnel stays were provided for hoisting collapsible lifeboats A and B off the roof and lowering them to the boat deck. This system appeared workable on the drawing table, but on a sinking ship things never go as planned.

Lightoller and lamp trimmer Samuel Hemming were struggling to shove collapsible B off the roof of the officers quarters and down to the port boat deck. Their intent was to install it in the davits originally used by lifeboat #2. Titanic increasingly rolled onto its port side while they tugged and pushed. By now the ship had gone from its early starboard list to an increasing death roll to port. Gravity was helping Lightoller's efforts, so Hemming went over to the starboard boat to lend a hand pushing collapsible A uphill off the roof. [7-5]

> *Mr. HEMMING: ...they were turning out the port collapsible boat. I went and assisted Mr. Lightoller to get it out. ...I went on top of the officer's house and helped to clear away the port collapsible boat on that house. After that I went over to the starboard side.* [U.S. testimony]

Collapsible B slammed down to the port boat deck. It has long been assumed that the hull landed upside-down, however there is no proof. Most likely, it landed right-side up and later, after it floated free, was overturned by the wash from a falling funnel. One of the ship's barbers, August Weikman was on the boat deck to wrestle the boat into the davits, but the sides had to be erected first.

Second Officer Lightoller turned to assist with collapsible A on the starboard side. Titanic's continuing roll to port made it ever more difficult to slide collapsible A down to the boat deck. Oars were turned into improvised skids, but the weight of the boat proved too much and they splintered. Steward Edward Brown was among the men Lightoller saw getting the boat off the officers' quarter roof.

"We slid it down to the boat deck, Brown said. "We got it about halfway and the ship got a list to port, and we had great difficulty. We could not get it right up to the davits, so we had to slacken the falls. She [*Titanic*] put the bridge right under. I found the water come right up to my legs here, and I jumped into the collapsible boat then. I cut the after all, and called out to the man on the forward end of the boat to cut her loose; she would float if we got the falls loose." [7-6]

During the struggle to get the collapsible boats off the officers quarters another drama played out inside. *Titanic*'s electric lights still glowed, but they were dimmer now and showed a reddish hue. Voltage was dropping and this loss of electrical power began to affect the ship's Marconi wireless transmitter as well. Distant operators noticed the radio signal growing weaker before it disappeared forever.

Evidence of those final minutes in Titanic's radio room was revealed when the remains of the ship's Marconi suite were explored by a remotely-controlled underwater camera. Deep inside the "silent room" the camera discovered the lid to the discharger box is still latched open. According to Parks Stephenson, an expert on early Marconi equipment, the open lid indicates that Bride and Phillips were making a desperate effort to adjust their transmitting apparatus as the ship gradually lost power. Bride most likely opened the box to make the adjustments while Phillips worked the key.

Titanic's radio silence was momentarily broken when the Phillips keyed the transmitter to test Bride's work. The operator aboard Virginian caught the distinctive tone of Titanic's transmitter once again, but he noted the power was "greatly reduced." There were two repetitions of the letter "V" used by radio operators as a signal when tuning their equipment.

During this tuning process Captain Smith appeared briefly in the Marconi office. "Clear out," he said. It was time to abandon their posts and fend for themselves. Instead, Phillips adjusted his earphones and tried again to summon help. "Mr. Phillips called once or twice more," assistant operator Bride told the British inquiry. "'The power was failing and I do not think we were getting a spark as there were no replies."

Bride was incorrect. It may have been weak, but Titanic's voice could still be heard. The steamer Virginian caught this last desperate plea from Phillips' telegraph key. The other ship's operator thought he heard the letters "C-Q" in Titanic's distinctive note. After that, the code was unintelligible from blurred and ragged spark. Suddenly, Titanic's signal stopped forever. The Virginian's operator thought the power had been switched off. He called the stricken liner, but got no reply.[7-7]

Lamp trimmer Hemming had been helping with collapsible A when water began climbing over the forward wall of the bridge. "I went and looked over the starboard side, and everything was black," he told Senator Smith. "I went over to the port side and saw a boat off the port quarter." Knowing that his survival was at stake, the seaman used a davit tackle to let himself into the water where he began swimming for the lifeboat.

Hemming got off the ship just before a sudden drop of the bow. This lurch was probably the first visible symptom of the hull tearing itself apart beneath the third funnel. The boat deck dropped so quickly that to people on deck it appeared a wave washed aft. The moving water was really a manifestation of the bow section dropping downward as Titanic began to break apart. The men around both of the collapsible boats found themselves swept overboard. Ship's barber Weikman was among them.

> *Mr. WEIKMAN: ...I was proceeding to launch the next boat when the ship suddenly sank at the bow and there was a rush of water that washed me overboard, and therefore the boat was not launched by human hands....I managed to get clear...and stared to swim...This was about 1:50 AM. ...because my watch stopped at that time by the water...[U.S. Testimony]*

The barber was not the only one washed off the boat deck by that "rush of water." One of the ship's postal clerks, J.S. March, was standing nearby. He was not as lucky as Weikman. Days after the sinking his body was recovered along with his stopped timepiece. It read 1:27 a.m., which was correct in April 15th ship's time. Apparently, March had set his timepiece back before retiring that Sunday night so it would be correct when he arose on Monday morning. When the 47 minute time change is taken into account, Weikman's and March's timepieces stopped at the same moment.

By now baker Joughin was on A deck in a pantry located at the base of funnel #3. "While I was in there I thought I would take a drink of water." As he refreshed himself Titanic gave up the fight to survive. "While I was getting the drink of water I heard a kind of crash as if something had buckled," Joughin recalled during the British inquiry. "As if a part of the ship had buckled. It was not an explosion or anything like that. It was like as if the iron was parting." No one in 1912 recognized how accurate Joughin was in describing the destruction of Titanic.

The British and American inquiries both erroneously concluded the ship sank intact. Only when a Franco-American expedition finally photographed the wreck in September, 1985 did it become obvious that the iron hull had been torn apart as Joughin described. What had been Titanic now lies in two pieces, ripped through exactly the area where baker Joughin stood when he heard the first crash of destruction.

Lightoller always denied that Titanic broke apart as it sank. Even so, it was the motion of the ship as it buckled told Lightoller it was no longer safe to stay aboard Titanic. He jumped off the front edge of the bridge roof into the freezing water. For a moment he considered swimming to the crow's nest, but then realized it was attached to Titanic and would sink with the rest of the ship.

Mr. LIGHTOLLER: Well, roughly, the crow's nest was level with the water when the bridge went under.

Lightoller's observation makes it possible to estimate the downward angle of the bow as the ship began to break apart. It works to be between 11 and 15 degrees. As late as when baker Joughin left the B deck pantry it was still possible to walk aft on solid deck. The destruction had not yet climbed that high in the hull. Although they now glowed red, the electric lights were still bright enough to reveal a frightening sight. "People escaping the wave at the front of the boat deck piled up against the railing where that deck ended overlooking the ship's after well deck. Some tumbled over the gates protecting the ladders leading down to the decks below. "When I got on top I could then see them clambering down from those decks. Their idea was to get to the poop." the baker remembered. Realizing the risk of being in a panic, so hung back. "Of course, I was in the tail end of the rush."

Assistant radio operator Bride almost reached collapsible A while it was still on the boat deck. Then, he decided to go climb onto the roof of the officers quarters. The sudden downward lurch of the bridge washed him away. Bride found himself in a confusing maelstrom of stinging cold water. One of the ship's large funnels slammed down, overturning Collapsible B and scattering the first group that tried to use it as a life raft. None survived. Bride was overwhelmed by the wave created by the falling smokestack.

In the maelstrom the collapsible boat washed over top of the officers' quarters where along the way it scooped up radio operator Bride. The wave then swung around to the starboard side where it moved aft on the boat deck, catching more victims. Among them was Col. Gracie.

> *...the water struck my right side. I crouched down into it preparatory to jumping with it, and rose as if on the crest of a wave on the seashore.*[7-8]

Baker Joughin was still dry. He paused for a moment before seeking a way down to the poop. "I was just getting towards the rail. The electric lights were burning right to the very last. I had my watch in my front pocket and I was transferring it to my stern pocket. I saw the time by my watch at a quarter-past two. I followed down getting towards the well deck." Titanic writhed even farther onto its port side. "I was not exactly in the well, I was on the side, practically on the side then. She gave a great list over to port and threw everybody in a bunch except myself. I did not see anybody else besides myself out of the bunch. She threw them over. At last I clambered on the side when she chucked them."

Collapsible B was now upside-down, but floating within an easy swim for those who found themselves in the water near where the forward end of the boat deck went under. Many had just reached what they thought was safety on the upturned hull when the second funnel gave an ominous lurch. Two shipboard friends, Jack Thayer and Milton Long were caught in the crowd on the boat deck. They noticed the #2 funnel tip forward accompanied by a rumbling mixed with what Thayer took to be muffled explosions. The youths decided to abandon ship.

When Thayer surfaced his friend was gone. Forever.

Despite the stinging cold water Thayer saw the second funnel lift off the deck and fall to starboard. Tons of falling metal missed him by a scant 20 to 30 feet as it toppled onto a mass of people who had been swept off the ship. The steel cylinder came down almost on top of both Lightoller and Collapsible B. "It fell within three or four inches of the boat. It lifted the boat bodily and threw her about 20 feet clear of the ship near as I could judge."

For ship's barber Weikman the collapse of the second funnel was a life-saving blessing. After being washed off the port boat deck he paddled around looking for something to make a raft. “I was about 15 feet away from the ship when I heard a second explosion,” he said in an Affidavit. “The explosion blew me along with a wall of water toward the dark object I was swimming to, which proved to be a bundle of deck chairs, which I managed to climb on.” It is possible these were the very chairs thrown overboard earlier by ship’s baker Charles Joughin. Weikman owed his life to them.

Marconi operator Bride had perhaps the most hair-raising experience of any survivor. The wave created by the fall of the first funnel pushed the boat fully across Titanic's centerline. Bride was spun around under water. While in the darkness beneath boat he thought it was collapsible A over his head. In reality, he was beneath overturned collapsible B. He could not see it, but the great ship was in its death throes. "It seemed a lifetime, really," he admitted in testimony before, "I got on top of the boat eventually."

Col. Gracie was still hugging the roof of the deckhouse near the 1st class entrance. He was virtually at the base of the second funnel when it toppled past him. Gracie never saw it. He was being pulled under by the sinking ship.

> *...My holding on to the iron railing just when I did prevented my being knocked unconscious. I pulled myself over on the roof on my stomach, but before I could get to my feet I was in a whirlpools of water...as I still tried to cling to the railing as the ship plunged to the depths.*[7-9]

Gracie’s ears popped from the pressure. Somehow, he kicked his way clear and swam to the surface without losing consciousness. He stuck a broken wooden plank under his arm for flotation and looked around to see only a “light-gray smoky vapor” on the sea. Behind his back the stern tipped up before sliding into the depths. In the cold and darkness Gracie did not notice. Instead, he focused on surviving and eventually managed to find Collapsible B with Lightoller, Bride and others standing on its overturned hull.

Jack Thayer and Col. Gracie apparently got wet at the same instant. After being rescued, the two survivors found their pocket timepieces had been stopped by the cold salt water at the same time, 2:22 AM. Robert Norman, was not so lucky. When his body was recovered the timepiece in its pocket showed 3:07 AM. Apparently, he had not adjusted his pocket watch from April 13th Civil Time. The correct time when the 47 minute setback is applied was 2:20 AM as shown in Table 7-2.

Greaser Thomas Ranger was assigned to the ship's electrical system, so was familiar with its operation. "The lights seemed to be going out," he told the BOT inquiry. The process started in the bow. Lights on the stern remained burning for a short while longer. "The lights right aft what were burning, on the after end what was floating," he said. Fuses protecting lighting circuits in the front of the ship "blew" as wires in the bow became immersed in salt water. Once the ship began to tear itself apart electrical cables leading forward across the break were stretched and broken. The section of hull behind the break regained an even keel for a few moments. Decks forward of the break were now dark Ranger told the BOT inquiry. "The lights gradually went out as the aft end of the ship went under," he recalled.

Major Arthur Peuchen laid on his oar for a moment as disquieting sounds came across the water. "We commenced to hear signs of the breaking up of the boat," the Canadian testified to the U.S. inquiry. "We heard a sort of a rumbling sound and the lights were still on at the rumbling sound, as far as my memory serves me. Then a sort of explosion, then another. It seemed to be one, two, three rumbling sounds. Then the lights went out."

Somewhere in that darkness ship's baker Joughin was among the hundreds clinging to the disintegrating wreck. He crawled out onto the starboard side of the hull and then up onto the starboard side of the poop despite the nearly complete darkness. "I eventually got on the starboard side of the poop, on the side of the ship. I was just wondering what to do next when she went," Joughin recalled. The Poop fell away from baker Joughin's feet and he floated free on the freezing Atlantic.

Classic renderings of the ship's last minutes show Titanic's upended stern pointing into the sky like an iron tombstone. Not so according the sole survivor who remained aboard to the very end. In sworn testimony he said such depictions, "...would be absolutely wrong. "She was not far out of the water at any stage that I saw. She went down in a glide. There was no great shock, or anything. She simply glided away. I do not believe my head went under the water at all. It may have been wetted, but no more."

From her lifeboat stewardess Annie Robinson caught a glimpse of the time. "I looked at my watch when the ship went down," she told the British inquiry. "It was twenty minutes to two. That was by altered time when we were in the boat." Robinson had set her watch back by the full 47 minute adjustment from April 14th hours and was keeping April 15 time. Converted to crew time by which the accident was recorded it was now 2:03 AM *Titanic* had succumbed to its wounds in only 2 hours 23 minutes.[7-10]

Maj. PEUCHEN: ...the quartermaster told us to stop rowing. We all thought we ought to go back to the boat but the quartermaster said, "No, we're not going back to the boat." he said, "It is our lives now, not theirs," and he insisted upon our rowing farther away.[7-11]

In truth, the lifeboats could not go back. The ship started rolling onto its port side just before the stern started to break free. Then, the stern tipped up like a steel tombstone before it began sliding into the depths. This writhing of the ship as it died was accompanied by sounds of explosions deep under water. Approaching that steel whirling dervish in a clumsy lifeboat would have been nearly impossible. Attempting it in a lifeboat handled by inexperienced and frightened passengers would have been suicidal. For their own safety, survivors in lifeboats could only finger their idle oars, avert their eyes, and listen to the screams of their loved ones trapped on the disintegrating wreck.

...there was no sound for what seemed like hours, and then began the cries for help of people drowning all around us, which seemed to go on forever.

--Emily B. Ryerson
First Class Passenger

Then the dreadful calls and cries. We could not distinguish the exact cry for assistance. Moaning and crying. Frightful. It affected all of the women in our boat whose husbands were among these; and it went on for some time, gradually getting fainter, fainter....

-- Maj. Arthur Peuchen
First Class Passenger

In the cold and dark baker Joughin paddled his way toward overturned collapsible boat B. Second Officer Lightoller was on the back of the boat trying organize efforts to use it as a makeshift life raft. After what seemed hours, enough room was found on the overturned boat for the baker to haul himself out of the water. Joughin had saved barber Weikman by throwing deck chairs overboard. In turn, Weikman's efforts to get collapsible B free of the ship helped save Joughin's life.

That's the way of it at sea.

Table 7-1
Comparison of Norman, Gracie, & Thayer Stopped Timepieces

Owner Of Timepiece	***Apr 14 Time***	***Crew Bridge Time***	***Apr 15 Time***	***GMT***
Norman (set to Apr 13 time)	*3:07 equates to 2:20 Apr 14*	*1:56*	*1:33*	*0518*
Col. Gracie	*2:22*	*1:58*	*1:35*	*0520*
Jack Thayer	*2:22*	*1:58*	*1:35*	*0520*

Table 7-2
Running Time (Duration) Of Sinking

Running Time	***April 14 Time***	***Crew Bridge Time***	***April 15 Time***	***GMT***	***Event Description***
0:00	*12:04 am*	*11:40 pm*	*11:17 pm*	*0302*	*Ship Strike On Iceberg.*
2:10	*2:14 am*	*1:50 pm*	*1:27 am*	*0512*	*Timpieces Of Weikman & March Stop*
2:16	*2:20 am*	*1:56 am*	*1:33 am*	*0518*	*Norman's Timpiece Stops 3:07 In Apr 13 Time*
2:23	*2:27 am*	*2:03 am*	*1:40 am*	*0525*	*Stern Disappears Per Annie Robinson*

CHAPTER 8
THE MORNING AFTER

The Big Myth: The rescue ship Carpathia steamed right to the spot where Titanic sank. Other ships came to the same spot later that Monday morning.

The Truth: Even before dawn on the morning of the sinking other mariners knew that Titanic had not foundered at the location in its distress messages.

Captain James H. Moore was both tired from his overnight vigil and chilled by the dawn of April 15, 1912. Six hours earlier his radio officer startled him with news that the world's largest ship which had radioed it was sinking after striking an iceberg. Without hesitation Moore turned his ship, *Mount Temple* around and started to *Titanic's* CQD position. Getting to the correct location required a nerve-racking night navigating around icebergs and through field ice. Moore stopped just before dawn for the safety of his ship. He would not chance a dangerous iceberg encounter during the remaining darkness.

In that first post-*Titanic* dawn he could see no sign of the sinking liner – no ship, no wreckage, no lifeboats, no bodies. To make sure he was in the right spot Moore asked his first officer to take a "prime vertical" on the sun. He explained the procedure to the U.S. inquiry, "This is a sight taken when the sun is bearing due east. That position gave me 50° 9 ½' West." To make sure of the accuracy of this longitude he asked for a second sight.

Mount Temple was exactly in the right spot. *Titanic* was not there and, obviously, had not foundered there.

Moore double-checked with his wireless operator to make sure he had the correct coordinates. Two sets had been received from the sinking ship. The first was 41°44' North, 50°24' West. Those coordinates had hardly been copied down when a new set arrived. "Before we had the course laid off I received another position, which read 41°46' North, 50°14 West. That was ten miles farther to the eastward, and it was that position that I laid my course for," Captain Moore said.

In the ruddy glow of dawn *Mount Temple* was east of *Titanic*'s second set of coordinates. There was no shipwreck to be seen. "I came to this great pack of ice. I went to the southeast to try to get around them because I realized that he (*Titanic*) must be somewhere eastward of me. The *Titanic* must have been on the other side of that field of ice, and her position was not right which she gave," Moore concluded. His assessment was absolutely correct.

Captain Moore continued hunting for the missing shipwreck. By 6 a.m. he had picked his way to the east of the pack ice where he sighted *Carpathia*. The rescue ship was also east of the floating ice where it was finishing the job of taking survivors aboard. Captain Arthur Rostron knew as well as Captain Moore that the rescue took place considerably east of Titanic's CQD coordinates. Yet, on the way to New York he told Joseph G. Boxhall, Fourth Officer of the ill-fated liner that the obviously wrong numbers as "splendid." Boxhall, of course, was the man who created them.

Titanic's first myth was born.

Captain Moore's accurate assessment of Boxhall's coordinates would quickly be forgotton. Captain Rostrons self-serving assessment would be repeated over and again until the discovery of the shipwreck at 41°44' North, 49°57' West. Rostron was wrong, but it did not matter. History had believed him long enough to insure his fame would propel him into commodor of the Cunard line. Even after the true location was learned, Captain Moore was never given due credit for noticing the error in Boxhall's work. Nobody cared why he did not find history's most famous shipwreck.

In New York City, the worst day of Phillip A.S. Franklin's worst week began in the worst possible way. Still groggy from being awakend out of a sound sleep, the head of White Star Line's office in New York was trying to make sense out of what the newspaper reporter on the other end of the telephone circuit was saying. “At about two minutes of two on Monday morning I was aroused by the telephone bell ringing,” he recalled for U.S. inquiry. “A reporter, I could not tell from what paper, said that they had just heard *Titanic* was sinking, and that she had sent out a call for assistance.” The men talked about the ship in the present tense because in their minds the ship was still afloat. They did not know that *Titanic* had been down for nearly a half hour.

“I immediately called up our dock and asked them if they had heard anything,” Franklin said. “They told me that several reporters had called them up, that reporters had been trying to give them some information about the Titanic. I said, 'Have you heard anything authentic?' He told me, 'No.' I then called up the Associated Press. They reported to me practically what the reporter had told me.”

Carpathia was not yet picking up passengers when Franklin became the first person connected with the sinking to attempt to put a positive “spin” on the story. “I then asked them whether or not they could not hold the matter and not give out such an alarming report until they could se whether it could be confirmed. They said, 'No, it has already gone out.'”

Franklin dressed and headed for the company office in downtown New York. Many of his employees had also learned of the story and were on hand hours before normal business hours. “We announced to everyone that these were rumors, but we could not confirm them,” he recalled for the U.S. inquiry. In fact, he did more. He trotted out the platitude that *Titanic* was “unsinkable.”

> Vice president Franklin of International Mercantile Marine says regrding reported accident to Titanic: “It is unbelievable that Titanic could have met with accident without our being notified...In any event, the ship is unsinkable, and there is absolutely no danger to passengers.
>
> Dow Jones News Service
> 9:22 am Monday, April 15, 1912

There was no doubt that *Titanic* could sink. But that dawn only the ship's more than 700 survivors now benefitting from Captain Rostron's hospitality aboard *Carpathia* knew the truth. Most of them were still under the emotional shock of losing loved ones in a most horrible fashion. Life would go on, but never go back to normal. Titanic's surviving bridge team members may have grieved for their lost comrades, but they still had pressing business. Nobody yet expected the U.S. Senate inquiry as there had never been any such proceeding in the past. The officers had to prepare themselves for the Board of Trade's inquiry which followed every major shipping casualty.

In the quasi-military hierarchy of a merchant ship, tradition passes command to the senior surviving officer. That was Second Officer Charles H. Lightoller. With Captain Edward J. Smith, Chief Officer Henry T. Wilde, and First Officer William M. Murdoch all dead, he was de-facto captain of the sunken liner.

Also among the survivors was White Star Line's managing director, J. Bruce Ismay. He clambered into collapsible lifeboat C at the last possible moment and was now sequestered in the small cabin normally occupied by *Carpathia*'s first class doctor. Ismay later claimed he was so shocked by the sinking and loss of life that he was under sedation during the entire trip to New York.

"I must say that at the time Mr. Ismay did not seem to me to be in a mental condition to finally decide anything," Lightoller recalled. "He was obsessed with the idea, and kept repeating, that he ought to have gone down with the ship because he found that women had gone down. We had difficulty arousing Mr. Ismay, purely owing to the fact that women had gone down in the boat and he had not."

Lightoller probably overstated the case to make his boss look good. It was more of that whitewash he spoke about in later years. The Second Officer also painted a very different picture of Ismay in some critical testimony. The two men met often and cogently discussed the problem of getting surviving members of *Titanic*'s crew out of the United States as quickly as possible. Ismay retained his faculties enough to converse via wireless with Franklin in the New York office.

Wednesday, April 17

ISLEFRANK, New York
Most desirable Titanic crew aboard Carpathia should be returned home earliest moment possible. Suggest you hold

Cedric, sailing here daylight Friday unless you see and reason contrary. Propose returning in her myself. Please send outfit of clothes, including shoes, for me to Cedric. Have nothing of my own. Please reply.

– YAMSI

This Marconigram was received in White Star's New York Office at 5:35 PM. "ISLEFRANK" in the address block was the code for company messages sent to Franklin. The signature, "YAMSI" was code for Ismay. By 8 PM Franklin replied.

Wednesday, April 17

ISMAY Carpathia
Have arranged forward crew Lapland, sailing Saturday, calling Plymouth. We all consider most unwise delay Cedric, considering circumstances.

FRANKLIN

So started an exchange of messages about *Titanic*'s crew and other matters such as the lifeboats. These were the only remaining intact pieces of the lost ship. Under so-called "Admiralty Law" governing ships at sea, they represented the remaining value of *Titanic* against which liability claims could be made.

Thursday April 18

ISLEFRANK, New York
Send responsible ship officer and 14 White Star sailors in 2 tugboats to take care of 13 Titanic boats at quarantine.

YAMSI

Thursday April 18

ISLEFRANK, New York
Please join Carpathia quarantine if possible.

YAMSI

"Quarantine" mentioned above is a physical location where incoming ships are required to stop for health inspections, payment of port taxes, and other bureaucratic paperwork. The term originated in the era when incoming ships were medically quarantined to insure they were not carrying infectious disease.

The ongoing series of messages made it obvious that Ismay still expected the company ship *Cedric* to be delayed in its departure until Titanic's crew could be placed aboard. The man goading him into this was none other than Second Officer Lightoller. "I think I am responsible for the telegram being sent," he told the U.S. Senate inquiry. "I know it was sent because Mr. Ismay told me it had been. Mr. Ismay apparently sent the telegram after I advised him. He then received a reply, as I understand from Mr. Franklin, which he read to me, and asked my further advice with regard to holding the *Cedric*. And, I advised him further. So, I believe Mr. Franklin replied and another was sent, further urging him to hold the *Cedric*."

Thursday, April 18

ISLEFRANK, New York
Very important you should hold Cedric daylight Friday for Titanic crew. Reply.

YAMSI

"Ismay asked me my opinion about it, and I frankly stated that it was the best thing in the world to do if we could catch the *Cedric*, said Lightoller. "Later on he remarked that owing to weather conditions it was very doubtful if we would catch the *Cedric*. I said, 'Yes, it is doubtful. It will be a great pity if she sails without us.'"

Lightoller claimed under oath that his motivation was only to return *Titanic*'s crew home as quickly as possible. He knew the men were only paid while working in a ship and that most were supporting families. Delaying them in America would put a financial hardship on the sailors and their dependents. Or, that's what Lightoller claimed.

The next message sent from Carpathia to Franklin hinted at a darker reason for returning the men quickly. Curiously it was also the only one in the sequence that does not carry Ismay's coded signature. This message said it would be "undesirable to keep *Titanic*'s crew in New York, an odd choice of word. For whom would it have been undesirable? And, why?

Thursday April 18

ISLEFRANK, New York
Unless you have good and substantial reason for not holding Cedric, please arrange to do so. Must undesirable to have crew New York so long.

(unsigned)

From the tenor of this message it would appear that Ismay and Lightoller were conspiring to prevent Titanic's crew from testifying before the U.S. inquiry. Such could not be the case. Senator William Alden Smith was still trying to organize history's first Congressional investigation. His success was not certain until noon on April 17th, so news of his efforts had not yet reached *Carpathia*.

The motivation for getting *Titanic*'s sailors on a quick trip home appears two-fold. One was to keep them away from news reporters. The second was to keep the men together against the needs of the upcoming Board of Trade inquiry everyone knew was coming. Such inquiries followed all major British shipping disasters.

"We discussed the pros and cons and deemed it advisable to keep the crew together as much as we could," Lightoller said of his meetings with Ismay. "We might then be able to choos our important witnesses and let the remainder go to sea and earn money for themselves." What neither man knew was that by keeping *Titanic*'s crew together they were also providing Senator Smith with the witness pool he needed.

Smith of Michigan was a populist senator with a penchant for taking on big business. He knew that although *Titanic* sailed under British colours, the money that made it possible was thoroughly American. International Mercantile Marine, parent company of White Star Line, was owned by New York financier J. Pierpont Morgan. Senator Smith could not miss an opportunity to metaphorically tweak the banker's outsized nose.

Singlehandedly, Senator Smith invented the Congressional investigation during the brief period while Carpathia carried Titanic's survivors to New York. He even managed to give his inquiry unprecedented subpoena powers even though no one knew if they could be applied to foreign nationals.

Ismay and Lightoller had no knowledge of the senator's efforts, but Franklin paid full attention to the developments in Washington, D.C.

By 2 PM on Thursday he knew the American probe was unavoidable. "We were here and we are hearing the criticism," Franklin recalled of that period of time. "But Mr. Ismay had no knowledge or information regarding that. We determined it would be a very unfortunate thing to attempt to hold the Cedric and hurry the crew on board or agree to Mr. Ismay's sailing under the present circumstances."

Thursday, April 18

ISMAY, Carpathia
Regret after fullest consideration decided Cedric must sail as scheduled. Expect join Carpathia at quarantine, but cannot remove boats, as everything arranged for steamer proceed dock immediately.

FRANKLIN

Sending the bad news about *Cedric* to Ismay was not sufficient. Franklin also had to find a way to warn his boss that something was afoot. But, he did not want anything on record that might be construed as an attempt to undermine Senator Smith's inquiry. The solution he found to this dilemma was a pair of blandly-worded messages with hidden meaning.

Thursday, April 18

ISMAY, Carpathia
Suggest senior surviving navigating officer prepare brief statement of facts ready for us upon arrival quarantine.

FRANKLIN

Thursday, April 18

ISMAY, Carpathia
Concise Marconigram account of actual accident greatly needed for enlightenment public and ourselves. This most important

FRANKLIN

Franklin's terse messages made it clear to *Titanic*'s crew aboard *Carpathia* that they better have their stories straight before landing in New York. Fourth Officer Boxhall was not privy to Ismay's cabin, but he was not prevented from meeting and talking with other survivors on the voyage to New York. His later testimony indicates he sought out key witnesses such as quartermasters Alfred Olliver and Robert Hichens. This is probably when he learned information later woven into the "port around" story that he claimed Murdoch told Captain E. J. Smith.

It was during the trip to New York that Boxhall and Hichens would have had the opportunity to discuss their roles in creating the accident. This is probably when the final two-point course change became transformed into the mythical "hard a-starboard" attempt to dodge the iceberg.

While *Carpathia* plowed through a stormy North Atlantic the story of *Titanic* underwent a sea change. From the harsh reality of a sinking ship arose many of the softer myths that have enchanted the public ever since. Even so, some of the events during the rescue cruise still defy understanding. As *Carpathia* neared its New York berth a Marconi company message was addressed to its operator, Harold Cottom. The message was also addressed to surviving Titanic operator Harold Bride. It promised a large financial reward for not talking to anyone until after meeting with company officials in New York.

Senator Smith learned of this message and saw it as another opportunity. He accused wireless inventor Guglielmo Marconi of gagging Bride to prevent him from telling his story of the sinking.

Senator SMITH: If his mouth were to be closed, or the mouth of this operator were to be closed so the details of that catastrophe could not be printed, would not the English Government and the British people be deprived of the knowledge which was in the exclusive possession of this operator?

Mr. MARCONI: Within every deference, I do not quite understand your question of what you are referring to.

Senator SMITH: I have not disclosed my whole purpose, and I am not going to. I am seeking to get what you know about it?

Mr. MARCONI: Yes. But, with every deference, I believe you are assuming – I may understand you wrongly – that I wished or instructed this man to withhold information.

The senator and the inventor continued their verbal skirmish. Smith carefully intimated, without saying directly, that the Marconi Company had deliberately ignored requests for information from no less than the President of the United States. The White House had sent questions about the status of certain passengers to *Carpathia* via the Navy warship U.S.S. *Chester*, but they went unanswered.

"I heard that through the papers," Marconi responded. "I asked the surviving operator – Bride – what he knew about it. He stated that the *Chester* had asked him for a repetition of the list of survivors names and that he told the *Chester* that this list had already been sent and acknowledged by a shore station.

Controversy over whether or not Bride was prevented from transmitting news about the sinking was fueld by wireless messages sent to him from the American Marconi Company. Bride received them aboard *Carpathia*.

MARCONI to CARPATHIA
Arranged for your exclusive story for dollars in four figures. Mr. Marconi agreeing. Say nothing until you see me.
F.M Sammis

Frederick M. Sammis was chief engineer of American Marconi. His mentioning of "Mr. Marconi" indicates the message originated at the highest levels of the company. However, Sammis did not want to be connected with the message. He told Senator Smith, "I only know about that exact message from what I have read in the newspapers. It was not I who originated this scheme or this arrangement at all." But, unlike in the case of the message from *Titanic* chief operator Jack Phillips to his parents, Sammis did not deny the contents. "The arrangement was made," he assured Senator Smith.

A short while after that message came a second one. This one was signed by the boss himself. And it's meaning was unequivocal.

MARCONI To CARPATHIA
Meet Mr. Marconi and Sammis at Strand Hotel, 502 West Fourteenth Street. Keep your mouth shut.
MARCONI

According to Sammis, the *New York Times* paid $1,000 for the stories of the two wireless operators. On the surface, this appeard little more than American checkbook journalism at its finest. Howeveer, when his turn came to testify, the man who invented Marconigrams denied sending this message to Bride and Cottam on *Carpathia*.

"I do not know anything whatever about any of those messages, Marconi told the U.S. Senate inquiry. "They are not in the phraseology which I would have approved of if I had passed them.

"I should, however, say that I told Mr. Sammis or Mr. Bottomly – I do not remember which – that I, as an officer of the British Company would not prohibit or prevent these operators from anything which they reasonably could make out of selling their story of the wreck."

Senator Smith seemed more intent upon embarrassing both the Marconi Company and IMM/White Star than shedding light on the involvement of wireless in the sinking. In London, a mirror image situation obtained. Polite deference was shown to the wireless company while its role in the flow of information was discounted. Even as they were probing the Titanic sinking, several of the men involved in the British inquiry became embroiled in what became known as the "Marconi scandal." The impact of this scandal on the British *Titanic* inquiry can only be speculated, but it hints of favorable bias toward the Marconi companies. Money was at stake in 1912 and truth has no bank account.

On the night it sank *Titanic* used cutting-edge technology to call for help. As it slept on the bottom it's spark gap transmitter became obsolete. Two world wars forced the development of better methods of long-distance communication. When the broken liner once again made headlines it was because of 1980s cutting-edge technology. And, just as in 1912, the discovery of the wreck by Dr. Robert Ballard in 1985 was surrounded by mystery, myth, and misdirection.

The so-called "Cold War" brought with it nuclear submarines able to probe the ocean depths. In particular, Russian submarines liked to lurk on the bottom in the vicinity of large wrecks. This made them extremely difficult to find for U.S. and British Navy vessels. It became necessary for the Allies to locate and plot the thousands of wrecks on the bottom of the North Atlantic. The names of the ships were irrelevant to this effort. But, two pieces of wreckage in close proximity were noted to be close to Titanic's last known position.

Titanic rested quietly beneath the Atlantic for seven decades. However, in 1967 one of its crew returned for duty. Fourth Officer Boxhall died 55 years after the accident at the age of 83. At his personal instruction his body was cremated and his ashes were scattered at 41°44' North, 50°14' West, the CQD position he calculated as the ship lay sinking so many years before.

Cold War tensions were at their peak in the 1960s when the U.S. Navy lost two of its finest nuclear subs, U.S.S. Scorpion and U.S.S. Thresher. Both sank in water too deep for then-available technology to survey the wreckage. By the mid-1980s Dr. Ballard had the necessary equipment. But, it was critical that the Russians not suspect the purpose of his mission. "I couldnt tell anybody," he recalled to reporters in 2008 when the story was revealed. "It was a secret mission." Secrecy demanded a cover story. "I felt it was a fair exchange for getting a chance to look for the *Titanic*."

Dr. Ballard had a good idea of where to look for history's most famous shipwreck. But, the ocean floor is expansive and almost devoid of landmarks in the area he planned to explore. So, he based his search on techniques perfected finding the two submarines. He would look for the tell-tale pattern of debris – the "debris field" – that seemed to lead back to other shipwrecks.

It was early morning on September 1, 1985 when an obviously man-made object appeared on the robot camera scanning the ocean floor. It was one of the single-ended boilers that fell out of boiler room #1 when the ship broke apart. At the time, nobody realized that finding loose boilers would ignite a disagreement that continues to this day. Until the Ballard expedition it was accepted that *Titanic* sank intact. Perhaps the most unexpected discovery on the bottom was proof that the hull split into two large pieces during the sinking. That started arguments over how and why the ship broke apart.

There are those who argue that the ship broke from the top down while others are just as vocal that the breakup came bottom to top. Some people are adamant that the break occurred with the stern raised high out of the water. While working on the documentary *Titanic: Achilles Heel* for the History Channel, I participated in a computerized study of the ship's hull girder. That study showed the failure probably took place with an 11 to 15 degree down angle by the bow. This confirmed what I see in the historical record which argues for about a

13 to 15 degree angle. The strain on the hull was greatest in this range.

Sorting out these arguments over a few adult beverages can be a pleasant enough way to spend an evening. However, they are of no real significance. By the time the hull began to break apart Titanic was too far gone to remain afloat much longer. The breakup may have hastened the inevitable, but that's all. The ship was already too full of water to remain on the surface.

The final word on the sinking probably came during the U.S. Senate inquiry. Florida senator Duncan U. Fletcher was examining the ship's second officer when the following exchange took place. The witness, Charles H. Lightoller, summed up the whole affair after Fletcher's rather florid question.

> *Senator FLETCHER. I will get you to state, not only from your actual knowledge of the immediate effect, but also from your experiences as a navigator and seaman, what the effect of that collision was on the ship, beginning with the first effect, the immediate effect; how it listed the ship, if it did; what effect it had then, and what, in your opinion, was the effect on the ship that resulted from that collision.*
>
> *Mr. LIGHTOLLER. The result was she sank.*

APPENDIX

APPENDIX A

QUO VADIS, BOXHALL?

One last time the old man prepared for sea. His plans were checked, everyone informed. He would be rejoining his shipmates on their interrupted voyage; a voyage that still haunted the remaining days of his life. At 77 years of age he admitted to spending his time reading and dozing off. "Being an old, old man one's memory becomes very poor," he wrote to an American friend in 1962. [A-1] He welcomed the gradual blurring of memories that came with age. Even so, a few troubling details of events a half century ago stuck in the seaman's mind. Those memories remained sharp, too sharp. They interrupted the rest of the former Fourth Officer of RMS Titanic by filling his mind with a long-ago mid-Atlantic night. Memories surged like an incoming tide: the cold air, the sloping deck, the screams of frightened people, and those white signals bursting overhead.

The old sailor recalled the look in the Captain's eyes as he said firmly, "get in the boat." A much younger man obeyed that order and moments later was adrift in mid-Atlantic. Soon enough he would be with his captain again.

Soon, but not yet.

Joseph Groves Boxhall was the sole survivor of a small cadre of four officers who commanded history's most famous sea tragedy. Each of man had borne his portion of the burden of those events so long ago. Over time their numbers dwindled. Three of the four could not longer shoulder their responsibilities. The lone fourth man intended to carry all four men's collective memories back to where they began. The weightiest of those burdens was his personal knowledge of how he carefully and meticulously navigated Titanic into an iceberg.

It was his role in the accident which forced Boxhall to become chief architect and builder of the mythical Titanic we all know so well. It is a matter of record that he lied to the British inquiry about writing and then posting a critical ice message. No other survivor was caught in such blatant perjury. His other testimony and later public statements reveal this was not the only time he confused history to hide his role in Titanic's fatal iceberg accident. In particular, Boxhall gave a variety of conflicting stories about his whereabouts during the critical minutes leading up to the accident. The resulting confusion allowed many of his mistruths to develop into myths which continue to plague historians. Even so, Boxhall was not an evil villain intent on distorting history. His motives appear understandably human and, perhaps, even noble.

Boxhall-Created Myths:

The iceberg popped into view only seconds before impact and was too close to avoid;

First Officer Murdoch's allegedly failed to "port around" the iceberg during an evasion maneuver;

And, that both reciprocating steam engines were reversed before impact.

All three of these cherished Titanic myths are false. Yet they have been treated as gospel because they came from the ship's fourth officer who was on duty at the time of the accident. If anyone knew the intimate details of what happened, it was Boxhall. He came on duty at 8 PM and remained on deck until he was sent away in a lifeboat. Perhaps he knew too much.

As part of his work that night he twice received instructions from Captain Edward J. Smith to alter the ship's course around ice. The first change of one point (11 degrees) proved to be inadequate. Half an hour later the captain ordered another course change and for the second time in a half hour Boxhall did as he was told. The result was that the unwitting fourth officer sent the ship to its doom on the iceberg. Of course, conning Titanic into the berg was not the sort of thing the aspiring young officer wanted on his record. It was irrelevant that Boxhall's actions were quite innocent and Captain Smith's intention had been to take his ship safely south of the ice. None of that mattered.

The thing that counted was the second course change executed by Boxhall which ultimately resulted in the ship foundering with more than 1,500 deaths. Even in 1912 it did not take a sea lawyer to understand the impact on his career if he told the truth.

Admitting that he conned the ship into the iceberg would also have forced Boxhall to say why he made that fatal course change. His explanation would have exposed Captain Smith's two failed attempts to steer clear of the ice. Had Boxhall not hidden his role in the accident, we would look upon the disaster completely differently today. If Boxhall had been more forthcoming, his words would have transformed the accident from an unfortunate result of ordinary perils of the sea into negligent human error. Even if criminal or civil court penalties did not result, the economic penalties in tort liabilities against the White Stare Line could have been astounding. But, Boxhall knew the future of White Star as well as continued employment of hundreds of his shipmates hung on his testimony. He chose his words carefully to the point of perjury in at least one instance.

Boxhall and Titanic's other surviving officers talked over the legal ramifications of the accident while on their way to New York aboard the rescue ship Carpathia. We know this from testimony of Second Officer Charles H. Lightoller who admitted a string of conversations with White Star managing director J. Bruce Ismay. The two men even sent wireless messages to White Star's New York office attempting to get Titanic's surviving crew out of New York before an American investigation could be organized. Their efforts failed and Ismay ultimately agreed to testify before Senator Smith's first-ever Congressional investigation. Ismay's acquiescence opened the door to subpoenaing other surviving crew members including Lightoller and Boxhall to appear before the U.S. Senate panel.

The fourth officer cloaked his personal role in the accident by taking advantage of the honest fact he was not on the command bridge during the minutes leading up to impact. One time Boxhall tried to explain his absence by saying he was having a cup of tea in his cabin. Preposterous! No officer standing watch would pop down to his cabin for a warm cup of anything.

Another time he suggested that he had been visiting the lavatory. Nature calls us all, and not always at convenient times. Boxhall might well have visited the lavatory, but his story is still unlikely. The four-hour duration of sailor's watches is designed around human endurance. An average man can perform at least four hours of duty without need to relieve himself. Although indelicate to discuss, sailors learn the value of emptying bowels and bladders before going on watch.

The lives of some 2,200 people depended upon Boxhall and the other officers performing their duties throughout the full four hours of their watches. That meant they were to remain on duty throughout there full watch and not slip away for tea or to the loo. Even so, during a 1962 interview with the BBC, the fourth officer told an intriguing story about when he heard the report of the lookouts' bell, "I was sitting in my cabin having a cup of tea." None of this matched his 1912 testimony to the U.S. and British inquiries where he said he was not in his room, but just coming out of the officers quarters when the lookouts rang their warning.

So, where was Boxhall?

We already know where. From his own words we know he was not sipping tea or using the lavatory. The fourth officer was performing his regular duties as assigned by company regulations. Boxhall was not missing from the bridge. He was working away from the bridge. The question that should be asked is not so much, "Where was Boxhall?" Rather, it should be, "What was Boxhall doing?"

The best clue to Boxhall's whereabouts during the minutes leading up to the accident came from relief quartermaster Alfred Olliver. He had steered the ship from 8 until 10 o'clock that evening before exchanging duties with fellow quartermaster Robert Hichens. From then on, "I was running messages and doing various other duties," Olliver explained to the U.S. inquiry. he also describe hearing the three strikes on the crow's nest bell warning of the fatal iceberg. "I happened to be looking at the lights in the standing compass at the time," he said.

Olliver probably did not use the term "standing compass" in his testimony. This wording was most likely an error by a stenographer unfamiliar with both the man's accent and nautical terminology. Olliver attended the ship's standard compass located on a 15-foot tall tower directly amidships over the first class lounge.

Titanic sailed prior to the invention of they gyro compass. Electronic navigation such as Loran or Global Positioning System was a half century or more in the future. The primary navigational instrument in 1912 was the magnetic compass. A mariner's compass does not point at the Earth's north pole. It suffers errors known to maritime navigators as variation and deviation. These errors throw off the reading so the compass points east or west of true north.

Variation is the difference between true north and the magnetic line of force controlling the compass magnets. It is geographic in origin and the same for all compasses in the same location.

Deviation arises from magnetic influences within its ship. Each compass on a ship has its own individual deviation error.

Navigators chart their courses in true directions (based on geographic north) because each compass in the ship has its unique combination of errors. So, it is necessary to perform a series of mathematical calculations to account for variation and deviation when determining the course to steer on the compass. Navigators uncorrect when going from a true course to a compass course; and correct when going from compass to true. The result of "uncorrecting" is the heading actually steered on the compass. It is seldom the same as the true course plotted on the chart.

Titanic had two steering compasses on the bridge and a third on the docking bridge at the stern. The ship's navigators did not have the time or inclination to compute three different courses for three steering compasses. The solution was to install a fourth compass, the *standard* compass. Once the ship was on course "per standard compass," (PSC) the reading on the steering compass was noted. This reading would never be quite the same as the standard instrument but that difference was of no consequence as long as the ship made good the desired PSC course. From then on the quartermaster followed the reading on his steering compass that corresponded to the desired heading on the standard instrument.

A possibility existed that the two compasses would get out of synch with each other. Or, that the quartermaster might mistakenly follow the wrong number on the steering compass. This is why nautical custom as well as company rules required comparing the two compasses every half hour around the clock. Steering a wrong course for half an hour in mid-ocean was of little consequence to an overall voyage of several thousand miles. However, catching errors quickly was necessary for the safest and shortest passage. White Star Line company rules were explicit about the importance of these compass checks.

104. ***Compasses, etc.***—*(a) The closest attention should be paid to the compasses, and the Commander should see that no opportunity is neglected to ascertain the errors, and to have the same noted in a Compass Book for comparison on the next passage.*

253. ***Steering and Compasses.***—*He (the officer of the watch) must pay particular attention to the steering and the course the ship makes. He must steady the ship on her course by standard every half-hour, and must compare the compasses every Watch, the comparisons to be entered in the Compass Comparison Book for reference. He will also ascertain the deviation as often as possible.* [B-1]

Specific times for each of the 48 daily compass checks were not designated by the company rules. However, it is traditional for the watch going off duty to clean up all of its unfinished business before turning the ship over to the new watch coming on duty. Most navies have strict regulations against changing watch while a ship is conducting a maneuver. Switching people in the middle of an evolution results in confusion that often as not causes accidents. The IMM rulebook was not quite that stringent, but it still prohibited the senior officer of the watch to leave the bridge until his relief was familiar with the ongoing situation.

251. ***Station.***—*At sea the station of the Officer of the Watch is on the Bridge, which he must on no account leave, either night or day, without being relieved.*

When the Watch is changed, the Officer who is being relieved will remain on the Bridge and in charge during the change...He is the responsible Officer until he leaves the Bridge, and must not leave the Bridge until the Officer relieving him has had time to familiarize himself with his surroundings.

Crew watches changed on the hour, at noon, 4, (also 6 for the dog watch), and 8 both day and night. Because of company rules and nautical tradition, the proper time to perform the required compass evolutions (checks and comparisons) would have been just prior to the hour and half hour. That way, the last check of each watch would be completed just before changing to the new watch. That fulfilled the need for the outgoing watch to complete all of its work prior to handing the ship over to the new watch.

Confirmation that compass checks were done on the hour and half hour comes from Boxhall's dead reckoning. The timing of the first one-point course change (from 266° to 255°) took place 11 hours 30 minutes after noon, April 14th. This indicates that the required half-hourly check was combined with the course change.

Considering the sub-freezing temperature that night, combining the two operations would have kept the men involved from facing two stints in freezing 22-knot wind on the exposed standard compass platform. An effort would have been made to have a single visit suffice for both the required half-hourly compass evolution and the course change.

Titanic's first course change to avoid ice was done at 11:30 PM using April 14th ship's time. That was not 11:30 o'clock for the crew which had already retarded their clock by 24 minutes to 11:06 PM (see Chapter 9). Thirty minutes later at 11:36 PM crew time quartermaster Olliver was once again on the compass platform. "I happened to be looking at the lights of the standing compass," Olliver testified. "That was my duty, to look at the lights in the standing compass, and I was trimming them so that they would burn properly." At night it was impossible to read the standard compass without light from the two tiny oil lamps that illuminated the dial.

Olliver's job was to prepare the standard instrument so that one of the junior officers could conduct the required routine compass check. As the fourth officer, this task fell to Boxhall. Meanwhile, Sixth Officer James Moody remained in the wheelhouse overseeing the steering of quartermaster Robert Hichens. Moody also kept the "scrap log" from which the ship's official log was transcribed at the end of the watch.

The quartermaster on the compass platform was already busy with his lamps as Boxhall stepped on deck from the officers quarters. At that moment lookout Frederick Fleet pounded out three distinct strikes on the crow's nest bell. It should be noted that Olliver was alone on the platform at that moment. The fourth officer had not yet arrived to conduct the compass evolutions.

Boxhall later recalled he was "just coming out of the officers quarters" when "I heard the bells." Those rings told every trained sailor aboard that a potential danger had been spotted dead ahead. "I was doing this bit of duty," Olliver said, "I heard three bells rung up in the crow's nest, which I knew was something ahead. I looked, but I did not see anything." [B-2]

Another member of Titanic's crew heard the crow's nest bell ring. Seaman Joseph Scarrott was relaxing in the crew's mess on C deck just under the forecastle. He was enjoying a "rope yarn Sunday" that required no work other than necessary for the safety of the ship. Sailors stood their Sunday watch around the galley coffee urn. Through the skylight came the sounds of the crow's nest bell.

Scarrott later testified that several minutes passed between that three-stroke warning and impact. "I did not take much notice of the three strikes on the gong, I could hardly recollect the time," he said honestly. "But, I should think it was – well shall we say about five or eight minutes; it seemed to me about that time.

His eight words – "shall we say about five or eight minutes" – are the most significant ever uttered by a survivor of Titanic. They are the only account by a member of the crew of the duration between when the iceberg was first reported and the moment steel met ice. Yet, Scarrott's words have always been ignored because they do not fit the cherished mythical accident. Everyone knows the berg "popped up" less than a minute before impact. Scarrott said otherwise. So, it has been necessary to discount what he said to preserve the myth that only 37 seconds passed between warning bell and impact.

Scarrott's "five to eight" minute estimate allows us to deduce what the fourth officer was really doing when he claimed to be sipping tea or using the toilet. Boxhall's routine duties at the standard compass that night would have taken a bit more than six minutes to perform, indicating seaman Scarrott got the duration exactly right. It took about 45 to 50 seconds for Boxhall to walk from the door of the officer's quarters and climb the platform. Once there, he and Olliver hunkered against the ship's 22-knot wind as the officer began the compass evolution. There was no voice communication with the wheelhouse. Instead, Boxhall pushed a button to ring a small bell near the quartermaster. A pre-arranged series of coded rings coordinated instructions from the standard compass platform with steering done in the wheelhouse.

After checking the compasses, Boxhall rang a new signal to begin Captain Smith's two-point course change to port. In the wheelhouse Hichens turned the bottom of the wheel to the right to apply what in 1912 was called "starboard helm." Turning the bottom to the right caused the top of the wheel to rotate left and the rudder followed. Titanic's bow began swinging two points to the left. This simple course change would later be transformed by Boxhall and Hichens into a dramatic "hard a-starboard" iceberg evasion maneuver.

No records survive of how long it typically took for this sort of compass work. Things undoubtedly went quickly that night. The men were experienced, the bell code system was familiar to them, and it was bitterly cold on that windy platform. Boxhall probably took about four minutes for the compass evolution before heading on his 50-second walk forward. Almost six minutes after lookout Fleet's bell first reported something ahead Boxhall was, "...just coming along the deck and almost abreast of the captain's quarters and I heard the report of three bells,"

During his testimony to either the U.S. Senate or British inquiry Boxhall did not identify the source of this second set of rings. In the United States he artfully changed the subject from the bell sounds to the meaning of a 3-stroke warning by the lookouts. "Three bells were struck. That signifies something has been seen ahead," Boxhall explained quite correctly. It was meaningless information the diverted attention from discussion of the origin of the bell sounds. Boxhall's quick verbal dodge created the impression that the three rings he heard when opposite the captain's cabin were the strikes on the crow's nest warning bell that he heard six minutes earlier when he came out of the officers quarters door. Not only was that implication not true, as will be seen it was not even possible.

Typically careless examination by Michigan Senator William Smith failed to spot the fourth officer's artful dodge. Historians continue to repeat the senator's mistake by not challenging the assumption that the bells Boxhall heard coming out of the officers quarters were the same ones he heard abreast of the captain's quarters.

The layout of Titanic's boat deck shows that the three strikes on the crow's nest bell Boxhall heard at the officers quarters door could not have been the three rings that sounded when he was abreast of Captain Smith's room. It was physically impossible. The two locations were separated by 45 to 50 feet of deck – the width of a typical American suburban housing lot. That was too much distance for them to be the same location. To believe Boxhall's story is to believe he could stand in two different places at the same time.

It's unlikely that Titanic's fourth officer had an out-of-body experience on the night of the sinking. Boxhall was not in two places at the same time. His testimony could only be true if he heard two different bells, each at one of two physically different locations. The first set of rings heard at the doorway was certainly the three strikes on the crow's nest bell. Therefore, the second set of three rings came from a different source. This second set of bells was examined in Chapter 4 when we studied First Officer Murdoch's maneuvers around the iceberg. As noted, by "double ringing" an engine order Murdoch would have caused the engine order telegraph bells to sound three times.

During his appearance before the U.S. inquiry Boxhall had an unguarded moment when he almost let the truth slip out. On the third day of testimony he first told Senator William Smith that he did not see the accident.

Senator SMITH: Could you see what Occurred?
Mr. BOXHALL: No, sir; I could not see what occurred.
Senator SMITH: Did you know what occurred?
Mr. BOXHALL: No, not at all. I heard the sixth officer say what it was.

Only a few questions later Boxhall's testimony changed dramatically. After giving his impression of the height of the iceberg he went on to accurately describe the iceberg at the moment it was doing its best to break open the after end of hold #2 and the forward end of hold #3.

Senator SMITH: Do you know whether it struck the bow squarely?
Mr. BOXHALL: It seemed to me to strike the bluff of the bow.
Senator SMITH: Describe that.
Mr. BOXHALL: It is in the forward part of the ship, but almost on the side.
Senator SMITH: On which side?
Mr. BOXHALL: It is just where the ship begins to widen out on the starboard side.

Senator Smith wandered through a slight diversion about how many feet aft of the bow the "bluff" was located before he allowed Boxhall to give a good description of the manner of contact between ship and iceberg.

Senator SMITH: But it was not a square blow on the bow of the ship?
Mr. BOXHALL: No, sir.
Senator SMITH: In ordinary parlance, would it be a glancing blow?
Mr. BOXHALL: A glancing blow.

For whatever reason, Senator Smith did not grasp that the witness had dramatically changed his story. Moments earlier Boxhall said he did not see what occurred. Now, he was accurately describing exactly those very events. Which of Boxhall's statements was true? Did he see the accident? or not? Smith never uncovered the answers to these questions and historians have been equally lax in the years since. How did Boxhall describe an event so perfectly if he did not see it happen?

It turns out that Boxhall did not contradict himself. His apparently paradoxical statements were both true. He did not initially see what occurred, but he did see the iceberg at the bluff of the bow. So, although the fourth officer's statements may appear to be contradictory, they are quite consistent with his route "going rounds" as officer of the Starboard Watch. These rounds were required by White Star line rules.

> *Opposite Art. 17* – WATCHES
>
> SEA WATCHES.—Regular sea watches must be kept... The Junior Officers, where five or more Officers are borne, will keep watch and watch with the seaman, the Third Officer having charge of the port watch, and the Fourth Officer the starboard watch... *They are also to go the rounds every hour during watch on deck* reporting having carried this out to the Senior Officer on watch. [emphasis by author]

During that 1962 BBC radio interview Boxhall confirmed that rounds were made every hour. "I had a set of stars that Lightoller had taken during the second dog watch. When I got these I said, "you, Moody go round the decks and come back at 9 o'clock. Even though Boxhall had the responsibility, his duties as navigator overrode making rounds of the watch. So, he passed that task off to the sixth officer. An hour later, Boxhall took making rounds upon himself. "At 10 o'clock I reported to the first officer that I was going round the deck." If company rules were followed, he should have made another set rounds at 11 o'clock and been starting his 12 o'clock (in time based on noon, April 14th) rounds at the moment when the ship struck the iceberg.

At impact Boxhall would have been inside the steel enclosure of the stairway to B deck. The entrance to that stairway was on the boat deck "just abreast" of the captain's quarters as he described. The fourth officer was fooled by the "slight impact" on the iceberg. "It did not seem to me to be very serious. I did not take it seriously," he admitted to Senator Smith. Boxhall was descending the stairway because of company rules that required him to make rounds of the men of the Starboard Watch once every hour. A moment later the fourth officer came out on B deck where his vision was not blocked. That was just in time to see the iceberg at the "bluff of the bow."

If it were not for a lie Boxhall told about Murdoch's report to Captain Smith, he probably could have admitted the truth about going rounds. But, while under oath he described in specific detail a conversation he never witnessed. To make that lie believable he had to create another lie to solve a problem. Boxhall knew there was at least one witness who could identify him as being in the well deck at the time when he claimed to be on the bridge listening to Murdoch. Boxhall solved this problem by never mentioning company regulations that required him to go rounds once each hour.

Late on a Sunday evening Boxhall's men were certain to be huddled around the coffee pot in the crew's mess on C deck. The fourth officer's path forward from the compass platform followed the starboard boat deck to a "crew only" stairway down to A and B decks. He descended an enclosed metal stair tower which blocked his sight forward. As Boxhall neared B deck he felt the ship's forefoot ride over the underwater portion of the berg. He could only feel the accident because his vision of the accident was blocked. "I could not see what had occurred," he testified honestly.

Seconds later, he burst through the doorway on B deck where he had full sight of the berg. "It seemed to me to strike the bluff of the bow, just where the ship begins to widen out on the starboard side," Boxhall said truthfully.

He watched the berg glide past before descending the open iron stairway down to the well deck. By now men of his Starboard Watch were streaming out of the forecastle to see what had happened. The crew's agitation apparently caused Boxhall to become concerned about passengers housed in cabins below the well deck. The fourth officer claimed that instead of pushing through the crowd into the crew's mess he decided to check on third class passengers in the bow.

The doorway into the crew's mess was next to the entrance to third class passenger cabins. "I went down forward, down into the third class accommodation," he told the British inquiry. "Through a staircase under the port side of the forecastle head which takes me down into D deck. And then walked along aft to just underneath the bridge, and down a staircase on the port side."

Boxhall came down on E deck at the head of the broad corridor known to the crew as "Scotland Road." He turned to his left, walked back across the width of the ship and then headed forward to yet another staircase. "You cross over to the starboard side of E deck and go down another accommodation staircase on to F deck. I went as low as I could possibly get," Boxhall said.

Titanic's fourth officer climbed back to the open well deck on the starboard side where he examined the ice deposited by the passing iceberg. He never resumed his rounds of his Starboard Watch men. One of the crew was picking up chunks of ice that had fallen from the passing iceberg. "I took a piece out of a man's hand," the fourth officer admitted, "a small piece about as large as a small basin, I suppose."

It was hard to tell one man from another in the darkness. Only uniform coats and caps identified officers from sailors. Seaman Frank Evans was approached by Boxhall although he recognized the man only as an officer. "I think it was the fifth officer, the fifth or sixth officer," Evans told the U.S. Senate inquiry. He was mistaken. Sixth officer James Moody was in the wheelhouse while Third Officer John H. Pitman and Fifth Officer Harold Lowe were both off duty and sleeping. So, the officer who accosted Evans had to be Boxhall. Recognizing Evans as one of his Starboard Watch men, the fourth officer issued an order. Evans recalled, "He told me to go down and find the carpenter and sound all the wells forward and report to the bridge."

All of all this activity – checking on third class accommodations, telling Evans to find the carpenter, and examining ice in the well deck – kept the fourth officer off the bridge for about six minutes after impact on the iceberg. Yet, Boxhall perjured himself by claiming that he was on the bridge when First Officer Murdoch explained the accident to Captain Smith. The story Boxhall told of overhearing Smith and Murdoch talk was an outright lie.

> *...I found the sixth officer and the first officer and captain. The captain said, "What have we struck?" Mr.*

> *Murdoch, the first officer said, "We have struck an iceberg." He followed on to say, "I put her hard a-starboard and run the engines full astern, abut it was too close. She hit it." Mr. Murdoch also said, "I intended to port around it. But she hit before I could do any more."*
>
> – Joseph G. Boxhall
> Compiled from 1912 Testimony

Over the years Boxhall's story changed, indicating why memories recalled 50 years after an event can be highly suspect. Or, the passage of time may have freed the person to speak with less constraint as Boxhall apparently did in a 1962 BBC radio interview. He recalled that Murdoch said, "I am running full speed astern on the port engine." It is possible that this radio interview was as close as he ever got to telling the truth. The pressure of staring into a microphone may simply have caused him to say "port" instead of "starboard" which was more likely what Murdoch ordered. If so, this indicates Boxhall knew he was not being truthful when he testified in 1912 that *both* reciprocating engines were run astern.

By claiming to overhear Murdoch's report to Captain Smith, Boxhall snared himself in his own web of deception. The truth was that he had been in the well deck with Evans at the exact moment when Murdoch made his report to the captain. To make believable his lie about being on the bridge required concocting yet another lie to explain why Evans saw him forward. The fourth officer needed a plausible story that moved him from the boat deck down to the forward well deck. One lie apparently begot another. Eventually, Boxhall claimed that his curiosity was raised by the iceberg accident to the point that he went charging off the bridge without permission from his seniors.

"I left the bridge then," he told Senator Smith, implying his motivation was personal curiosity about the iceberg. To the BBC he said, "I slipped down to have a look. Nobody told me to go." This would never have happened. A junior officer who departed his duty station without permission would have been derelict of duty unless already performing a task that routinely took him away.

Boxhall got lucky. Senator Smith's ignorance of nautical customs and the responsibilities of ship's officers prevented him from asking why the fourth officer deserted his post. If Senator Smith had been a better interrogator, he would have discovered the simple reason why the fourth officer could not explain why he left the bridge. Boxhall was never there in the first place. And, that revelation would have exposed Boxhall's biggest lie – that he overheard First Officer Murdoch give his report to Captain Smith. At that moment, the fourth officer was well out of earshot seven decks below checking on the third class passengers.

Testimonies from other members of the bridge team confirm that Boxhall was nowhere to be seen when Smith questioned Murdoch. Proof is not in what the witnesses said, but what they did *not* say. None of the other eyewitnesses recalled Boxhall being present.

Second Officer Charles H. Lightoller who arrived moments after impact did not report Boxhall's presence on the bridge, although he did see Captain Smith and First Officer Murdoch talking.

"Runner" quartermaster Alfred Olliver saw his counterpart, quartermaster Robert Hichens, Murdoch, and Smith. Just as when he was on the compass platform, Olliver never mentioned Boxhall as present on the bridge.

From his post at the wheel, quartermaster Robert Hichens saw the captain, heard Murdoch's voice, and spoke of Olliver taking the time of the accident at Sixth Officer Moody's direction. He never mentioned Boxhall.

Forgetting to mention Boxhall could be explained as a simple oversight for a single witness. However, for all three eyewitnesses to make exactly the same oversight was highly unlikely. The only reason all three would have failed to mention Boxhall was that the fourth officer was not there. From two of the eyewitnesses who were there we learn that Captain Smith quietly asked Murdoch, "What was that?" Quartermasters Olliver and Hichens overheard this same conversation.

"An iceberg, sir," was the direct reply.

"Close the watertight doors."

"They are already closed," Murdoch reported.

Captain Smith went to the far end of the starboard bridge wing to look for the iceberg in *Titanic*'s wake before summoning Olliver. "The Captain gave me orders to tell the carpenter to go and take the draft of water," Olliver recalled. The runner quartermaster went down to the wide corridor known as "Scotland Road" on E deck where he found the carpenter already at work in accordance with Boxhall's orders passed by seaman Evans. "He was down below in the working alleyway already doing it. He says 'All right, I am doing it,'" Olliver told the U.S. inquiry.

Despite being off the bridge, Fourth Officer Boxhall willingly described a conversation he did not witness. "The captain said, 'what have we struck?' Mr. Murdoch, the first officer said, 'We have struck an iceberg.'" Up to this point Boxhall seems to have been quoting the recollections of Olliver and Hichens. Then, he added something not contained in any other eyewitness testimony about the conversation between Murdoch and the captain.

"Mr. Murdoch followed on to say, 'I put her hard a-starboard and run the engines full astern, but it was too close. She hit it." After a moment Boxhall added, "Mr. Murdoch also said, "I intended to port around it, but she hit before I could do any more."

No other eyewitness heard Murdoch use the words "port around" in conjunction with the iceberg. An intention is something never done. By saying that Murdoch "intended" to port around the iceberg (swing the stern clear by turning the bow to the right, toward the iceberg on the starboard side), Boxhall made it seem that the proper helm order was never delivered. This was not the case. Runner quartermaster Olliver had been there to hear the order. He was certain that Murdoch ordered a hard a-port (right) turn and that the helm was put over in compliance with that order.

"I know about the wheel," Olliver testified to the U.S. inquiry. "What I knew about the helm is hard a-port. I know the orders I heard when I was on the bridge was after we had struck the iceberg. I heard hard a-port, and there was the man at the wheel (Hichens) and the officer (Moody). The officer was seeing it was carried out right."

There was another important point on which Boxhall and Olliver did not agree. The fourth officer claimed he witnessed Murdoch operate the switch to close the ship's automatic watertight doors. He actually interrupted a question by Senator William Smith to interject, "I saw him close them."

Quartermaster Olliver entered the bridge a heartbeat or two before the ship struck after completing the walk back from the compass platform as Boxhall. By now the fourth officer was out of sight in the enclosed stairway. First Officer Murdoch was alone, standing at the switch that closed the doors. "As I entered the bridge I saw him about the lever," Olliver told Senator Smith. As noted earlier, although Olliver specifically mentioned Sixth Officer Moody and the other quartermaster, he never spoke of Boxhall on the bridge while Murdoch was closing the doors.

It was about six minutes after impact when the fourth officer really climbed back to the bridge. That was well after Murdoch delivered his report to the captain who was now in conversation with J. Bruce Ismay, head of White Star Line. The fourth officer gave those men a report filled with information that was as true as it was misleading. "I came right up to the bridge," Boxhall testified, "and reported I could find no damage."

Only Fourth Officer Joseph G. Boxhall could have explained is brazen claim to have been part of events that took place while he was away from the bridge. Unfortunately for history he remains forever silent. We know for certain he never spoke openly about his final visit to *Titanic*'s compass platform. Nor did he speak of the White Star Line requirement for him to make rounds of his Starboard Watch. We are left to speculate on his personal motives.

Providing deliberately false information was not outside Boxhall's personal ethics. During the British inquiry he perjured himself by denying he ever saw an important ice warning posted in the officers' chartroom. Fifth Officer Harold Lowe inadvertently exposed the fourth officer's deception when he described a 3x3-inch "chit" of paper on the officer's chart table. "What I saw was that a chit was stuck in the edge of the frame with the latitude and longitude down," Lowe said.

The fifth officer's testimony forced Boxhall to admit the truth. He wrote that chit with his own hand and posted it on the table. Boxhall lamely explained his amazing gaffe as a simple lapse of memory. "The mentioning of it has refreshed my memory," he said, "and I remember writing it out. It is the position of the *Caronia*'s ice. I copied it off the notice board to save taking the telegram itself down. I copied it on a chit and took it into the Captain's chartroom, and put it on the chart. And that is the ice that I must have put down between 4 and 6 in the evening."

Nothing more was said about Boxhall's perjury. Perhaps Lord Mersey understood that *Titanic*'s fourth officer was only following company policy. Boxhall was an employee who remained loyal to paragraph 3(a) in the company rulebook.

> 3. **Company's Affairs Confidential**—(a) Knowledge of the Company's business and interests shall be regarded as confidential, and shall not be the subject of conversation with passengers and/or strangers. If it should come to the knowledge of the Management that anyone connected with the ships in whatever capacity has made use of any expression tending to injure the character of the ships, or any of the Company's employees, or the interests of the Company in any particular...that person shall be at once dismissed from the service.

Boxhall's willingness to risk perjury on behalf of his employer seems to have been rewarded. He rose steadily through the ranks even after the company's merger into the Cunard organization. He became Chief Officer in the largest liners afloat. Even so, Boxhall was never given a Cunard ship of his own.

The Olliver Problem:

It is Olliver's testimony about trimming the lamps of the standard compass which reveals the second course change that actually caused the accident. Yet, Olliver never mentioned that Boxhall ever visited the tiny platform located between the second and third funnels. His words gave the impression that he left the compass just as the ringing of the lookouts' warning bell was fading into the night and then went straight to the bridge.

> *Mr. OLLIVER: ..I heard three bells rung up in the crow's nest. ...I looked, but I did not see anything. I happened to be looking at the lights in the standing compass at the time...and, I was trimming them so they would burn properly. When I heard the report, I looked, but could not see anything, and I left that and came was just entering on the bridge when the shock came. I knew we had touched something.*

At first glance, this testimony would make the short duration of 45 to 60 seconds between warning bell and impact seem plausible. However, to understand what Olliver said it is necessary to parse the questions which prompted his testimony. He was asked "Where were you when the collision occurred?" And, to this was added, "Just state what happened?" These questions asked not what the quartermaster was doing over the minutes leading up to impact. Rather, they were specifically aimed at discovering what Olliver was doing at the moment is struck on the iceberg.

The witness spoke truthfully when he said, "I...was just entering the bridge as the shock came." It would appear, however, that he felt the need to explain why he was not on the bridge which was his normal duty station. So, he explained that he had been on an errand to the compass platform, which was true.

But, the question did not ask what he was doing on the platform. So, Olliver dutifully skipped the intervening details and went straight to his appearance on the bridge. Because of the wording of the questions there was no need to explain about why Boxhall came to the platform or the actions taken. All that Olliver needed to say was that he had been on an errand to the standard compass and that was why he was just entering the bridge when the ship struck the iceberg.

APPENDIX B

THE MYTHS OF TIME

What time was it? This seemingly innocent question has a diabolically complex answer. Yes, *Titanic* struck on the iceberg at 11:40 o'clock, but that is only half of the necessary information to identify when it happened. The other half is knowing the reference clock by which that 11:40 time was measured. At the moment of the accident three "times" were in use aboard ship. One referenced the ship's noon position that Sunday, April 14th. A second was based on the ship's projected noon longitude for the next day, Monday, April 15th. And, yet a third "time" lay halfway between April 14th and 15th. This odd halfway time was created specifically to meet the needs of the crew for an orderly "midnight" change of watch.

Three time references for a single event sound confusing, but there was even a fourth. While ship's time was used for everyday events the navigators used Greenwich Mean Time (GMT) for their work.

It took me years of research to realize that the 11:40 o'clock time of the accident was not measured in April 14th ship's time as conventional wisdom claims. When I wrote my first book on the sinking, *The Last Log Of The Titanic,* a decade ago I also accepted the convention that "the clock" had not been set back prior to the accident. I naively assumed that "11:40 PM" was in the ship's time established by *Titanic*'s noon longitude that Sunday. This seemed a safe assumption because historians went blindly along with the official 1912 inquiries that no clock setbacks had been made.

Although the conventional view that the accident took place 11 hours and 40 minutes after noon had universal acceptance, it left many questions time-related questions unanswered. George Behe, a meticulous *Titanic* researcher, pointed out that American Colonel Archibald Gracie recalled the time of the accident as "midnight." George never suggested any reason for Gracie's odd observation. I ascribed this oddity to Gracie's sleepy eye. But, trying to explain the colonel's time led me to discover he was not alone in being 20 to 25 minutes "wrong." Looking back it's embarrassing to admit that Gracie was correct and that my eye was clouded about the issue of time.

It is now obvious that all of the apparently erratic time observations are exactly a "half bubble off." That was as it should have been because the "full bubble" was the 47 minute setback of ship's time scheduled for the switch from April 14th to April 15th. Crew time had to be that "half bubble" off because it was designed to split those 47 minutes equally between the watches. (Note: in this book it is assumed the Starboard Watch was given 24 extra minutes while the Port Watch got 23.)

Gracie's "midnight" was separated from the 11:40 PM time of the accident by about half of the 47 minute setback. And' 23 or 24 minutes was the extra time each of the crew Watches were to serve that night. The significance of this time error was so obvious that it lay hidden in plain sight for nearly a century.

Unraveling the enigma of time became the genesis for this book. It was key to understanding the reason Fourth Officer Joseph G. Boxhall went away from the bridge just prior to the accident. This knowledge exposed Captain Edward J. Smith's two attempts to avoid ice that night. In turn, that helped explain with elegant precision why the ship's two sets of distress coordinates were wrong. Most unexpectedly, an understanding of *Titanic* timekeeping confirmed the legend that a mirror was displayed in the forward grand staircase where a clock dial should have been.

Understanding *Titanic*'s clocks requires knowledge of how time is reckoned in general. This means plodding through some rather dull "book learning" before getting back to the more exciting detective work. Timekeeping is based on the Sun, and more precisely noon when the Sun is directly overhead. The Earth turns almost exactly one revolution (360 degrees) each 24-hour day, noon to noon. Expressed as angular rotation this is 15 degrees of longitude every hour. Midnight comes 12 hours after noon, or 180 degrees of rotation of the Earth. [9-1]

Shipboard time was originally measured noon to noon. Prior to electronic navigation it was impossible to observe midnight because the sun is on the other side of the Earth. Only at high noon is the sun is visible, so that moment was chosen as the starting point for reckoning time. Each ship used it's local apparent noon (LAN) to reckon time. This meant that the clock in any one vessel always showed a slightly different ship's time from the clocks in other ships. (This discrepancy did not apply to GMT which was always the same for every ship everywhere on Earth.)

The invention of the chronometer allowed navigators to use the apparent rotation of the Sun around the Earth for measuring longitude. The "Prime Meridian" (also called the "Greenwich Meridian") became the starting point. When teaching navigation classes, I accentuate the "long" in "long-i-tude" for my students. This makes it easier for them to grasp the idea that longitude is a measurement of how long (in time) it has been since noon at Greenwich. The difference in hours, minutes, and seconds at the Prime Meridian to high noon at the ship's location was easily translated into angular rotation of the planet.

Every minute of time is the equivalent to a quarter degree of rotation of the Earth. Rotation is closely associated with reckoning longitude and establishing local time. New York City lies approximately 74 degrees west of Greenwich, so Local Apparent Noon in Central Park comes four hours fifty-six minutes after noon on the Prime Meridian at Greenwich.

Originally navigators used the celestial day (starting at noon) for keeping track of calendar dates. Under this system a Sunday would become Monday at noon. Ashore, the civil day which starts at midnight was adopted to make the change of date take place overnight when people were asleep. *Titanic* and other ocean liners adopted the familiar midnight-to-midnight civil day simply because it was familiar to their guests. A so-called civil day starts exactly twelve hours prior to high noon on the observer's longitude. This is "midnight" marking the start of the new day.

Civil midnight occurs when the sun crosses the meridian 180 degrees away from the observer's noon meridian. This means the sun is directly below the observer's feet. People are not so precise when they use the term "midnight" in everyday speech. *Titanic*'s passengers and many of its crew considered "midnight" as both the end of the old and the start of the new day. However, to understand *Titanic* timekeeping it is necessary to keep in mind that midnight is never the end of one day. Rather, it is *always* the start of the next.

Things become complicated when a ship steams either east or west on the ocean. The duration from noon to noon is shortened or lengthened according to the distance covered each day. Days measure shorter for a ship heading east. Westbound ships like *Titanic* experience longer days. This phenomenon is the basis for modern "jet lag." In 1912, however, lag was not a problem because speeds on the ocean were so much slower than jet planes.

In theory, local apparent time changes continuously as the ship steams east or west. Constantly adjusting clocks to match the ship's longitude would have been an impossible task. And, even if it could have been done, the process would have been confusing to passengers. Instead, ship's time was adjusted once each day to match the vessel's noon longitude (called "local apparent noon" or "LAN"). For passenger convenience the clock hands were reset and the date changed at midnight marking the start of the new day.

Titanic's noon meridian on Sunday, April 14th was 44°28' West. That put high noon aboard ship 2 hours 58 minutes behind Greenwich. Local apparent noon on *Titanic* came at 2:58 PM (1458 hours) Greenwich. If the ship had sat still, noon on April 15th would have come again at 1458 hours GMT. Of course, the ship was steaming westward at about 22 knots. With each mile *Titanic* steamed westward, its clocks got "ahead" of local apparent noon for the its actual longitude. This required shipboard clocks to be set *back* to match the LAN of each day.

If daily setbacks of the ship's clocks had not been made, life aboard *Titanic* would have been wildly out of synch with New York when the ship arrived. It would have been noon for the ship's passengers and time for lunch, but on Broadway it would have been 7:00 am breakfast time. To avoid this problem *Titanic*'s clocks were set back about an hour each day during the voyage so ship's time would match New York clocks upon arrival. The setback for the Sunday of the disaster was calculated to be 47 minutes.

For the crew, setting back the clock meant 47 minutes extra work because the day had become that much longer. Since "midnight" *always* starts the new civil day, those extra 47 minutes had to be "tacked on" to the end of Sunday. (The extra minutes were part of Sunday, not Monday.)

Adding extra minutes to the day brings the problem of naming them. For instance, 12:15 o'clock occurs twice daily at 15 minutes after midnight; and 12:15 after noon. We call one "AM"and the other "PM." However, what is the time 15 minutes after 12:00 o'clock at night if the date has not changed? By definition it cannot be either "AM" or "PM." We have no common descriptive word for the 47 extra minutes added to *Titanic*'s Sunday.

There is an easy way to avoid this problem of naming the extra minutes. It's called the 24-hour system ("military time" in the United States) which eliminates "AM" and "PM" designations. In the 24-hour system Sunday, April 14th in *Titanic* could continue past 2400 through to 2447 hours. Unfortunately, *Titanic* did not use this elegant system for keeping ship's time. Historians are trapped into using the confusing "AM" and "PM" o'clock system because that is how time was described by surviving officers and passengers.

Table 9-1
Comparison of "AM / PM"
To 24-Hour Timekeeping

AM/PM System	24-Hour System
8:00 pm	2000 hrs
9:00 pm	2100 hrs
10:00 pm	2200 hrs
11:00 pm	2300 hrs
11:40 pm	2340 hrs
12:00 pm	2400 hrs
00:00 am	0000 hrs
Midnight	Midnight
1:00 am	0100 hrs
2:00 am	0200 hrs

Even so, the 24-hour system makes time computations so transparent that it will be used here. Readers who are unfamiliar with it may want to dogear this page for ready reference. Table 9-1 shows often-quoted times in both the "AM" and "PM" system and the corresponding 24-hour notation. White Star Line recognized the ambiguities of using “AM” and "PM" for ship's time. To avoid confusion the company required entries in log books be made in both Greenwich Mean Time (GMT) and local ship’s time. GMT is the same for all ships everywhere in the world.

> 116. **Time to be Kept.**—Seventy-fifth meridian time must be used for time of arrival at and departure from Sandy Hook Lightship, Five Fathom Bank Lightship, and other points of arrival and departure in the United States and Canada. Greenwich Mean Time must be used in Abstract Logs after the English or Irish land is made. When passing points and ships at sea, either eastbound or westbound, *Greenwich Mean Time, as well as ship’s time, must be used.*[9-2] [Emphasis by author.]

Paragraph 116 contains a significant omission. It says logs must be kept in ship’s time, but does not specify precisely how it was to be reckoned. The only guidance given shipmasters was to restrict clock changes to between 10 PM and 6 AM. Save for an offhand remark by Second Officer Charles H. Lightoller during the U.S. inquiry we would have no hint of how time was adjusted in *Titanic.* He stated that all clocks were to be “correct” for April 15 noon at midnight marking the start of the new day. The second officer mentioned only one resetting of the clocks, which has mislead most historians to assume there was a single setback each night. Like so many other *Titanic* myths, this “one change” setback is dead wrong.

A single setback would have forced one of the ship’s two watches to serve all of the 47 extra minutes that Sunday. For instance, a single setback could have required Fourth Officer Joseph G. Boxhall and his Starboard Watch to have stayed on duty until 12 hours 47 minutes past noon, or 2447 hrs. The clocks would then have been rest to show 0000 hrs and the Port Watch would have taken the deck. At the same instant the date would have changed from April 14 to April 15. Under this one-setback system the Port Watch would have had no extra time and all 47 minutes would have been worked by the Starboard Watch.

One thing certain, the crew did not expect either Watch to serve all 47 extra minutes. The two watches were to share equally in the extra duty. Another detail gleaned from crew testimony is that the clocks were scheduled to be set back again after the Port Watch came on duty. Once that second setback occurred, *Titanic's* clocks would have shown April 15th hours based on the predicted noon latitude for Monday.

Two setbacks were necessary because sailors kept track of their watches by a system of coded bell strikes. Instead of saying something happened at "10 PM," sailors would say "four bells." Each new watch started at 8 bells of the previous watch. One bell was then struck for every passing half hour. Two bells meant the first hour of the four-hour watch had been worked. Four bells announced the halfway point of the watch. An immutable part of this system was that 8 bells always marked the change of watch.

Table 9-2
Standard Pattern Of Ship's Bells

Running Time of Watch	Number Of Bells	Ringing Pattern
0:00	0	(8 bells of previous watch)
0:30	1	Ding
1:30	2	Ding-Ding
1:30	3	Ding-Ding..Ding
2:00	4	Ding-Ding..Ding-Ding
2:30	5	Ding-Ding..Ding-Ding..Ding
3:00	6	Ding-Ding..Ding-Ding..Ding-Ding
3:30	7	Ding-Ding..Ding-Ding..Ding-Ding..Ding
4:00	8	Ding-Ding..Ding-Ding..Ding-Ding..Ding-Ding

Note #1: Dog watches in Titanic followed British naval tradition. The first dog watch (4-6 PM) ended at "4 bells." The bell sequence for the second dog watch (6 to 8 PM) then re-started so that it also ended at "4 bells." This tradition eliminated "8 bells of the second dog watch," the infamous time of a mutiny during the Napoleonic wars.

Note #2: Seven bells was struck at 7:20 and 11:20 AM each day to allow the off-duty watch to have breakfast and lunch.

Generations of sailors have recognized 8 bells as change of watch. It would have been extremely confusing if extra time were added to the end of a watch after 8 bells. Few sailors carried expensive and fragile pocket timepieces in 1912, so most men would have been unable to know when 8 bells *plus* 23 minutes had passed. Simple crew convenience meant that any time change system had to maintain the honored tradition of 8 bells marking the end of each watch. It turns out that this was the reason White Star Line regulations allowed clock adjustments to start at 10 PM each night.

Ten pm is the midpoint of the 8 to 12 PM watch. Adding extra time in the middle of a watch was least disruptive to the ship's bell system. At 10 PM the crew's bridge clock would have been turned back to 9:36 PM This increased the normal 30 minute duration of the 4th bell to 56 minutes. Even so, when 4 bells was finally struck, the Starboard Watch knew it had the usual two hours remaining on duty before the "midnight" change of watch. Table 9-3 shows both the traditional sequence of bells and the modified sequence by which *Titanic*'s setback of ship's time took place.

Table 9-3 also shows why a double setback was necessary to create an 8 bells crew "midnight" halfway between April 14th time and the new day of April 15. It allowed the Starboard Watch to serve its extra 24 minutes prior to the crew's "midnight" change of watch at 8 bells. The Port Watch would then have served its extra 23 minutes immediately upon coming on duty. In this way, both Watches would have served their extra time during Sunday, April 14th so that all 47 minutes were accounted for prior to true midnight marking the start of April 15th. A double setback placed "crew midnight" at 2424 hours, exactly 23 minutes before true midnight at 2447 hrs April 14th which would have been the same as 0000 hours April 15th.

Table 9-4 shows why the "midnight" change of watch had to come 24 minutes after 12:00 o'clock in April 14th time or 23 minutes before 00:00 o'clock in April 15th hours. It also shows how the crew clocks were retarded in two stages, each equal to the extra time served by its respective Watch. Hence the name "two-stage" for this method of time keeping. Table 9-4 also shows the "midnight" change of watch had to come 24 minutes after 12:00 o'clock in April 14th time or 23 minutes before 00:00 o'clock in April 15th hours. It also shows how the crew clocks were retarded in two stages, each equal to the extra time served by its respective Watch.

Table 9-3
Ship's Bells 8-to-12 PM Watch
Night of Accident

Bells	**April 14 Time**	**Crew Bridge Time**
1	8:30	8:30
2	9:00	9:00
3	9:30	9:30
4	10:00	10:00 Becomes 9:36
None (Already Struck)	10:24	Second 10:00
5	10:54	10:30
6	11:24	11:00
7	11:54	11:30
None Bells Struck to Crew Time	0.5	11:36
Accident	**12:04**	**11:40**
8	12:24	Midnight Becomes 11:37 At Change of Watch
None	12:47 Becomes 00:00 April 15	Midnight To Become 00:00 April 15

Table 9-4
Time Of Crew Change of Watch

Time Of Crew Change Of Watch	Starboard Watch Extra Minutes	Port Watch Extra Minutes	Comments
12:00 PM April 14 Passenger Midnight	0	47	WRONG Only Port Watch works extra.
12:24 PM April 14 Crew Midnight (Correct Two-Stage Setback)	24	23	RIGHT Both watches share extra time.
12:47 PM April 14 Civil Midnight 0:00 April 15	47	0	WRONG Only Starboard Watch works extra.

It is now possible to define the 11:40 o'clock time of the accident based upon the testimonies of crew members. There was universal agreement among survivors that the accident occurred about 20 minutes prior to their "midnight" change of watch.

> Edward Buley (seaman): *I was in the watch on deck, the Starboard Watch. At 12 o'clock we [were to be] relieved by the other watch.* *(U.S. Inquiry)*

> Frank Osman (seaman): *I was waiting for one bell, which they strike, one bell, just before the quarter of the hour, before the four hours, when you get a call to relieve.* *(U.S. Inquiry)*

Likewise, Port Watch survivors said impact came five minutes before their wake-up bell which was to be sounded 15 minutes before the crew's midnight change of watch. Adding five and 15 minutes places the time of impact at 20 minutes before the crew's "midnight" change of watch, or 11:40 o'clock for the crew. It is significant that all surviving crew agreed *Titanic* struck on the berg at about 11:40 o'clock with reference to the crew's "midnight" change of watch.

This agreement was evident in the testimonies of seaman George Moore and off-duty lookout George Symons. Roused by the commotion after impact, Symons began dressing. The wake-up bell was just sounding 15 minutes before change of watch when he arrived on deck. Moore corroborated the time when the crew was roused out to begin dealing with the emergency.

George Symons (lookout): *There was an order came to the forecastle door by the boatswain to "stand by, as you may be wanted at any moment." By the time I got on deck it must have been about one bell, a quarter to twelve. (U.S. Inquiry)*

George Moore (seaman): *Sunday night about a quarter to 12 I was on watch below and turned in.... About 10 minutes to 12 the boatswain came and piped all hands on the boat deck, and started to get out boats. (U.S. Inquiry)*

Although he slept through the accident, quartermaster Arthur Bright was awakened as usual 15 minutes before change of watch. He dressed and went aft to his duty station on the poop.

Arthur Bright (quartermaster): *At 8 o'clock I turned in. One of the watch on deck came and called me and told me that the ship had collided. I went out to the after end of the ship to relieve the man I should have relieved at 12 o'clock, a man by the name of Rowe.* (U.S. Inquiry)

Another lookout, George A. Hogg, was also asleep at impact. The commotion afterward caused him to go on deck for a few minutes. When he returned below, his fellow lookout told him it was time to relieve the men on duty.

> George A. Hogg (lookout): *I waked up at 20 minutes to 12. I rushed up on deck...and I went below again. I asked the time, then, of my mate Evans, and he said, "It is quarter to 12. We will get dressed and get ready to go on lookout. I dressed myself, and we relieved the lookout at 12 o'clock, me and my mate Evans.* (U.S. Inquiry)

Seaman Frederick Clench was among those awakened by the impact (he claimed to be a very light sleeper). He went on deck to look around before going below again to smoke a pipe before going on duty.

> Frederick Clench (seaman): *I went on deck...and saw a lot of ice. I should say about 10 minutes...after I was awake...I went down below and put my Guernsey on, my round hat on, and after that I sat down on a stool having a smoke. Then ...I heard the boatswain's pipe call all hands out on deck. (U.S. Inquiry)*

The crew was quite certain that *Titanic* struck on the iceberg five minutes before the warning bell rousing out the Port Watch. Some members of the off-duty Port Watch first came up to see the cause of the consternation, then went below to prepare for going on duty. At the appointed time, they migrated to their duty stations for the crew's "midnight change" at what should have been 8 bells.

Titanic's iceberg encounter took place 20 minutes before change of watch. This timing of impact required the Starboard Watch to have already served its extra 24 minutes because it is impossible to subtract 24 minutes from the remaining 20 minutes before change of watch. The result would be negative time, something which cannot happen. However, if the extra 24 minutes had already been served, then there is no problem with the accident occurring 20 minutes before 8 bells and the crew's "midnight" change of watch.

Although 24 minutes cannot be subtracted from the remaining 20 minutes before the crew's "midnight" change of watch, we can use addition to our advantage. We can change crew time to stright April 14th hours by simply adding back the 24 extra minutes already served by the starboard watch. Adding 24 minutes to the crew's 11:40 o'clock time of the accident yields 2404 hrs in April 14th time. This proves the familiar 11:40 o'clock time of impact was not measured in April 14th time, but on a clock retarded by 24 minutes to crew time.

O'clock Crew Time Of Accident

11:40 Crew + 24 min = 2404 hrs April 14 Time

or

2404 hrs – 0024 Stbd Extra = 2340 hrs Crew Time

The math leave no doubt that *the quoted 11:40 time of the accident was not in April 14th hours*, but in an altered time reference halfway between April 14th and the forthcoming April 15th hours. I call this "*crew time*" to differentiate it from all other references for reckoning time. Crew time was designed to insure that 8 bells would take place exactly at "crew midnight" as they are supposed to.

Was "crew time" the official time used in the ship's logbook? No one knows, but the recording of the accident at 11:40 PM crew time suggests that it was. In the end whether or not 11:40 o'clock was official ship's time or not really doesn't matter. All of the times cited for the accident are exactly the same instant in history. Time itself does not change just because you twist the hands on a clock. All of the times quoted for the accident refer back to the same hour and minute in GMT.

Greenwich Mean Time (GMT) of Accident

2404 hrs April 14 = 11:40 o'clock Crew = 0302 GMT

If it had not been for the accident, the Starboard Watch would have stood another 20 minutes on deck until crew "midnight," or 2424 hrs April 14th. The first task facing the Port Watch after the change would have been to reset the crew clocks a second time. The hands would have gone back from 12 o'clock by 23 minutes to 11:37

o'clock. The crew clocks would then have displayed time based on *Titanic*'s predicted noon latitude for the new day, Monday, April 15th. The Port Watch would have served its extra minutes from 2424 to 2447 hours April 14th. At true midnight, the Port Watch would have begun its regular four hours on duty.

Planned Second Resetting of Crew Clock (If No Accident)

12:00 Crew Time - 23 min = 11:37 April 15th Hours
(Crew Clock Is Now Showing April 15th Time
Even Before Civil Midnight)

At 0000 hrs April 15th *Titanic* would have begun the new day, but neither Monday nor the second resetting of the crew clocks to 11:37 o'clock ever took place. The accident intervened and launching lifeboats became more important than timekeeping. However, the crew understood that if things had gone normally they were to reset their clocks again after change of watch. Setting the crew clocks back an final 23 minutes would have accounted for all 47 extra minutes of duty. It would also have made the crew clocks show the correct time for April 15th. This need for an additional setback was mentioned by boatswain's mate Albert Haines to the U.S. Senate inquiry.

> ***Albert Haines***: *I was standing by, down below. It being Sunday night, the men did not work. The men were in the mess room and I was outside. The right time, without putting the clock back, was 20 minutes to 12. (U.S. Inquiry)*

Historians favoring the mythical single-setback system misinterpret Haines' statement by claiming he said the crew clocks had never been set back. As we have seen, however, statements by multiple members of the crew prove that the first 24 minute setback must have been completed before the ship struck on the berg. This first crew setback was not the official resetting of ship's time to April 15th hours. Ship's time and date remained based on April 14th noon even though the hands of crew clocks were retarded by 24 minutes. All of the extra 47 minutes had to be worked before the date and time could change to Monday, April 15.

Haines knew the ship's clocks would go back another 23 minutes at the crew's "midnight" change of watch. He also knew that this second setback was the one that would adjust them to ship's time for April 15th. This explains why he said, "without putting the clock back, (it) was 20 minutes to 12."

Quartermaster Robert Hichens correctly stated that he remained on duty in the wheelhouse until 12:23 o'clock. His words are widely cited as proof the accident happened on unaltered April 14th time. In fact, what he said proved exactly the opposite. Sailors traditionally come on duty a minute or two before change of watch. It is unacceptable to come on duty late. Normal practice would have seen Hichens relief taking over a minute before crew "midnight." Hichens statement indicates he was relieved on time by his opposite number of the Port Watch. Any clock showing April 14th ship's time would have read 12:23 as the crew's midnight change began to take place.

Hichens got his 12:23 reading from a special clock mounted on the back wall of the wheelhouse. This dial was not connected to *Titanic*'s Magneta master clock system (see below). It was intended to keep unaltered April 14th hours during the transition period while the Magneta system was being set back from April 14 to April 15 time. Keeping one clock on the "old time" insured that certain routine duties were performed exactly every 30 minutes no matter how ship's clocks were changed.

Junior Officer In Charge of Crew Watch

30 Minute Interval Tasks

Comparing Steering to Standard Compass

Report of Crow's Nest Lookouts

Hourly Task

Rounds of Ship by Junior Officer

It was the 30 minute or 1 hour interval between the above tasks that was critical and not the time of day when these duties were executed. For most of the day they would have been done on the even hour or half hour as displayed on all clocks throughout the ship.

After 10 PM, the ship's clocks were being retarded so a special reference clock was needed to maintain the required intervals.

Quartermaster, Thomas Rowe, stood watch on the poop deck. If the main steering system on the bridge failed, Rowe was handy to take over from the ship's docking bridge. He also made routine checks on the ship's taffrail log (distance measuring instrument) and made sure passengers did not skylark on the safety railings. Rowe stated that he looked at his pocket timepiece to note the time of accident as "20 minutes to 12." His statement proves his timepiece matched the crew clock by which the time of the accident was recorded. He then went on to say, "I remained until 25 minutes after 12, when I saw a boat on the starboard beam."

Rowe's relief, quartermaster Arthur J. Bright, testified that he went on duty at the appointed midnight change of watch. The men talked about the iceberg and other odd events of the night for about a half hour before both men were surprised to see one of Titanic's lifeboats in the water.

One-setback proponents twist the actions of Rowe and Bright by claiming that while Bright may have arrived at midnight, the change of watch did not take place until more than 20 minutes later. The problem with this solution is that no boats were launched at 2425 hrs (12:25 o'clock) in April 14th ship's time. The launching of boat #7, the first to go, did not occur until about 2449 hrs.

Rowes timepiece, however, had been set back 24 minutes to crew time. Within reason, that 2425 launching of boat #7 would have taken place about "12:25" for him, proving Rowe was keeping crew time. Working back, if we subtract the time he and Bright talked after change of watch, Rowe's timepiece would have shown "midnight." And, going back another 20 minutes we arrive at 11:40 o'clock which is what Rowe's timepiece recorded.

Rowe's Time of Boat #7

2449 Launch Boat #7 = 12:24 on Timepies
12:25 - 24 Minutes = 12:00 on Timepiece
12:00 on Timepiece - 20 min = 11:4 0 Crew Time of Iceberg

Table 9-5 hows how the times cited by Hichens, Rowe, and Bright work perfectly within the two-setback method of sharing extra duty between the Port and Starboard Watches.

The fatal flaw of the single setback lies in its failure to share the extra 47 minutes between the first and second officers. If the time were set back only once, then Second Officer Lightoller would have worked no extra minutes. His relief, First Officer Murdoch, would have been forced to serve all 47 minutes because his shift spanned Civil Midnight. Anyone who has served a military knows senior officers never serve extra duty when junior can handle it. "Rank has its privileges."

Any proposed method for changing the clocks which puts the burden of extra time solely upon a senior officer must be rejected out of hand. The two officers should have either shared the extra time evenly, or the full burden should have fallen on the shoulders of the second officer. While there is admittedly no historical proof for the two-setback system (Table 9-6) proposed here, it is the only system that shares the extra time in proper nautical fashion.

Table 9-6 shows it was necessary to set back the crew clocks at 10 PM to share the extra time among the first and second officers. This explains why White Star regulations allowed ship's clocks to be changed as early as 10 PM. Fiddling with the clocks any earlier in the evening would have been disconcerting to passengers. But, 10 PM was also the latest possible moment when time could be added to the second officer's watch before the first officer came on duty.

Senior officers (Chief Officer, First, and Second Officers) changed two hours out of step with the crew to make sure that continuity of events was not lost. Junior officers remained on duty during each change for the seniors and senior officer provided continuity across changes of juniors. Because of this system, the senior officers changed at 2, 6, and 10 AM and PM each day.

Table 9-5
Comparison Of Hichens/Rowe Times

Event	April 14 Passenger Time	Rowe's Timepiece (Crew Time)	Greenwich Mean Time (GMT)
Impact on Berg	12:04 am	11:40 pm	0302 hrs
Hichens Relieved At Wheel	12:23 am	11:59 pm	0321 hrs
Crew Change of Watch	12:24 am	Midnight	0322 hrs
Launching Lifeboat #7	12:49 am	12:25 am	0347 hrs

Table 9-6
Time Change System Used In Titanic

Event	Duration From April 14 Midnight	Time Based On Noon April 14	Crew Bridge Clock	Time Based On Noon April 15	Greenwich Mean Time (GMT)
Crew Clocks Retarded by 24 Minutes (1st Setback)	-2:47	10:00	10:00 Becomes 9:36	(Never Used In *Titanic*) 9:13	0058 hrs
Officers Change of Watch	-2:23	10:24	10:00 Officers Change	9:37	0122 hrs
11:30 pm Course Change	-1:17	11:30	11:06	10:25	0228 hrs
April 14th Midnight	0:00	12:00 Passenger Midnight	11:36	11:13	0258 hrs
Iceberg Accident	0:04	12:04	11:40	11:17	0302 hrs
Hichens Relief	0:23	12:23	11:59	11:36	0321 hrs
Crew Midnight Clocks Retarded 23 Minutes (2nd Setback)	0:24	12:24	12:00 Becomes 11:37	11:37	0322 hrs
Boxhall CQD Time	0:27	12:27	11:40	11:40	0325 hrs
Civil Midnight Apr 15	0:47	12:47 (Disappears As 0:00 April 15th)	0:00	April 15th To Have Begun Here As 0:00 Midnight	0345 hrs

Although the two-setback system would have been transparent to the crew, it might have confused passengers. This appears to be the reason why *Titanic* was designed to carry two master clocks. Having two systems allowed the crew to live in one "time zone" and the passengers in another. According to *The Shipbuilder* magazine (Vol. VI, Midsummer, 1911), the clocks were supplied by the Magneta company. An oddity not explained in the *Shipbuilder* article is why two master clocks were necessary. The 48 secondary clocks displayed throughout the ship were half the number that could have been handled by a single master clock alone.

> MAGNETA CLOCKS
>
> The clocks, of which there are 48 throughout each vessel, have been supplied by the Magneta Time Co., Ltd., and are all actuated electrically on the Magneta system, which obviates the use of galvanic batteries. They are controlled by two master clocks placed in the chart room, so that they may work in complete unison and each register exactly the same time... .
>
> As is well known to ocean travelers, the ship's clocks gain over half an hour each day when going westwards and lose a corresponding amount when returning to Europe. To allow for this difference in time the master clocks are set each day at noon by the officer in charge, who puts them backwards or forwards according to the longitude.

Corroboration that *Titanic* was *supposed* to carry two master clocks as described by *The Shipbuilder* article can be found in a handwritten note on page 30 of the Harland & Wolff notebook kept in the company's drawing office as a quick reference during construction:

ELECTRIC CLOCKS. 2 master clocks
48 secondary clocks.

The Harland & Wolff document reaffirms that *Titanic* should have enjoyed a clock system capable of providing two "time zones," one for the crew and another for passengers. However, the double master clock system may not have been fully functional for *Titanic*'s only voyage. There is apocryphal evidence that the slave clock dial was never installed in the forward grand staircase. Many people over the years have claimed a circular mirror was fitted as a substitute.

Supporting the mirror story is the oddity that not one first class survivor recalled observing the time displayed on the main stairway clock either during the voyage or on the night of the sinking. Yet most passed beneath it several times daily and many huddled on the stairway before going to the lifeboats. Why did all of them fail to look at the clock? Or, was that famous dial never installed and a mirror fitted after all?

Another oddity of the sinking is that so many surviving passengers recollected events in crew time halfway between April 14th and April 15th ship's time. Passengers had no need of a two-stage setback for their clocks. They should never have experienced the crew's two-stage timekeeping system. A simple 47-minute setback would have been sufficient for passengers. Why, then, did so many passengers seem to use crew time?

The simplest answer to these questions is that the Magneta Clock system was only partially operational. If so, this explains why there was a mirror instead of a secondary clock on the main grand staircase. And, the need to organize the operation of the ship would explain why passengers were forced to use two-stage crew time during *Titanic*'s maiden voyage.

If *Titanic* had only one Magneta master clock functioning, then clock dials throughout the ship would necessarily have been retarded on the two-step process of the crew. The reason is contained within the *Ships' Rules* published by the International Mercantile Marine Company and governing White Star Line ships like *Titanic*. Paragraph 259 allowed for the 10 PM setback of the clocks to crew time. It also required clocks in various parts of the ship to agree for the ship's safety.

> **259. Ship's Time.** – The Officer of the Watch will see that the ship's time is changed between the hours of 10 PM and 6 AM, the clocks to be set for Noon before 6 AM. The Engine Room Clock must at all times agree with the Clock in the Wheelhouse, and must be corrected accordingly.

The requirement that the engine room and wheelhouse clocks show the same time to synchronize the “bell book” with the ship's official log kept on the bridge. The bell book was a written record of every order sent down from the bridge. It was maintained in the engine room. The need for synchronization of bridge and engine room clocks was so important that it was covered yet again in another White Star Line rule.

> **305. Engine Room and Deck Clocks to Agree. –** When passing points of departure or arrival, he will see that the Engine Room and Deck times agree.

Titanic was too large and complex for the First Officer to easily check his bridge clock against an instrument in the engine room. There were also additional secondary clocks scattered around the ship which synchronized the actions of the engine room crew with those of the deck crew and bridge officers. All of these dials had to be adjusted simultaneously. The need for automatic clocks controlled from the bridge was obvious.

Titanic’s dual master clock system should have allowed the crew to have it’s two-stage setback while the passengers experienced only one. However, for some never-revealed reason only one master clock appears to have been connected to all of the slave clocks in both passenger and crew spaces. Everyone aboard *Titanic* shared the same time because the need to the synchronized the bridge and engine room clocks overrode passenger convenience.

Readers should not fear they have been needlessly dragged through the dull and complex business of shipboard timekeeping. This recitation of facts and testimony was necessary to prove that the time reference for the famous 11:40 PM was not Local Apparent Noon (LAN) of April 14th. Rather, it was 11:40 PM in crew time retarded by 24 minutes. The accident took place 12 hours 4 minutes after noon that Sunday. It is impossible to write a correct history of *Titanic*’s accident and sinking without taking into account these important 24 minutes.

Table 9-7
Witness Time Comparisons

Witness	Event	Time Claim	Apr 14	Crew Time	Apr 15	GMT	Notes
Abelseth, Olaus	Impact	**11:45**	12:04	**11:45**		0307	Clock 5 Min. Late
Bishop, Mrs.	Impact	**11:45**	12:32	12:08	**11:45**	0329	Steward 20 min. after impact
Collins, John	Impact	**11:15**	12:04	11:40	**11:17**	0302	Set To 4/15 Hrs
Gracie, Col. A	Impact	**Mid-night**	**12:04**	11:40	11:17	0302	
Hardy, John	Impact	**11:40**	12:04	**11:40**	11:17	0302	Based On His Duties
Hogg, George	Impact	**11:40**	12:04	**11:40**	11:17	0302	
Moore, George	Impact	**11:45**	12:04	**11:40**	11:17	0302	Impact prior to crew wakeup bell
Osman, Frank	Impact	**11:40**	12:04	**11:40**	11:17	0302	Waiting For Wakeup Bell
Peuchen, Maj Arthur	Impact	**Mid-night**	**12:04**	11:40	11:17	0302	Leaving Smoke Room
Pickard, Berk	Awake	11:50	12:42	12:18	11:55	0340	
Ryerson, Emily	Impact	**12:00**	**12:04**	11:40	11:17	0302	Time She Looked Out
Scarrott, Joseph	Impact	**11:40**	12:04	**11:40**	11:17	0302	
Weikman, A.H.	Impact	**11:40**	12:04	**11:40**	11:17	0302	Barber Shop Clock on Crew Time

Wheelton, Edward	Impact	**11:40** to 11:45	12:04	**11:40**	11:17	0302	
Widgery, James	Impact	**11:35**	12:04	**11:40**	11:17	0302	Clock Slow By 5 Min.
March Post Clerk	Unk.	1:27	2:14	1:50	**1:27**	0511	Stopped When Washed Off Ship
Weikman, A.H.	Wash Off	1:27	2:14	1:50	1:27	0511	
Boxhall, Joseph	Ship Sinks	**2:20**	**2:20**	1:56	1:33	0518	Observe
Minahan, Daisey	Ship Sinks	**2:20**	**2:20**	1:56	1:33	0518	Over Heard
Gracie, Col. A	Breaku p	**2:22**	**2:22**	1:58	1:35	0520	Stopped Timepce
Thayer, Jack	Breaku p	**2:22**	**2:22**	1:58	1:35	0520	Stopped Timepce
Robinson, Annie	Ship Sinks	**1:40**	2:27	2:03	**1:40**	0525	Observe In 4/15 Time

APPENDIX C

REPORT ON THE LOSS OF THE ""TITANIC"." (S.S.)

THE MERCHANT SHIPPING ACTS, 1894 TO 1906.

PUMPING ARRANGEMENTS.

The general arrangement of piping was designed so that it was possible to pump from any flooded compartment by two independent systems of 10 in. mains having cross connections between them. These were controlled from above by rods and wheels led to the level of the bulkhead deck. By these it was possible to isolate any flooded space, together with any suctions in it. If any of these should happen accidentally to be left open, and consequently out of reach, it could be shut off from the main by the wheel on the bulkhead deck. This arrangement was specially submitted to the Board of Trade and approved by them.

The double bottom of the vessel was divided by 17 transverse watertight divisions, including those bounding the fore and aft peaks, and again subdivided by a centre fore and aft bulkhead, and two longitudinal bulkheads, into 46 compartments. Fourteen of these compartments had 8 in. suctions, 23 had 6 in. suctions, and three had 5 in. suctions connected to the 10 in. ballast main suction; six compartments were used exclusively for fresh water.

The following bilge suctions were provided for dealing with water above the double bottom, viz., in No. 1 hold two 3 1/2 in. suctions, No. 2 hold two 3 1/2 in. and two 3 in. suctions, bunker hold two 3 1/2 in. and two 3 in. suctions.

The valves in connection with the forward bilge and ballast suctions were placed in the firemen's passage, the watertight pipe tunnel extending from No. 6 boiler room to the after end of No. 1 hold. In this tunnel, in addition to two 3 in. bilge suctions, one at each end, there was a special 3 1/2 in. suction with valve rod led up to the lower deck above the load line, so as always to have been accessible should the tunnel be flooded accidentally.

In No. 6 boiler room there were three 3 1/2 in., one 4 1/2 in., and two 3 in. suctions.

In No. 5 boiler room there were three 3 1/2 in., one 5 in., and two 3 in. suctions.

In No. 4 boiler room there were three 3 1/2 in., one 4 1/2 and two 3 in. suctions.

In No. 3 boiler room there were three 3 1/2 in., one 5 in., and two 3 in. suctions.

In No. 2 boiler room there were three 3 1/2 in., one 5 in., and two 3 in. suctions.

In No. 1 boiler room there were two 3 1/2 in., one 5 in., and two 3 in. suctions.

In the reciprocating engine room there were two 3 1/2 in., six 3 in., two 18 in., and two 5 in. suctions.

In the turbine engine room there were two 3 1/2 in., three 3 in., two 18 in., two 5 in., and one 4 in. suctions.

In the electric engine room there were four 3 1/2 in. suctions.

In the store rooms above the electric engine room there was one 3 in. suction.

In the forward tunnel compartment there were two 3 1/2 in. suctions.

In the watertight flat over the tunnel compartment there were two 3 in. suctions.

In the tunnel after compartment there were two 3 1/2 in. suctions.

In the watertight flat over the tunnel after compartment there were two 3 in. suctions.

Bilge and Ballast Pumps. - The ship was also fitted with the following pumps: Five ballast and bilge pumps, each capable of discharging 250 tons of water per hour; three bilge pumps, each of 150 tons per hour capacity.

One ash ejector was placed in each of the large boiler compartments to work the ash ejectors, and to circulate or feed the boilers as required. This pump was also connected to the bilges, except in the case of three of the boiler rooms, where three of the ballast and bilge pumps were placed. The pumps in each case had direct bilge suctions as well as a connection to the main bilge pipe, so that each boiler room might be independent. The remainder of the auxiliary pumps were placed in the reciprocating and turbine engine rooms. Two ballast pumps were placed in the reciprocating engine room, with large suctions from the bilges direct and from the bilge main. Two bilge pumps were also arranged to draw from bilges. One bilge pump was placed in the turbine room and one of the hot salt-water pumps had a connection from the bilge main pipe for use in emergency. A 10 in. main ballast pipe was carried fore and aft through the ship with separate connections to each tank, and with filling pipes from the sea connected at intervals for trimming purposes. The five ballast pumps were arranged to draw from this pipe. A double line of bilge main pipe was fitted forward of No. 5 boiler room and aft of No. 1.

APPENDIX D

THE OLYMPIC - CLASS STANDARD COMPASS PROBLEM

White Star Line reacted to the loss of *Titanic* by making a significant improvement to the bridges of *Olympic* and *Britannic*. On both ships a standard compass was installed atop the wheelhouse in an open-air enclosure often called by sailors a "flying bridge" or "monkey bridge." It was built on the flat wheelhouse roof. The design of that space indicates Harland & Wolff must have anticipated the installation of a flying bridge. In Titanic, the wheelhouse roof was devoid of ventilators and other paraphernalia as if Harland & Wolf expected to move the standard compass of *Olympic* and *Titanic* to this traditional location once White Star Line came into line with the normal practice of the shipping industry.

White Star appears to have been quite alone in the industry in its placement of standard compasses. On most of its ships that instrument was located amidships just as on *Titanic* and *Olympic*. The standard instruments of most ships owned by other companies were placed adjacent to their steering wheels. The usual location was on the roof of the covered bridge or wheelhouse. A few ships carried their standard compasses on platforms in front of their bridges. A wheelhouse rooftop location allowed easy verbal communications among the bridge team members. Voice communications were possible between the officer of the watch and the junior officer conducting compass checks.

Curiously, *Olympic*'s original standard compass was left *in situ* after the new instrument was installed. This strongly suggests a lawyer at work. By leaving the old standard compass in place White Star Line made it unlikely the compass change made to *Olympic* would be noticed and even less likely that it would be linked to the *Titanic* disaster. There may have been fear that moving *Olympic*'s compass could have been viewed as proof the company knew the original location was negligent.

Existing records from *Olympic* during the post-refit period show that readings of the former standard compass continued to be taken every half hour as before. However, this was the only practical purpose served by the old compass, and that was simple misdirection to hide the role played by the location of *Titanic*'s compass in the tragedy. A ship can have only one "standard" compass and no more. For navigational purposes, the new compass atop the wheelhouse would have been the only functioning "standard compass" aboard *Olympic*. However, the original compass was still consulted every half hour and its reading recorded in the ship's Compass Comparison Book until well into the 1920s.

Even more curious was the installation of an unnecessary compass platform was installed between the second and third funnels of Britannic, even though that ship received an expanded flying bridge. It would appear that even Britannic was made part of the cover-up of *Titanic*'s standard compass problem.

NAUTICAL GLOSSARY

Aft – Toward the stern of a ship. A person "goes aft" when he walks toward the stern.

All Stop – An engine order calling for the propellers to be brought to a stop. This does not cause the ship to immediately come to a halt. It will continue coasting ("shooting") forward for some distance.

Amidship – The location at or near halfway from the bow to stern; or pertaining to a location halfway from the bow to stern.

Below – To go to a lower deck, particular to a deck within the hull itself. Any space inside the hull below the weather deck.

Bilge – The lowest portion of the hull, often where water collects. Specifically, the point where the flat bottom of the hull curves to meet the vertical sides.

Binnacle – Any housing for a nautical compass. In *Titanic* the binnacles were made of polished wood and brass. The one in the wheelhouse also contained a clinometer for measuring any list of the hull.

Bow – The front of the vessel, but by extension any part of the vessel near the front. Sometimes "bows."

Bottom – The portion of the hull that extends horizontally from the keel outward to where it meets the vertical sides of the ship.

Bridge ("Captain's Bridge") – The main control station of the ship. It contained the steering wheel, compass, engine telegraphs, and other equipment necessary for navigation.

Bulkhead – Any "wall" placed across the width of a ship. In *Titanic* the word usually refers to the watertight bulkheads that divided the hull into 16 separate compartments.

Bunker – any storage area or bin reserved for the stowage of fuel (coal) for the ship's boilers.

Captain – A largely honorary title bestowed upon the master of the vessel. May also honor anyone who holds a master's license whether or not he has held command.

Carpenter – In 1912 the ship's carpenter was no longer just a woodworker. He was responsible for minor repairs while under way, checking ballast tanks, and other duties.

Companionway – A small hatch or hatchway with a stairway ("ladder") leading to lower deck. Often a small hood over a hatchway on a weather deck to prevent entry of spray or water.

Crash Stop – An emergency maneuver in which the ship is halted by applying full reverse thrust of all engines.

Crow's nest – A small platform located on a ship's mast for the purpose of sheltering a lookout.

Davit – Any of a number of small cranes specifically intended for launching small boats, particularly lifeboats. *Titanic* was fitted with radial davits requiring one for each end of the lifeboat.

Deck – Any horizontal surface intended for walking on a ship. *Titanic* had nine decks: boat deck; Promenade deck (A); bridge deck (B); shelter deck (C); saloon deck (D); upper deck (E); middle deck (F); lower deck (G); orlop deck; and tank top deck.

Dead Reckoning – A process of navigation in which the ship's position is determined by its movements (speed and direction over time) since its last known fix. Term derived from "deduced reckoning."

Engineer – In a ship, any member of the crew detailed to service or maintain the engines. Also a licensed officer rank, such as Chief Engineer.

Even Keel – said of a vessel that is drawing the same amount of water at the bow and stern. Most ships are trimmed so that the bow draws slightly less than the stern.

Falls – The ropes of a block and tackle system; specifically the ropes between blocks of a tackle supporting a lifeboat.

Field ice – Frozen seawater floating in a loose formation.

Fireman – In 1912, any member of the crew serving the fireboxes of the boilers or tending fuel in the coal bunkers.

Fix – Navigational term for the exact position of a vessel while under way. Near shore compass bearings of landmarks are used. Offshore, in 1912 the only way to obtain a fix was to use a sextant and the sun or stars in a process called *celestial navigation.*

Floe (ice floe) – An area of field ice large enough to pose a danger to navigation.

Forecastle – the raised deck at the very bow of the ship. *Titanic*'s forecastle contained galley and dining areas for the crew. It also provided a weather break for the third-class promenade space on the forward well deck.

Foredeck – The forwardmost upper deck of a ship.

Forepeak – A small, triangular compartment at the very bow of a ship, usually kept void but in *Titanic* it was used for some stores and supplies.

Forward – Toward the bow of a vessel.

Founder – For a vessel to sink completely.

Funnel – The nautical term for a boiler smokestack. *Titanic* had four funnels, three of which served the boiler rooms and the fourth ventilated the engine rooms and galley.

Greaser – A non-skilled member of the engine room crew. Term comes from the job of applying grease to moving parts of engines.

Growler – A colloquial term applied to smaller icebergs.

Hard a-port – In 1912 parlance this was a helm order to move the ship's tiller to port causing the rudder to swing to starboard and the ship to steer to its right.

Hard a-starboard – In 1912 parlance this was a helm order to move the ship's tiller to starboard causing the rudder to swing to port and the ship to steer to its left.

Helm – The steering wheel or, by extension, any of the other equipment used to steer the ship. In *Titanic* the helm consisted of the wheel, an hydraulic telemotor, and a steam steering engine that moved the rudder.

Hogging – A condition in which the keel of a vessel is raised upward in the center so that the bow and stern ends are lower.

Iceberg ("berg") – A large portion of polar or glacial ice that has become detached and has floated out to sea. Icebergs are made of fresh water, so they float with only one-eighth of their mass above the surface of the ocean.

Knot – a measurement of speed equal to one nautical mile per hour.

List – Any transverse lean of the ship that raises one side of the deck while lowering the other. Initially, *Titanic* listed to starboard after the iceberg accident. (See "Tip.")

Lookout – A trained member of the crew specially charged with the duty of observing by sight, hearing, and any other means. Lookouts report anything unusual they observe to the bridge.

Maiden Voyage – A ship's first paying trip after passing its builder's sea trials.

Make water – when water enters the hull through damage, the ship is said to be "making water."

Marconi – Gugliemo Marconi was one of the inventors of wireless telegraphy and gave his name to the company which owned and operated the wireless equipment aboard *Titanic.*

Marconigram – A proprietary name for any wireless message sent via the Marconi Company.

Master – The person in legal command of a vessel. All ship's masters must hold appropriate licenses from their governments. Holding a Masters License does not guarantee one the position of captain. Many of *Titanic*'s officers held licenses even though they served in an inferior position to Captain E.J. Smith.

Mile, nautical – A measurement of distance at sea equal to one minute of latitude, or approximately 6,076 feet. (Often rounded to 6,080 feet for convenience.)

Officer – Any member of a ship's crew operating under an Officer's License from an issuing government. Usually applied to deck officers who navigate ship. In *Titanic* there were eight deck officers:

Master – Captain Edward J. Smith
Chief Officer – Henry Wilde
First Officer – William M. Murdoch
Second Officer – Charles H. Lightoller
Third Officer – Herbert Pitman
Fourth Officer – Joseph G. Boxhall
Fifth Officer – Harold G. Lowe
Sixth Officer – James H. Moody

In addition to these well-known deck officers there were thirty-five men broadly classified as "engineers" aboard *Titanic*. Among these were Chief Engineer Joseph G. Bell, twenty-four engineering officers, two boilermakers, a plumber, and a clerk.

Orlop deck – In *Titanic*, two short deck extending no father aft than boiler room #6 and located between the tank top and lower deck (G). Similar orlops were located aft of the turbine engine room. The forward upper orlop was used as a mail room.

Pack ice – Freshwater ice broken from glaciers that covers wide areas of the polar seas, broken into large pieces that are driven (or "packed") together by wind and current.

Plates (plating) – The flat pieces of rolled metal bent or shaped to become part of the ship's hull. They are attached to the frames and may for either the bottom or sides of the hull.

Port – The left side of the ship when facing forward, or pertaining to the left side of the ship when facing forward.

Quartermaster – Job rating of the seaman who actually steered the ship. Additional duties included errands for the officer of the deck.

RMS – Abbreviation for "Royal Mail Ship." Identified British liners that carried mail for the Royal Post Office. Such ships were required to maintain 16-knot speeds on the Atlantic.

Rounds – A colloquial name given to hourly inspection trips of the on-duty deck crew by the junior officer in charge of those men. Also, nightly tour of ship by the Chief Officer.

Saloon – Any large public room given primarily to passenger use, hence *saloon deck*. Does not refer to sale or consumption of alcoholic beverages as it does ashore in the United States.

Scantlings – The collective term for all of the specifications relating to strength, weight, and size of materials used in construction of a ship, particularly its hull.

Seaman – Any member of the deck crew, regardless of sex, who handles lines, steers, or stands lookout. Ordinary seamen are of lower rank than able-bodied seamen.

Secure – To stop any action, including to shut down equipment (such as ship's engines) when not needed. To tie off a rope.

Sound – To measure the depth of liquid in a tank or in the bilge of a ship. Sounding is also done when damage is suspected to learn of water ingress.

Starboard – The right side of the ship when facing forward, or pertaining to the right side of the ship when facing forward.

Steerage – (a) The ability of a vessel to be controlled by its own rudder. Usually expressed as a minimum speed for such control. (b) Term for third-class passengers, probably because they were formerly housed in the least desirable sections of the ship near the stern where the tiller and steering equipment are located.

Stern – The very back of a vessel, but also any part of the hull or deck at the back of the vessel.

Stokehold – In coal-fired ships the area of a boiler room where the work of stoking furnaces was done. By extension any boiler room of a ship.

Stoker – A member of the crew detailed to shovel coal from bunkers into the fireboxes of the boiler furnaces.

Stoker Plates – special deck plates raised above the tank top on which the stokers work. The stoker plates are raised enough to allow easy access to furnace openings.

Superstructure – Deck houses or other structures built on top of the ship's hull. In *Titanic,* everything above the shelter deck was considered superstructure.

Tank Top – the inner bottom of a double-bottomed ship. It forms the top of the ballast tanks inside the bottom, hence the name. The tank top is normally the lowest deck of a ship.

Telegraph, Engine Order – A mechanical device used to send orders from the bridge to the engine room.

Tiller – A lever attached to the rudder post by which the movements of the rudder may be controlled from inside the ship. In *Titanic* the tiller was replaced by a large quadrant gear driven by a steam-powered steering engine.

Tip – Any upward or downward movement of the bow not caused by wave action. *Titanic*'s bow *tipped* downward as the ship sank. Tipping should not be confused with listing which is a transverse lean of the ship.

Topsides – The vertical portion of the hull from the waterline upward. Does not include superstructure.

Trimmer – A member of the crew detailed to adjust the level ("trim") of coal in bunkers; or to move coal from bunkers to the stokers for feeding into furnaces.

Triple-Expansion – Any steam engine having at least three cylinders arranged so that the exhaust of the first feeds into the second, and then into the third. Each time the steam expands, providing more power to the propeller. *Titanic*'s triple-expansion engines had four cylinders; one high pressure, one medium pressure, and two low pressure.

Watch – a period of time on duty, usually four hours, during which crew members had responsibility for tending the ship.

ENDNOTES

Chapter 1: A Tale Of Fire

1-1 Tonnage capacities are estimated based on 44 cubic feet per ton of bunker coal.

1-2 Hayler, William B, *Merchant Marine Officer's Handbook*, Cornell Maritime Press, Centreville, MD, 1989, page 423.

1-3 Parr, S.W. & Kressmann, F.W., The Spontaneous Combustion of Coal, *The Engineering Magazine,* vol. 43, no.5, August 1912, page 836.

1-4 "Drawing Office Notebook," Harland & Wolff, page 7. The auxiliary bunker spaces of Hold #3 are identified as "No. 3 Bunker" in the notebook.

Chapter 2: Dodging Ice

2-1 In sailing ships the tradition had been for officers to stand on the windward side, whether port or starboard.

2-2 Rappelyea, George W. Ph.D., *Navigation Wrinkles for Combat Motor Boats,* Higgins Industries, New Orleans, 1944, 2nd ed., page 8. This manual was prepared for operators of U.S. Navy PT Boats and other small craft during World War II.

2-3 Original online at:
http://www.bbc.co.uk/archive/titanic/5049.shtml

2-4 The computed course from "the Corner" to Nantucket Lightship in 1912 was 265.5°. The half degree could easily have been read on the Kelvin compass fitted in *Titanic*'s wheelhouse. However, First Officer Lightoller testified the ship steered 266°, which works perfectly when reconstructing the ship's dead reckoning.

2-5 Bowditch, Nathaniel, LL.D., *American Practical Navigator*, U.S. Navy Hydrographic Office, H.O. Pub No. 9, 1926, pages 12 - 13.

2-6 British Board of Trade Inquiry, question 15646.

Chapter 3: Dancing With Death

3-1 British Board of Trade Inquiry, question 343.

3-2 Technically a compass point is 11.25°. A compass card divided into single degree increments cannot be read to a fineness of more than 0.5°, so the quarter degree was often discarded in discussions of a "one point" turn. There was no practicable way to achieve closer accuracy in 1912.

3-3 Parry, Capt. William Edward, R.N., F.R.S., *Journal of a Second Voyage For The Discovery Of a North-West Passage From The Atlantic To The Pacific,* John Murray, London, 1824; reprinted by Greenwood Press, New York, 1969, page xix.

3-4 Bowditch, Nathaniel, LL.D., *American Practical Navigator*, U.S. Navy Hydrographic Office,, 1926, page 265.

Chapter 4: Not A School Bus

4-1 Three strikes on the lookouts' bell reported something dead ahead; two strikes something to port; and one stike a danger to starboard.

4-2 *Olympic*'s maneuvering data suggested that turning using full rudder would have caused the ship to move about 1,300 feet forward ("advance") and about 120 feet tward the direction of the turn ("transfer"). The bow would have been angled about 24 degrees into the turn.

Chapter 5: Killer Gravity

5-1 The S.S. *Willis B. Schoonmaker* (ex-*Schoonmaker*) is preserved as a museum ship in Toledo, Ohio. Tours of the ship do not include the forepeak where ice damage occurred. The author has been given access to this area where he found the original hull plates and frames *in situ* with no visible damage.

5-2 Hayler, William B, *Merchant Marine Officer's Handbook*, Dornell Maritime Press, Centreville, MD, 1989, page 410.

5-3 Baker, Elijah III, *Introduction To Steel Shipbuilding*, McGraw-Hill Book Company, New York, 1953, 2nd ed., page 65 - 66.

5-4 Noel, Capt. John, USN (Ret), *Knight's Modern Seamanship*, 1984, Van Nostrand Reinhold Company, Inc., New York, page 81.

5-5 Beesley, Lawrence, *The Loss of the S.S. Titanic,* Houghton Mifflin, 1912; reprinted Mariner Books, 2000, page 46.

5-6 British Board of Trade Inquiry, questions 2346 - 2601.

Chapter 6: Final Destination

6-1 Robeert Froude, a prominent naval architect himself, was the son of William Froude (1810-79), a pioneer naval architect who worked with I.K. Brunnel developing bilge keels to reduce rolling of vessels and later developed *Froude's Number* which is used to predict the behavior of full-size hulls from tank test models.

6-2 Beesley, Lawrence, *The Loss of the S.S. Titanic,* Houghton Mifflin, 1912; reprinted Mariner Books, 2000, page 41.

6-3 *Daily Sketch*, London, Tuesday April 16, 1912, "The Man At The Wireless."

6-4 *Daily Sketch*, London, Wednesday April 17, 1912, "Not From Wireless Man."

6-5 *New York Tribune,* New York, Tuesday April 16, 1912, "London Hears Late of Loss of Titanic."

6-6 As told to Mary Margaret McBride, *The Saturday Evening Post*, August 7, 1926, page 141-2.

6-7 *Daily Sketch*, London, Wednesday April 17, 1912, "Mysterious Messages."

6-8 *Dow Jones News Service*, sent at 3:01 PM New York, April 15, 1912.

6-9 As told to Mary Margaret McBride, *The Saturday Evening Post*, August 7, 1926, page 141-2.

Chapter 7: Death Of A Titan

7-1 Affidavit dated May 1, 1912 and entered into the record of the U.S. Senate Inquiry.

7-2 Testimony before U.S. Senate Inquiry, day 13.

7-3 *ibid.*

7-4 British Board of Trade Inquiry, questions 4245 - 4267.

7-5 It appears the collapsible lifeboats were neither numbered nor lettered on *Titanic*. The familiar letters "A" through "D" by which they have become known seem to have been first applied during the British Inquiry to clarify testimony.

7-6 British Board of Trade Inquiry, questions 10529 - 10540.

7-7 Extracts from the reports of the seamers *Olympic, Baltic, Mount Temple, Caronia, Virginian,* and *Asian* submitted to the Board of Trade by W.W. Bradfield, manager, The Marconi International Marine Communication Company, Ltd., pages 4 and 5 (Available at www.marconicalling.com).

7-8 Gracie, Col. Archibald, *The Truth About Titanic,* Mitchell Kennerley, 1913, Reprinted in *The Story Of The Titanic*, Jack Winocour, ed., Dover Publications, New York, 1960, page 139.

7-9 *ibid*, page 148.

7-10 The traditiional duration of the sinking is 2 hours 40 minutes. This was created by using the wheelhouse clock to establish the time of the accident at 11:40 PM. Then, the time of the foundering was taken as 2:20 AM from when Boxhall, Pitman, and others saw the lights go out on the upending stern. When the two times are converted to Greenwich Mean Time (GMT) they become 0302 hours for the accident and 0525 hours for the final disappearance. The difference is thus only 2 hours 23 minutes, which represents the actual duration of the sinking.

7-11 U.S. Senate Inquiry, day 4.

Appendix A: *Quo Vadis,* Boxhall?

A-1 Letter from Joseph G. Boxhall to Joe Carvalho of Massachusetts regarding the 50th anniversary of the *Titanic* sinking. Carvalho donated the original to the *Titanic International Society* archives. They are available online at:
www.encyclopedia-titanica.org

Appendix B: The Myths of Time

B-1 The apparent rotation of the sun around the Earth is not exactly 24 hours due to the elliptical orbit of the planet and the inclination of the Earth's axis. As a result, the solar day is slightly longer or shorter than the mean day of 24 hours. Navigators must account for this difference to obtain precise celestial fixes. However, the day-to-day difference is slight enough that it can be ignored in this discussion.

B-2 International Mercantile Marine Company, *Ship's Rules and Uniform Regulations,* issued July 1st, 1907, page 24. Taken from personal copy of J. Bruce Ismay now filed with papers from New York Limitation of Liability hearings.

SELECTED BIBLIOGRAPHY

PRINTED BOOKS

Ballard, Robert D. *The Discovery of the Titanic.* New York: Warner Communications, A Warner/Madison Press Book, 1987.

Beesley, Lawrence. *The Loss of the S.S.* Titanic: *Its story and its lessons.* Boston: Houghton Mifflin, 1912, rpt. 2000. See also Winocour, *Story of the* Titanic.

Brown, Capt. David G. *The Last Log of the* Titanic. Camden, Maine: Inter-national Marine/McGraw Hill, 2001.

Bryceson, Dave. *The* Titanic *Disaster As Reported in the British National Press April – July, 1912.* New York: W.W. Norton, 1997.

Caren, Eric, and Steve Goldman. *Extra* Titanic, *The story of the disaster in the Newspapers of the Day.* Edison, J.J.: Castle Books, 1998.

Lightoller, Charles H. Titanic *and Other Ships.* Nicholson & Watson, 1935. See also Winocour, *Story of the* Titanic.

Stenson, Patrick. *The Odyssey of C.H. Lightoller.* New York: W.W. Norton, 1984.

Winocour, Jack, ed. *The Story of the* Titanic *as Told By Its Survivors.* New York: Dover Publications, 1960. This volume includes: Gracie, *Truth about the* Titanic, in entirety; Beesley, *The Loss of the S.S.* Titanic, in entirety; and portions of Lightoller, Titanic *and Other Ships.*

WEB SITES & ONLINE

www.encyclopedia-titanica.org – a goldmine of research papers, passenger and crew biographies, and other facts about the ship and its fatal maiden voyage. Excellent discussion forum.

http://marconigraph.com – This site by Parks Stephensonprovides a forum for some of the leading researchers in the field of maritime history. The reader should be familar with ships of the Cunard and White Star Lines, most notably Lusitania and Titanic. Excellent source of early Marconi radio information.

www.titanicinquiry.org – The transcripts of both the U.S. Senate and British Board of Trade inquiries can be found here in searchable format. Some material from New York limitation of liability hearings is also presented.

www.titanic-titanic.com – lots of good research information and a forum for contributors.

www.titanic-model.com – primarily intended for model builders, but this site has research papers and data not available anywhere else online.

http://www.bbc.co.uk/archive/titanic/5056.shtml – Hear the aging Boxhall on this web site which archives radio interviews presented by the BBC over the years.

Index

7967144R00137

Made in the USA
San Bernardino, CA
23 January 2014